Brimfield Rush

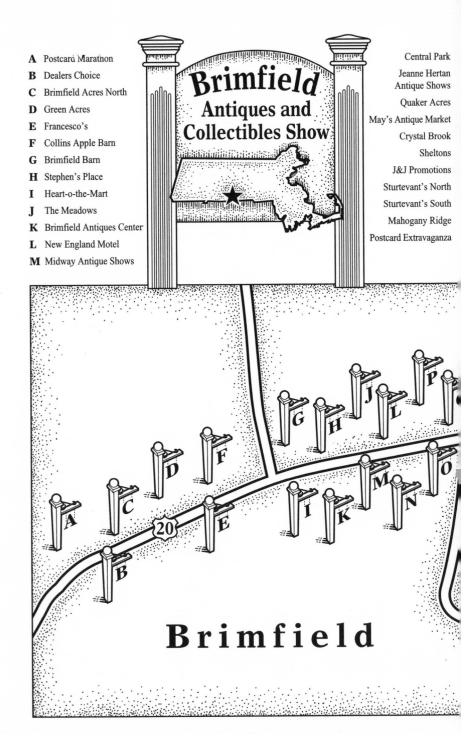

A Postcard Marathon
B Dealers Choice
C Brimfield Acres North
D Green Acres
E Francesco's
F Collins Apple Barn
G Brimfield Barn
H Stephen's Place
I Heart-o-the-Mart
J The Meadows
K Brimfield Antiques Center
L New England Motel
M Midway Antique Shows

Central Park
Jeanne Hertan Antique Shows
Quaker Acres
May's Antique Market
Crystal Brook
Sheltons
J&J Promotions
Sturtevant's North
Sturtevant's South
Mahogany Ridge
Postcard Extravaganza

Brimfield
Antiques and
Collectibles Show

Brimfield

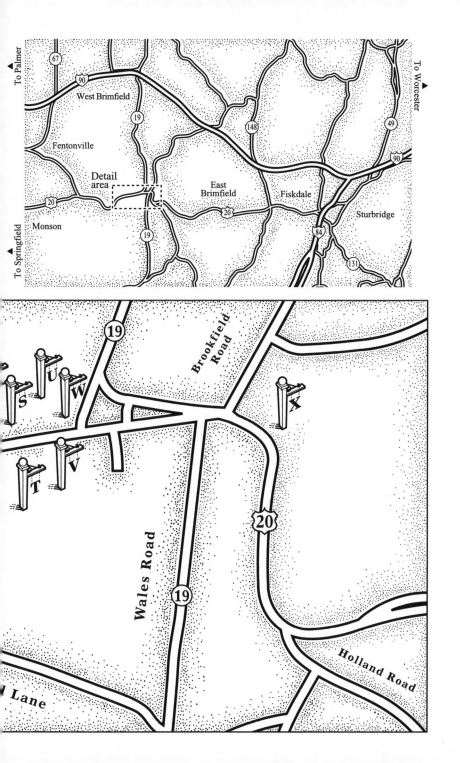

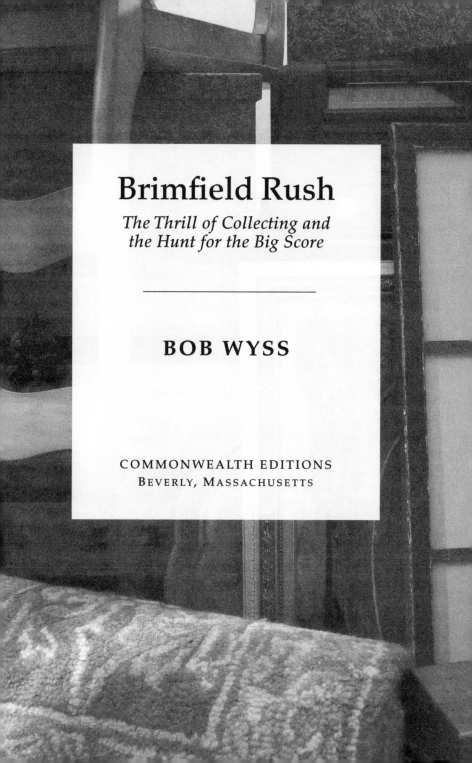

Brimfield Rush

*The Thrill of Collecting and
the Hunt for the Big Score*

BOB WYSS

COMMONWEALTH EDITIONS
BEVERLY, MASSACHUSETTS

First edition

ISBN-13: 978-1-933212-04-3
ISBN-10: 1-933212-04-7

LIBRARY OF CONGRESS CATALOGING-IN-PUBLICATION DATA

Wyss, Bob.
    Brimfield rush : the thrill of collecting and the hunt for the big
score / Bob Wyss.— 1st ed.
        p. cm.
    Includes bibliographical references.
    ISBN 1-933212-04-7 (alk. paper)
    1. Antiques business—Northeastern States. 2. Antique dealers—
Northeastern States—Anecdotes. 3. Flea markets—Massachusetts—Brimfield (Town) I. Title.
    NK1133.28.W97 2006
    745.10973´075—dc22

                                                    2005027671

Cover design by John Barnett.
Interior design by Rachel Reiss.
Map by Jeffrey M. Walsh.
Author photo by Dianne Sprague.
Printed in the United States of America.
Published by Commonwealth Editions,
an imprint of Memoirs Unlimited, Inc.,
266 Cabot Street, Beverly, Massachusetts 01915
www.commonwealtheditions.com

10 9 8 7 6 5 4 3 2 1

For my wife and partner Dianne Sprague

Contents

Introduction

"Look at that!" exclaims Caryn Greco, so excited that she interrupts her husband's concentration. For a moment James Greco cannot make out what his wife is pointing at. Rusty old tools, blackened pots and pans, aging porcelain and glass containers are heaped on a table and stacked with other relics of America's past. Piles grow rapidly as men empty the truck. Similar scenes play out around them. A new field at the Brimfield Antiques and Collectibles Show has opened and dealers frantically yank out goods while buyers eagerly scan each booth for bargains.

And then, through the tumult, James sees it.

"Oh my goodness!" he cries. James is so thrilled he is tingling. He knows any overt expression of enthusiasm could be costly. Still, it is tough to restrain his excitement. What he has spotted is a skeleton—a full, human skeleton, with every bone from the skull to the phalanges wired, intact, in place. The bones are yellowed with age. They look beautiful to James.

Stuart Phelps, the dealer who has just removed the skeleton from his truck, brings it close to where the Grecos, a handsome couple in their thirties, are standing. James Greco recognizes Phelps, a longtime dealer from Belfast, Maine.

1

He asks Phelps about the skeleton's origin. Phelps bought it earlier in the year at an antiques auction in Skowhegan, Maine. It had been brought in by two antiques pickers, experts who find antiques and sell them wholesale at auction or to other dealers. Phelps explains that it was from an Odd Fellows Hall in Berwick, or perhaps in South Berwick, Maine. It came with a wooden case. The dealer points it out among the pile of antiques and debris—a long box made of what looks like worn, aged pine. The shape is familiar: it looks like a coffin. The dealer does not know very much about the skeleton or what the Odd Fellows used it for— perhaps it was part of some kind of ceremony held by the fraternal organization. He does, however, have other evidence of its provenance.

Greco cannot believe it when Phelps pulls out a bill of sale. It is dated January 26, 1876, and attests that Dr. Joseph E. Lord, of 13-15 Tremont Street in Boston, bought the skeleton from Codman & Shurtleff, a leading nineteenth-century supplier of medical equipment that was later bought out by Johnson & Johnson. Phelps is certain this bill of sale will help clinch any deal for the skeleton. He came into its possession in an odd way. Besides the skeleton, other items from the Odd Fellows Hall included several boxes of documents and mementos. Phelps had bid on several of the boxes but lost out to another dealer. Weeks later that dealer called, trying to sell one of the boxes to Phelps. Inside it he had found the bill of sale, and they both knew that kind of documentation instantly made the skeleton more valuable. Provenance means everything in the antiques world. Phelps eventually agreed to buy the bill of sale for $100. The document also identifies the skeleton as French in origin. Greco knows French skeletons were the best on the market at that time. They are much better than the skeletons of East Indians or Chinese, who tended to be more malnourished, with smaller and more brittle bone structures.

What a find! He has to have it. For ten years James has been searching auctions and flea markets for a human skeleton. That is one reason he keeps coming back to Brimfield. Caryn Greco also knows they should buy it. They live twelve miles away in a house built two hundred years ago for the physician Joseph Cady. Their dining room had once been Doctor Cady's operating room. For years they have been restoring the house. Once, when they pulled up the original floor to repair it, they found bones underneath. They did not even want to guess the source. They got rid of them quickly. While they were troubled by the discovery of the bones, the Grecos felt that the skeleton would be a perfect addition to the dining room, along with the other vintage objects they collect, including apothecary bottles and a leech jar. Perhaps some day, if they can find it, the room can also house a nineteenth-century amputation kit.

James Greco fears he will pay for sounding so excited.

"How much do you want for that?" he asks.

"Eighteen hundred," Phelps replies.

Greco fights to keep his face impassive. He is pleased. He has seen other skeletons of this vintage go for up to $3,200 at auction.

"What is your best price?" Greco uses a common Brimfield bargaining ploy.

Phelps pauses. "Sixteen hundred," he replies.

Brimfield prices, and how far they may fall during haggling, vary depending on a few conditions. As a general rule during negotiations, a seller is usually willing to come down in price by 10 to 20 percent. But timing is important too. When a show like this one first opens, prices may already be unusually low. Dealers never know for sure the value of objects in their possession and sometimes they underestimate demand. Some dealers base prices solely on what they paid for a group of objects. Once they have recouped their money, the price on the remaining items may go down.

Greco gently tries to move the price down further, but he can't. Finally, he says that he will take the skeleton for $1,600, if Phelps will throw in a Mettlach Hires Root Beer mug that he picked up just before he saw the skeleton. He estimates that the mug is worth $300.

Phelps agrees.

For forty-nine weeks of the year the town of Brimfield, Massachusetts, is a quintessential New England village of 3,300 residents, complete with white clapboard Congregational church on the spacious town green. It's sixty-five miles west of Boston, near the foothills of the Berkshire Mountains, and usually the major action is at the Woodbine, the combination coffee shop and grocery store where some locals gather daily. That all changes three times a year on the second Tuesday in May, July, and September, when Brimfield's population swells twenty to forty times.

Of the hundreds of antiques shows that run every year, Brimfield is the greatest. It has earned that reputation partly because of its size: It draws some three thousand dealers and tens of thousands of buyers from across the country and the world to its one-week shows. It is also famous for the vast range of antiques and collectibles found inside its tents and atop tables set up in dusty fields. There is a saying at

Brimfield, "If you can't find it here, you can't find it anyplace." Ultimately it is not size or breadth that distinguishes Brimfield but intensity. Brimfield is not a single antiques market but a collection of more than twenty different fields spread out for a mile along Route 20, or Main Street. Fields open on different days. Each time a new one opens, buyers race for bargains.

Walking the fields of Brimfield it is clear that America is a nation of pack rats. Our tendency to hoard must be deeply imbedded, extending back generations. Parents, grandparents, and great-grandparents and beyond were even worse than we are. Much of what they saved is worthless. Some of it, however, is spectacular. Much of what one finds at flea markets and antiques shows around the country was merely utilitarian in its time. Much is junk, or reproductions, or in some cases outright fakes. Buried in all this are items of value, not only monetarily but intrinsically. They are rare.

Another universal characteristic on display at Brimfield is the lure of a good bargain—or a great score. A successful discovery not only produces financial rewards but it is also an intellectual victory, a validation of one's superior ability over one's peers. It is that quest that keeps drawing crowds back to Brimfield, though there are some who worry that the crowds may be thinning, that the best deals all may soon be on the Internet.

This book follows several dealers and collectors at the Brimfield antiques market, from May 2003 to May 2004. It is not just a tale of some very smart and resourceful buyers and sellers or of their triumphs and failures. It is a story of history, culture, and heritage and how we can rediscover values lost amid the rubble of time.

May

Deals are my art form. Other people paint beautifully on canvas or write wonderful poetry. I like making deals, preferably big deals. That's how I get my kicks.

DONALD TRUMP

CHAPTER 1

Opening Day

JOE LASKOWSKI AND Rachel McKay awake at about five on this Tuesday morning in their small nylon tent. It is still dark and cold, and the beige walls of the tent are dripping wet from the night's drizzle. Joe was a little amazed last night when Rachel told him that this was the time they would need to awake. However, he did not argue. After all, Rachel knows Brimfield; she has been coming for years. Joe has been here only once, for a couple days last fall when he was first getting to know her. Waking up is not as difficult as Joe had feared because the cold, hard ground kept sleep away for much of the night. The tent is pitched at a field called Heart-O-The-Mart which opens tomorrow. Tomorrow Joe and Rachel will try to sell some of the paintings they brought, but today they are searching the fields for lost art.

They do not look like art dealers, let alone Brimfield dealers. Rachel is thirty-two, with her trademark blue jeans and casual shirt. Her shoulder-length hair and deep brown eyes soften the look cast by her rugged apparel and definitely make her appear younger. Joe is six feet tall and 214 pounds, and he looks as though he could have played football in high school, especially with his balding pate so closely cropped. He also looks younger than his thirty-seven years. They may seem more youthful because they are surrounded by much older associates both here at Brimfield and on antiques circuits. It is rare to see young antiques dealers, and usually they are related to a parent who is trying to pass on the family business. Rachel is the daughter of a dealer, although there is no family business she is going to inherit. Antiques dealers usually learn the business over the years, and for most it is a second career, often supplemented by the luxury of a pension.

The couple are quickly out of the tent and soon walking east on Route 20. The coming dawn is chilly and damp, but the Brimfield market is awake and alive. Cars, trucks, trailers, tents, and tables stretch a half mile behind them, a half mile ahead. A side lane opens up every twenty or thirty steps and runs a quarter mile or more. Buyers and sellers are moving around, beginning their dance, their ritual of barter. Stuff is everywhere: rumpled bear fur rugs and shiny antique slot machines, brightly colored African beads and rusting old farm apple corers, a worn antique horse-drawn buggy and a cumbersome red-and-white barber pole. The scene looks as if an army from the nineteenth century has bivouacked, with the soldiers bringing all the clutter they could possibly find in their attics, cellars, barns, and sheds.

At a field called Sheltons, on the eastern end of the market, sleepy dealers are opening tent flaps and sipping coffee that steams in the chill of the morning air. A dealer mostly selling French crystal, bronzes, glassware, and china tells Joe that he has some paintings in the back of his van. Joe sifts through the canvasses in the half light and finds a darkly colored surrealist oil with a clock, face, and lips. The signature is Pierre Alechinsky. It is dated 1956, one year after the famous Belgian-born artist moved from Paris to Japan and eight years before he painted his most famous piece, *Last Day*. It is hard to believe that an oil by Alechinsky, whose work can fetch $100,000, is sitting here in this dealer's van priced at $275. It is much easier to suspect that the painting is a fake. Still, you never know, thinks Joe as he turns it over, looking for potential flaws. He cannot find any, not that that means much. He stares at it some more. Finally, he asks the dealer for his best price. They settle on $200. Despite Rachel's strong skepticism, Joe cannot resist. He loves to research paintings, to comb his growing library of art books. He knows right where to look to find out more about Alechinsky. Besides, it's only $200. "You never know," he tells Rachel.

They linger for a moment at the tent of another dealer, Mike McClintock. They are only dropping by to say hello. Joe and Rachel both live in the Philadelphia area, and they go regularly to McClintock's gallery in nearby Lambertville, New Jersey. Rachel once worked briefly for McClintock, both at his gallery and here at Brimfield. It was McClintock who introduced Rachel to Brimfield. The couple move on. Most of the others roaming the fields this early on opening day are professional antiques dealers too, along with a few very committed collectors and a few interior designers. The more casual buyers are rare. They will show up later in the week.

Joel Schiff, one of Brimfield's most famous collectors, is approaching them on the road. He walks on his one leg and two sturdy crutches. He has a short ponytail, hidden by a pirate's cap, and a fake parrot perched on his shoulder. Rachel and Schiff greet each other. Brimfield regulars know that Schiff cannot pass a single booth without inquiring, in a chant that takes on a singsong quality, "Any cast iron, any cast-iron cookware here?" Dealers who have never sold a single piece of cast iron are still questioned not once, but often twice, at every show. Behind his back, some roll their eyes or make fun of Schiff's interest in cast iron. They joke about how his apartment back in New York City is still standing despite the weight of all the iron Schiff has stored in it. Yet those who talk to Schiff soon find themselves in an erudite discussion of social history, economics, and culture.

Throughout the morning Joe continues to strike deals. He finds three Coulton Waughs, more impressed by their look than by the artist's name. Not that it hurts to have a signed artist with an established track record. Joe is familiar with Waugh, he knows that Waugh is really known more as a cartoonist, that he did an obscure comic strip called *Dickie Dare* from 1933 to 1957. Waugh was also an author, a historian of cartooning, a teacher, and an accomplished artist. These three paintings are quick, abstract oil sketches, and the dealer is asking $150 apiece. Joe works the price down to $300 for the three.

The scattered rain with which the cold morning began is ending with a brilliant rainbow and now the sun is beginning to chase away the chill. Joe and Rachel walk with the crowd, which is moving slowly toward the western perimeter of Brimfield, where the Dealer's Choice field opens at eleven. While anyone can walk onto many of the fields, others are fenced and the owners charge an admission fee. Here it is five dollars. Fields such as this create a huge crowd at their opening, but there is a drawback. Such fields are considered picked over and dead within three hours of their opening. Rarely do buyers return. Fields such as Dealer's Choice respond by closing after only a few hours. Until the new fair opens in July, they will revert to pastures, back yards, or parking lots for the few permanent residents and businesses on Route 20.

Joe is carrying the three Waugh paintings as the gates open at Dealer's Choice, and he has to be careful to protect them from the press of the crowd. By this point Joe has begun to realize he would need to go to ten or maybe even twenty auctions to find the wealth of art he is discovering at Brimfield. The crowd is so huge that Joe and Rachel are forced in opposite directions. He finds a dealer with a still life he likes. The dealer wants $250. Joe isn't comfortable with the price. He suggests $200. Now the dealer hesitates. Joe says he is not familiar with the artist, Allen McCurdy. The dealer agrees to the $200. Joe asks if the dealer has a *Davenport*. They huddle in the back of the dealer's truck and look up McCurdy in the fat *Davenport Art Reference and Price Guide*, which is the size of the Manhattan telephone directory and lists recent sales. Neither knows much about McCurdy and the book does not add much. It does indicate that a still life, similar to the one they have been looking at, sold at auction twelve years earlier for $3,960. Joe now definitely wants the painting.

The dealer looks at him. "I'm having a change of heart on this," he says.

Joe stares at him in disbelief. This dealer is a short, scruffy little fellow and he is not quite looking Joe in the eye.

One reason may be that Joe has at least five inches on him. Joe knows, they both know, that a moment ago they had a deal. "You can't back off now," cries Joe.

"You had a chance to buy it at two hundred and you didn't do it," whines the dealer. He still is not looking at Joe. The dealer looks worried, but he wants to hold his ground. His apprehension is understandable. Joe can look imposing; that's why recently he was hired to be a security guard at a big tattoo convention in New Jersey.

Joe's appearance can help him negotiate many things, but it is not going to help him buy the McCurdy for $200.

"No, what you are doing is unfair," says Joe hotly to the dealer. Then he walks quickly away.

Minutes later Joe is still fuming about the missed opportunity and how the dealer mishandled the transaction. There are rules and codes in the antiques business, but sometimes they get tricky. Later, another Pennsylvania dealer who knows Joe and Rachel says that the incident reminds him of when his wife got caught in a similar ethical dilemma. Howard and Linda Roberts are general antiques dealers based in the suburbs west of Philadelphia. One day they bought several items at an estate sale, including a painting in the attic. Linda Roberts liked the winter scene, and she paid $25 for it. When they got back to their shop, Linda placed it on a wall. Normally they consulted with an art expert, but this time there was no time for that before a couple came in and inquired about the painting. Linda said they could have it for $900. They said they would think about it, and left. Shortly afterward, another couple came in and asked about the painting. Since it had not sold at $900, Linda Roberts lowered the price to $800 and she sold it. It was not until she was writing it up that the buyers insisted she list the piece by the artist's name. It was George Sotter. When she listed it, she knew it was familiar and she suspected she had made a mistake. But she had already agreed to sell it, she was writing it up, and she did the ethical thing, she completed the sale. It was a costly decision. Minutes after the couple left with the painting, the first couple came back to the shop wanting to buy the painting for $900. They accused Linda of making up a story about selling it. The man asked her: "Do you know what that was?" George Sotter was a Pennsylvania artist, part of the Bucks County School that painted mostly landscapes of the rolling eastern Pennsylvania countryside. While not a leading artist of the school, he and others were becoming increasingly popular. Six months later the Roberts read that the Sotter painting had sold at auction for $85,000.

Joe knows he is partly to blame for losing the McCurdy painting. "I usually buy on sight," he explains. "You need to trust your instincts and it was a good painting. But even though I knew it was good, I didn't know the artist." That lack of faith in his own judgment cost him.

He does not have much time to fret. Within a few minutes he finds a seascape by a California artist. It is a beach scene, with a heavy tint of orange, red, and yellow, and the seller wants only $125 for it. Cash. Joe has run out of cash and is writing checks to dealers who will take them. Brimfield is so much a hard currency market that two ATMs are brought in on trailers for each show. In previous years as much as $500,000 has been taken out of one of those ATMs by the end of the week, according to David Lamberto, the manager of one of the fields that has a cash machine.

Joe asks the dealer to hold the California painting. Within minutes he finds a dealer he recognizes and he quickly comes to terms on one of the Coulton Waughs, selling it for $200. That is a hundred percent profit in less than an hour. Then Joe goes back and buys the California painting for $125. And that's how the show goes. Tomorrow he will sell the California painting to another dealer for $250.

Dealers call these quick sales "flips." They happen almost continually at Brimfield. There is a good reason. Brimfield is a dealer's market, a wholesale market where nearly everyone seems to be a middleman intent not only on buying but also on selling. Flips work because true dealers never worry too much about how much a piece is worth. Rather, they work to get some money out of it. "If you buy something for ten dollars and sell it for twenty, it might sell again for forty or sixty or a hundred," explains Mike McClintock, the art dealer from New Jersey. "One of the problems with too many new dealers is that they buy something for ten dollars and then they try to sell it for a hundred and ten when it is only worth a hundred. Making sure there is still money in something is never wrong. I have sold one painting five different times, making money every time I acquired it and then sold it again."

Rachel worries that perhaps Joe is buying a bit too recklessly, until they find the painting signed by Eugene Boudin. Joe holds it up. It is an Impressionist, a twilight scene on a river with a boat slowly gliding by. He looks at Rachel.

"What do you think?" he asks.

"I wouldn't buy it," she replies.

He is about to say something more, but the dealer is watching them carefully. Joe puts the painting back down, without asking the price. Boudin was a nineteenth-century French painter known for his fluid style. The brush strokes on this painting are chunky and harsh, the scene flat and lifeless. Joe's heart wants to buy it, wants him to believe that he has found a lost masterpiece, but his eye is telling him the painting has significant problems. It's too bad. Boudins can sell for up to $800,000.

They both see a second painting carrying the Boudin name. It has the same problems. A tag says "ask about price." Joe and Rachel look at each other and move on.

By early afternoon Rachel takes a break while Joe runs on ahead for the opening of the last field of the day, Brimfield Acres North. She is sitting under a dining canopy at Dealer's Choice drinking a juice when she notices an older man who is holding what looks like a violin. She asks if he is looking for more violins.

"I'm looking for fiddles," replies Karl Ferret.

Rachel asks what the difference is between a violin and a fiddle.

"Price," says Ferret. A violin is constructed of traditional materials in a prescribed and orthodox method. A fiddle may be made similarly, with whatever materials the maker could find. But the biggest difference between the two is the way the instruments are played and the melodies they produce. Violins play a range from classical to pop while fiddles are devoted more to folk and ethnic music, from Swedish to Irish to Cajun to American bluegrass. Ferret, who is seventy, has been repairing fiddles as a sideline since he was seventeen and playing them for nearly as long. He comes to Brimfield and walks for eight hours a day, poking around for old, tired instruments that he can fix. "I like the low-end, not the expensive instruments and I don't like big concerts, I like parlor playing," he says. "It's a passion of mine."

As the two part after the fifteen-minute conversation, Rachel is reminded of just how diverse Brimfield can be. She has always enjoyed this ability to stumble into a conversation with a stranger and learn something different and exotic. At Brimfield that happens with almost everyone she talks to. She makes a note to herself to later seek out and talk to Ervin. She does not even know his last name, but she does know that he sells a range of weapons and other exotic artifacts, from knives, swords, spears, helmets, shields, and other instruments of war to pottery and beads. In years past she has sat under his tent while he has told stories of some of his discoveries. She's heard that he found a dagger on the fields today that he thinks is either Greek or Etruscan, more than twenty-five hundred years old. But that will come later, because now she has to find Joe and see what she can find on the last field of the day. The bargains are there, she's sure. She just has to find them.

CHAPTER 2

From the Silk Road
to the Brimfield Rush

WHEN THE FIRST civilizations dawned eons ago, one of their signatures was great markets and bazaars. The lure of these markets spread commerce and wealth—by way of the Silk Road from Babylon to Xian, Marco Polo's Spice Route from Venice to Cathay, the camel paths from Marrakesh to Timbuktu, or the sea routes from Lisbon and Barcelona to Goa, Veracruz, and beyond. Great exotic markets, or souks, still flourish at the Grand Bazaar in Istanbul, the Devaraja Market in Mysore, the Asian Bazaar in Kathmandu, and the Namdaemun Market in Seoul. A sense of these ancestral bazaars can still be found on the frenzied trading floors of commodity markets on Wall Street or at quaint country auctions. But one can get only a taste, because so much of the world's retailing fervor is controlled by indistinguishable capitalistic monoliths, by faceless identical shops stretching from strip malls to Fifth Avenue, or by the antiseptic click of a computer mouse. It is the Brimfields of America that keep the homogenization of retailing in check and that maintain a fleeting link to the days when barter in an open field moved mankind from cave to metropolis.

In the Western world the most universal name for such bazaars has become "flea market." No one knows for sure the origin of the name, but its first known usage was at the Sunday market in Paris, which in the 1890s took the name Marché des Puces, or Market of Fleas. Versions of this Parisian market date back centuries, and its specialty has long been "old or used" merchandise. The most common story of the name's origin is that much of the material sold at the market was acquired either by theft or pulled from the trash by Parisian rag pickers. That meant that the goods were not clean, either because they had been illegally acquired or because they literally were dirty, infested with vermin and fleas. A variation of this tale is that market activity would be disrupted when the police arrived, causing buyers and sellers to disappear like fleas escaping or fleeing.

America has a long history of outdoor markets, dating from the years when the nation was young and rural. Venues were often centered on country fairs, farmers markets, and livestock auctions. Some happened only once a year while others were weekly, such as the trade days that flourished throughout the South beginning in the late nineteenth century. Another name popular in the western United States is "swap meet." That name may have begun during the Great Depression, when men would sometimes meet in garages and filling stations to exchange tools and other parts that they could not afford to purchase. These gatherings were often held on the weekend and eventually they moved to vacant lots. As these markets grew, they also drew women, who traded more common household necessities, from kitchen utensils to spare clothing.

In the South one of the survivors of the trade days is in Ripley, Mississippi. The First Monday Sale and Trade Days began in 1893. We know a great deal about it because of research by the Center for the Study of Southern Culture. The trade days in Ripley were initiated by local merchants on the courthouse steps, although they are now at the county fairgrounds outside of town. Most early transactions amounted to trade or barter because rural farmers in northern Mississippi were cash-poor. A hound dog might be traded for a shotgun or plow tools for a mule. Researchers were told of an old farmer in overalls who waved a large pipe over his head and walked the grounds seeking to swap it for a billy goat. Another tale, perhaps fictional, told of a farmer who traded a shotgun for a hunting dog, traded the dog later for a sewing machine, and then made more trades before finally settling again for a shotgun. It was only when he got home, according to the story, that the farmer realized the shotgun was the same one he had brought that morning to the market.

Gordon Reid called his first gathering in the pasture behind his Brimfield home a "station-wagon tailgate" sale. It was the summer of 1959 when he convinced sixty-seven dealers to set up for the one-day event. Hardly anyone had ever heard of an outdoor antiques sale, and they questioned whether they could make money. Reid believed there was a market for quality furniture, art, and other heirlooms that dealers were finding in New England attics and sheds. The 1950s and 1960s were not a time when antiques were especially prized. But Reid had been in the business long enough to know their value. Gordon Reid had joined the auction business begun by his father, Robert, in the 1930s. Together Gordon, his brother, Raymond, and their father developed a booming business up and down the Connecticut River Valley through the 1930s and 1940s. Robert Reid was known as a flamboyant, colorful auctioneer and folks were drawn to his sales. One year he and his sons conducted 241 auctions. Gordon Reid was a born auctioneer. Pamela Beall, who moved to Brimfield in the late 1960s and later became town clerk, remembers the first auction she attended at his Brimfield barn called Auction Acres. "When I bid the first time, Gordon Reid asked for my name. He had to ask only once; he remembered it the rest of his life," she recalls.

Reid, his wife Madelyn, and their three children moved to Brimfield in 1946 to set up their auction business. They found a town of about three thousand people that had been established fifty years before the founding of the republic, a community whose best claim to history was that it was part of the Revolutionary War pathway used by General Henry Knox to haul cannons from New York's Fort Ticonderoga to Boston to fight the British. Small New England towns often have a timeless feel to them. Gordon Reid worried that time was running out not only for Brimfield but also for similar villages throughout New England. In 1973 Reid told an old family friend, Fred Dole: "Each time we sold out a herd of cattle, we were selling ourselves out of business. Once a farm was sold to a developer, it was never operated again. The other day I sold the contents of an attic in Thompson, Connecticut. That attic will never be full of antiques again. We had two virgin attics last year. This is the first one this year. In time, there won't be any attics full of antiques anywhere in connection with estate close-outs."

In 1959 Gordon and Madelyn Reid visited flea markets in Salisbury and Higganum, Connecticut, and they told everyone that they traveled thousands of miles circling around New England asking friends to come to the antiques flea market they were going to host on their farm in Brimfield. "They thought we were crazy," Reid recalled years later, "but they came as a favor to us."

Francis X. Breen brought three grandfather clocks and a mandolin to that first Reid show in the summer of 1959. Based in Wilton, New Hampshire, Breen was a true Yankee peddler who would sell everything from apples and eggs to antique furniture. Dealers set up in the morning. One dealer, who was selling bells, played tunes from the chimes all morning. In the afternoon Reid held an auction in his barn. Breen's son, Tom, remembers that his father returned home with $500, a sizable amount of cash in 1959.

Over the next few years the number of dealers and buyers slowly grew. The Reids worked hard to make the shows a success. Madelyn Reid recalled making endless sandwiches in the house to supply the dealers so that they could stay at their booths. Later, when the Reids bought tents and had the food catered, Madelyn would take any ripped tents back to the house and mend them. "We couldn't afford the fifty dollars to have them fixed," she explained. Dealers came because everyone in the antiques business knew Reid, who drove a car sporting the license plate SOLD. Reid was also deft at dealing with community complaints about the shows, especially since he had long been entrenched in Brimfield, serving at one time as a town selectman and participating in the Men's Club at the First Congregational Church. He was also lucky: it rained only a couple of times in the show's first fifteen years. Slowly the crowds grew.

In those years, Reid would look out a front window and see a convoy of antiques dealers lined up on the road waiting for the Reids to open at six in the morning. Reid knew the show was a whopping success when an antiques dealer from California got off the bus and knocked on his door at four-thirty in the morning on the Friday the show was to begin. By 1970, Reid was hosting three shows, each two days in length, in May, July, and September, and each was drawing seven hundred dealers and ten thousand buyers. The show's reputation was moving from regional to national and soon to international.

Part of its appeal was the quality of the merchandise at Brimfield. "You could always see the very best of a given form," said David Rose, a Massachusetts antiques dealer. "I remember one time two guys brought in a formal Victorian wicker wire plant stand," he said. "It was absolutely the best piece of its type I had ever seen."

Tractor trailers would arrive from California, Texas, and the South and load up throughout the day. The market was sought after because of all its Victorian oak and walnut, wicker, glass, and china. Buyers were eager to buy. Doc LeVarn, an antiques dealer from New Hampshire, remembers pulling onto the Reid field and "you would sell a bunch of stuff that you did not even have to unload from the truck. People would come up and ask what you had and they would pay for it right there. Or they would come the night before with their flashlights and say they wanted something."

Friday was technically dealer's day, when the dealers were supposed to be setting up, but there were no restrictions on selling. Smart buyers came on Friday too, or Friday night, which was often called bargain night. On that evening Brimfield never seemed to close. Beall, the Brimfield town clerk, recalls: "We would have parties at our house and people would come in after shopping and say, 'You would not believe what I just bought at the flea market.' They would show an old sword, a gun or other antique they had just bought out on the fields. It was a magical time."

Buyers toted flashlights, sellers hung kerosene lanterns, and any dealer who fell asleep in his car or van might be jarred awake by a knock on the car door or window in the middle of the night. The Woodbine stayed open all Friday night to feed the hungry. "It never seemed to slow down," agreed David Rose. "We always kept somebody up the entire night because the trading would continue at all hours. You could make your best sale at three in the morning. And sometimes it wasn't because the buyer was necessarily sober. Sometimes a dealer would wake up the next morning and say, 'When did I buy all of this?'"

The phenomenon was not lost on Gordon Reid's neighbors, many of whom decided after a few years to cash in. Lois Shelton, who grew up across the street from the Reids, remembered putting up a sign in the late sixties advertising parking for a dollar. Within ten minutes she had parked twenty cars and netted twenty dollars. "I was astonished," she said. "I had never made money so quickly. I immediately went across the street and spent it." Other neighbors also were parking cars and profiting nicely. That discovery was an early harbinger of the changes to befall Brimfield.

In November 1974 Gordon Reid Sr. died at sixty-five of a heart attack. The loss hit Madelyn Reid hard. "We had worked together for thirty-seven years, every single day of our married life. We were together morning, noon, and night," she told a reporter. She asked her son and two daughters and their husbands to help. At the time none were living in Brimfield. Gordon Reid Jr., who was called Punchy, left his job managing a radio station near Providence, Rhode Island, and ran the May 1975 show. Judy and Jacques Mathieu moved back from Florida, while Jill and her husband, Peter Lukesh, helped from their home near Boston. Almost immediately a family feud began. The two sisters and their husbands converted an old cornfield about a half-mile down Route 20 into a new market, Antique Acres, and competed openly with their brother. "We—my sisters, my mother and I—had what is probably the most widely publicized family squabble since the Hatfields and the McCoys," said Punchy Reid a few years later. Neither side ever really explained why it happened. Fred Dole, the longtime family friend, said he never asked about it. Judy Mathieu, who serves as the family spokeswoman, will not discuss it.

The family rivalry doubled the number of dealer spaces at Brimfield. That was just the beginning of the expansion. A long waiting list to get onto the Reid field had been in place; everyone wanted to deal at Brimfield. The expansion began innocently enough with dealers selling out of their cars before the Reid fields opened. Owners who had been renting their lots out for parking realized they could make far more money by renting dealer spaces. Beginning in 1975, and continuing for the next twenty years, more and more fields opened. Lois Shelton said she began renting spaces because she was tired of chasing dealers off her property. Neighbor

Diane Sturdevant said she was weary of people "peeking in my dining room window." "It's been a zoo," said another neighbor, Richard Ethier, at the time. "At least now that we have joined them we get something out of it." Others, such as Don Moriarty, who sold the Woodbine and plunged into debt, and Dick May, a local contractor, bought land along Route 20. "Interest rates at the time were quite high and we did not have a lot of financial resources," says Moriarty. "But I never thought it was a gamble."

By 1981 there were 11 field owners renting space to a total of 2,350 dealers and drawing crowds of 50,000. As its reputation grew, Brimfield drew more and more buyers not only from the United States but also from Europe, South America, and Asia. Brimfield veterans still talk about the Japanese dealers who walked down the aisles, selecting, recording, and buying huge quantities of specialty antiques, and the Argentinean who one year purchased everything he could find that said Coca-Cola. Many remember the first two decades of the Brimfield shows as the golden years, when dealers and buyers would sit around campfires at night playing guitars and singing. Action was available all day and all night, not only antiques but also big card games, parties, and hookers.

Others watched this growth with mounting concern. "This is not at all the way Gordon envisioned it," said Madelyn Reid in a 1980 newspaper article. "If this had happened when he was alive, he might have chucked the whole thing," agreed Punchy Reid. It certainly was not what most Brimfield residents had expected. Many complained of the riffraff the market drew, which caused everything from long traffic jams on Route 20 to a higher incidence of burglaries in local homes. Perhaps most distressing was that the number of days the shows were open kept getting longer. "Everyone wants to have an opening day, and that's the reason the shows just got longer and longer," says Shelton. "Things started expanding by opening on Friday across the street, and then we opened on Thursday. The dealers would come in on Wednesday to set up and after they were doing that for awhile we said, 'Well, maybe you should come in on Tuesday.'" It did not hurt that field owners could raise their rent for each additional day the dealers hung around.

The growth also upset residents and town officials. "Flea markets are like poison ivy," said then-selectman Richard Raymond. "When it gets to the crotch, that's when you scream." It was getting there. Residents gathering each spring for that unique New England institution, the annual town meeting, spent the increasingly heated sessions debating an ever longer list of concerns over the flea market. The warrants ranged from banning the market to strictly regulating it. Some field operators were being hauled into local court for violating the town's zoning ordinances by running a flea market in a residential zone. "You were at the mercy of whoever was on the board of selectmen or the building inspector at the time," says Shelton. "If they came in and did not like what they saw, they could close you down."

By the early 1980s some of the town's anger was beginning to dissipate. In 1977 the town fathers finally realized, just as had many of Gordon Reid's neighbors, that it made more sense to cash in on rather than fight the shows. That year a new bylaw was adopted restricting the number of days the antiques fair could be open and also assessing a three-dollar fee on every dealer. A couple of years later the town raised it to five dollars, and then to ten. With cash suddenly pouring in, the fleas were considered far less a problem. "Hey, if we have to be the flea market capital of the world, it's time the town got something out of it," said then-selectman Jean McGann.

Most field operators and dealers grudgingly accepted the new fee system and restrictions, but not Punchy Reid. He only got angrier each time the town raised its price. Finally, he sued. By then, Reid seemed to be fighting with everyone. His feud extended to his mother. Some suggest the break occurred when Reid tried to add a fourth show in October 1981 over her strong objections. The show was a failure—attendance was terrible. Stories about Punchy Reid's drinking and his erratic behavior were all over town, including rumors about his taking an ice pick to the tires of a lost motorist who pulled into Reid's driveway looking for directions. "He was a tough guy to deal with," said Fred Dole, whom Madelyn Reid asked to help out on the field after her husband's death. Dole lasted only one summer with Punchy Reid and then began working with the Reid sisters. "He had a drinking problem, and when he began to drink, he became difficult," said Dole. In 1982, Punchy Reid announced he was moving to New York. "The town of Brimfield doesn't want us," he said, "so we don't want them."

The idea of having a farewell party in honor of Brimfield arose at a lobster boil early in the week of the September 1982 show. As Gerry Dooley remembers it, about fifty dealers had each pitched in ten bucks for all the lobster, corn on the cob, and potato salad they could eat on Tuesday night. When everyone was stuffed, they still had $200 left. The logical solution was to have another party: hot dogs and beer,

Dooley's booth, 6 P.M. Friday. Everyone agreed to invite everyone. This might be the last Brimfield show, and if it was, Brimfield was going out with a glorious wake.

By now Punchy Reid was determined to leave Brimfield. A headline in the local newspaper that week had announced: "This flea market could end an era." Reid had bought a hundred and fifty acres in Duanesburg, New York, sixteen miles from Albany. Next year he would stage his first antiques show a week before Brimfield was to open. He was talking as many dealers as possible into coming to New York. "He said he wanted to bury Brimfield," recalled Tom Breen, who had gone to the first Brimfield as a youngster with his father.

Dooley thought Punchy Reid's plan was crazy. Yet he himself was considering going to Duanesburg next spring. Dooley liked to gamble. Reid wanted Dooley in New York not just for his ability to hawk Taiwan-manufactured junk but also for his pranks.

It had been Dooley who one night had ripped up a supply of feather pillows and layered the down stuffing on the roofs of a row of tents. The night dew quickly pasted the fine layers of down onto the tarpaulins, and at dawn the rays of the rising sun struck the first tent, slowly drying the feathers and freeing them to rain down on bewildered buyers and sellers. It took hours for the sunlight to move down that row of tents and hours for the blizzard of feathers to subside.

Early Friday evening Dooley dug a huge pit behind his tent and dumped what he felt was about a cord of firewood into it. He doused the logs with Coleman fuel and they ignited with a roar. For a moment Dooley and others watched in awe. He wondered how he was going to cook on such a fire. Antique copper buckets were soon filled with water from the creek that passed Punchy Reid's field. Quickly the potatoes and corn were boiling and the dogs were ready to be roasted. By now it was after six and Dooley began to worry whether enough people were going to show to eat the chow. That's when he heard what sounded like a low bellow. He looked up, and he saw a wave, a throng of humanity pouring through the gate onto Reid's field. In a few minutes Reid arrived, his pickup loaded with booze, with cases and kegs of beer and countless bottles of cold duck champagne.

Reports of what happened over the next twelve hours are clouded by a haze of bravado fueled by junk food, endless swills of alcohol, blaring music from impromptu sound systems, and the high flames of a bonfire on a starry summer night. Dooley's fondest memory was of dancing the cancan with two women on top of a bus. The rotund dealer had no idea how any of them scampered on top of the vehicle or how they got down. It was not clear how many times the cops came, but it was clear that they were stymied by the size of the crowd and by the realization that they had no way to jail five hundred drunken revelers. Plus someone kept feeding wieners to the police dogs. The Brimfield firefighters were squirted with streams of cold duck. They may have responded playfully with small blasts from their fire hoses. They also trained the hoses on the blaze, dousing it with enough water to create a small lake inside the pit. As soon as they left, Punchy found some cardboard barrels full of trash and threw them in the hole. Dooley splashed the remaining Coleman fuel on the debris and lit it. Slowly the fire rose again. But it needed more fuel. According to legend, this was the moment when Dooley and friends began burning antiques. Joel Schiff still remembers it as the moment Dooley sacrificed his antiques, moving forever into the retail world where he sold only new or surplus items. He was sad to see it happen. But Dooley says this is not quite what happened. It began when a dealer remembered an old blanket chest he had been trying to sell all summer. It had a rotted back and no one wanted it. The dealer tossed it into the flames. Another dealer produced an antique wagon wheel with several busted spokes and in it went. "Pretty soon we had anywhere from three to five thousand dollars' worth of antiques that were burning in the fire," said Dooley. "We were contributing them to the Great Bonfire God."

Some sacrifices were prevented. A dealer who sold player pianos actually stopped several drunken revelers who had been wheeling one of his instruments toward the fire. He spent the rest of the night guarding his pianos from another onslaught. Another dealer who sold carved wooden decoys threw in a duck because, he explained, it had a cracked rear. Someone else pulled it out. It was christened Fred Fowler, the duck with the singed ass. Dooley kept it for years as a remembrance of the party, until someone chopped off Fred's head.

When the sun finally peeked above the horizon at dawn, anyone arriving would have thought that some horrific plague had swept across Brimfield, striking down the innocent in their tracks. Men and women had collapsed amid vomit and piss on the town green, around the town hall, across Punchy's field, and on down Route 20. Groggy and hung over, as the sun rose and the heat built, they awoke and tottered slowly away. Sales that Saturday were horrible. In hindsight, the size and ferocity of the party were overwhelming to many of the participants. The magnitude of what became known as "The Party" may have owed to an unusual confluence of events, as the power and wealth of the great show collided with the fear of Brimfield's demise. "People were worried," said Dooley. "No one knew what was going to happen. So we had one big rip-snorting take-the-dragon party."

No one doubted that Punchy Reid meant to destroy Brimfield. "I do feel that my leaving will have a definite impact upon the Brimfield Flea Markets," he warned. Others shrugged off the threat. Buttons appeared around Brimfield in 1983 that said simply: "Gordon who?" "My brother is building an entirely new show in Duanesburg," Judy Mathieu told a reporter that year. "He will have to work very hard to be successful."

Practically from the time he arrived in New York Punchy encountered problems. Reid was immediately confronted by what was called the Woodstock Rules—a complex, intimidating set of regulations developed after the famous nearby 1969 rock concert. Lois Shelton believes that Reid might have prevailed if he had not been so revengeful. "His whole point was that he wanted to kill Brimfield," she said. "He could have been a success out there, but he was so anxious to dilute Brimfield that he started to cut corners. The [Duanesburg] field was not really in a position to be opened, even though he had these grandiose plans on what he wanted to do out there. When the first show opened, there were not enough services for the dealers. There were no phones, there were not enough rest rooms, and there was not enough food." Worse yet, it rained, turning his fields into a muddy quagmire. Dealers got stuck and buyers stayed away. "I lost my shirt in that show," recalled Gerry Dooley. "It was a muddy mess where everyone had to be pulled out of the mud by trucks," said Shelton. "When it rained the next show, he was finished." Gordon Reid Jr. lived on quietly at what he called his Pine Grove Farm. He got along better with his neighbors, even when they kidded him and called him "The Rain-maker." He died in January 1990 at age forty-eight.

It rained in Brimfield too during Punchy's Woodstock summer, but the crowds kept coming. "We have a full house of dealers," Judy Mathieu reported after the September 1983 show. During the year the two sisters took back control of their father's field and soon returned it to its original Friday and Saturday schedule. They called their company J&J Pro-motions, the name they still use. As part of their agreement, Madelyn Reid was no longer involved in the shows. She died in March 1987. It took a few more years for the town to control just which days the shows could run, but eventually the field promoters agreed after they began to realize that a regular schedule would help them. Too many times a tour bus of buyers pulled in to Brimfield a day after the show had closed or a dealer arrived on his normal day for setup only to discover that the field had opened a day early.

However, cooperation from both dealers and field own-ers can vary. Monday has become the day on which dealers can only set up and a town ordinance prohibits any selling. Police sometimes patrol the fields on Mondays and issue ci-tations to dealers selling in violation of the ordinance. The citations are not a great deterrent. A former Brimfield police chief, Jack Jovian, explained: "I had one guy complain to me that he had bought a rug from a dealer, he had a bill of sale, and now the seller was reneging." During the conversation the chief learned the buyer had made the purchase illegally on Monday. The buyer was not concerned. "Look," the buyer told the chief, "I was going to make twenty thousand off that rug by the time I sold it to someone else, so I really was not worried about your twenty-five-dollar fine." The result is that field owners do not pay attention to what is happening on their fields, and buyers and sellers make deals while watching out for the police. Buyers are careful, usually asking a dealer if he or she is interested in making a sale tonight. Or they come to an arrangement, but the cash and merchandise are not transferred until the next morning. The selling continues deep into the night. Flashlights and lanterns are turned off when dealers hear that a uniform is walking the aisles.

Within the antiques industry Brimfield is famous. It has been studied by the Smithsonian Institution, filmed by television networks ranging from HGTV to the BBC, and promoted around the world. Other shows strive to compare themselves with Brimfield, from one in Atlanta that calls itself the Brimfield of the South to another in Newark, England, that maintains it is the Brimfield of Europe. Today there are hundreds, if not thousands, of flea markets and antiques shows and they come in all flavors and colors. There is a show in the Rose Bowl in California and one off the boardwalk in Atlantic City. Shows can run once a year, like one in Miami Beach each January that draws wealthy customers from Europe or South America. Others operate daily year-round, such as the big flea market just up the highway in Fort Lauderdale that hawks surplus items such as flashy tube socks. One flea market, held one weekend each summer, stretches along 450 miles of Route 127 from Covington,

Kentucky, to Gadsen, Alabama. The only show that even begins to match the legend of Brimfield is Round Top, in Texas. Like Brimfield it occurs for only one week twice a year (not three times) and it is spread across numerous fields. But it is decidedly more retail than wholesale, producing quality goods for the burghers fat on oil and real estate who drive in from Houston and Dallas. Sometimes a buyer's ignorance about antiques can make dealers wince, but only inwardly, especially when a customer pulls out his wallet. A Texas dealer who goes to both Round Top and Brimfield concedes that the Massachusetts show is decidedly more big league. "Round Top starts later and it is more laid-back," he says. "The buyers are not as fanatical or as knowledgeable as they are here at Brimfield. If you want to find the people who know antiques, you come here."

Despite its reputation, Brimfield is facing a new challenge. In the last few years attendance has been falling in both the number of dealers setting up and in buyers attending. It's not just happening at Brimfield. Antiques shows throughout the country are smaller, with fewer dealers, fewer goods, and fewer buyers. With the reduced demand come lower prices. Dealers always like to complain, but many say they are making less money. Some blame this decline on an ailing economy and a post-9/11 nervousness. Most are convinced that there is a bigger culprit, one that has affected everyone in the antiques and collectibles market—the Internet.

The Internet and companies such as eBay have been threatening the retailing of America since their arrival in the mid-1990s. During the early boom years of the dot.coms, many predicted the demise of physical markets. Then came

the high-tech crash and many traditional retailers and mar-
keters were reassured that their future was not lost. That is
not the case, however, with antiques, collectibles, or markets
such as Brimfield. The giant electronic marketplace eBay has
only become more powerful each year. By the May 2003
Brimfield show, eBay was enormous, with eighty-five million registered users and twenty billion dollars in sales. Up
and down the dusty lanes of Brimfield, the Internet and
eBay elicit a mixture of admiration, respect, reservation,
scorn, and distrust, sometimes from the same people.

Buyers and sellers embrace eBay. No longer do they have
to drive hundreds of miles and bake under a hot sun or get
drenched in a downpour. Increased access, however, also
has produced increased competition. Now dealers and buyers are not only competing with whoever shows up at a field
but also with anyone who clicks on an Internet site. Prices
have begun doing strange things, first rising and then de-
clining as electronic, and then physical, markets are over-
whelmed with far more pieces of Depression glass or Steiff
bears than anyone knew existed or had seen before. Prices
have fallen so far that some antiques dealers are struggling
to make money. Some say that the increased volume and increased knowledge brought by eBay makes it harder to find
big scores. Others say there are more scams and fake goods,
not only at Brimfield but also on eBay, than ever before.

Buyers, collectors, and field owners at Brimfield are
worried and concerned about the future. Can Brimfield survive this threat? It has survived others, from a field owner
who tried to move the whole show to New York to local residents who consider it a nuisance and would like to see it
permanently closed down. But those perils were easier to

understand and to overcome. eBay is so huge, so amorphous, so complex. There is a rumor at the show that someone from eBay is coming here, someone in the hierarchy who is intent on building a better relationship between the biggest electronic marketplace and the largest physical antiques market. Don Moriarty hopes to talk to him and so does Tim May, Dick May's son. Tim May has been taking over more of the business from his father, while trying to build his own website. Moriarty has allowed eBay access to his field in the past. Moriarty is unafraid of eBay. "My feeling is that eBay will help Brimfield more than it will hurt," he explains. "eBay can't produce products, it is only a marketplace. This is where people come to buy the products, some of which they will sell on eBay and elsewhere."

Perhaps. But not everyone is convinced that Brimfield and America's great antiques shows have the magic they once had.

CHAPTER 3

The Rush

WHILE JOE AND Rachel were out Tuesday looking for bargains, Howard Roberts spent the day stocking his tent at the New England Motel field, named after the quaint 1950s-style motel that is almost hidden by the city of tents, booths, and antiques. Now it is Wednesday morning, just before six, and the rush is about to begin. Wednesday is a morning of rushes. The New England Motel opens in just minutes. Roberts, whose tent is at the front gate, is surprised at how thick the crowd is this year.

Some people come to Brimfield intent on finding bargains or prizes. Others such as Roberts come primarily to sell. The hardcore buyers and sellers all share the same desire to discover something precious but they vary in where they favor finding it. Roberts prefers searching homes abandoned by their owners through death or other reasons. He especially finds that basements and attics can yield the most fantastic stuff.

Although Roberts has his shop in Malvern, Pennsylvania, he spends much of the year at antiques shows, and

Brimfield is one of his favorites. "Brimfield is a great show," he says. "It's a chance to take just about anything to the show. I can sell anything here."

There was the ocean-liner deck chair and the twelve-foot propeller from a World War I aircraft that included a picture of the pilot and the tale of his exploits. And of course there were the three life-size toy soldiers he had acquired from a toy store that was going out of business. Roberts sold the three to a couple who had a huge estate that they decorated each year with a bigger and bigger Christmas display.

This year Roberts's Brimfield merchandise is a grade below his standard. He has a Texas-style hat rack with cow horns; a mounted sailfish; a traffic light blinking green, yellow, and red; a physician's surgical instrument kit from the late nineteenth century; and a Philadelphia museum case with the drawers holding displays of flax, cotton, sugar, hemp, salt, and other materials. He almost brought a twelve-foot-tall Santa Claus. But the huge figure weighed a ton, and he would have had to rent a larger truck just to get it here.

No one knows what will show up at Brimfield. A year ago John Mathews brought a modest oak cabinet, lashed to the roof of his Volvo station wagon. Mathews had found it three days before at a yard sale in Long Island. He saw it at ten-thirty on a Saturday morning, long after the professionals should have picked through every sale on the island. He was not even shopping, he was on his way to the post office, but he knew he was coming to Brimfield, so he stopped and asked the price. It was $85. It was a nice piece, six feet high and thirty-three inches wide, and when he got it home he carefully searched, unsuccessfully, for any indication of who had made it. On Tuesday he drove onto the Dealer's Choice field at Brimfield ninety minutes before the gates opened. Immediately a dealer saw the cabinet and asked how much he wanted. Mathews was surprised. He was really a collector, not a dealer. He was only here because his friend Bill Grotheer had invited him to set up. Plus, his specialty was stoneware and country furniture, not oak.

"What do you think?" he asked Grotheer.

"I don't know anything about it," replied Grotheer.

Mathews was going to ask $500, but the cabinet was very heavy and he did not want to take it home with him. "Give me three hundred fifty and you can have it," he told the dealer.

The first hint that he might have made a mistake came a moment later when another dealer spotted the cabinet and was upset to learn it had already been sold. He began cursing loudly. That brought other dealers to look at it as the new buyer carried it away. Later in the morning the cabinet sold for $13,000. Word was that later in the week that buyer doubled his money when it was sold again.

The cabinet had been made by Gustav Stickley, one of the most renowned furniture makers of the late nineteenth and early twentieth centuries and a leader of what became known as the American Arts and Crafts Movement. A similar Stickley piece had recently sold at auction for $20,000, and several dealers had seen pictures of it in antiques trade publications and recognized Mathews's cabinet as a twin. "I knew it was attractive," said Mathews later. "I went through that thing inside and out and I could not find a manufacturer's marker. But somehow they found it."

Somehow they always do, especially during the rush.

Even before the bell chimes at six on this Wednesday morning, and the crowd surges through the gate of the New

England Motel field, Roberts sells 125 old *Sports Illustrated*s. Then the crowd is gone. This field has a second gate in the back. It's a given that the crowd from each gate will run past the other in the first moments of the rush.

Over the years the Brimfield rush has become legendary in the antiques world. At some booths buyers have been known to line up eight deep and literally throw hundred-dollar bills at dealers who cannot keep up with the pace. Sometimes competitors who know each other race to reach the same booth. One year a television network wanted to capture the magic of Brimfield's rush. A cameraman secured a very tall stepladder inside the gate, so that he could get a good shot of the crowd as it lunged through the gates at May's. Somebody in the May family recalled suggesting to the cameraman that while this might yield a good picture, it might not be a wise place to perch. The crowd may be composed of adults, but when the gates open, they run like children. Sure enough, when 9 A.M. came, the crowd bowled right over the ladder, sending camera and cameraman down. No one was seriously injured.

No buyer relishes the rush more than the one-legged collector of cast-iron cookware, Joel Schiff. Schiff is up as early as four-thirty and is near the front of the crowd at fields such as New England Motel that have an opening hour. When he arrives before dealers set up, he is annoyed. "It was never like this years ago," he complains one day. "People used to be raring to go. Now they stroll in with their coffees and sit down in their chairs and take their time. It's becoming like a Southern market."

The latter phrase is said with derision, although Schiff concedes he may be exaggerating. At other shows, especially in the South and the West, the peak buying period is midday. The pace can be agonizingly slow, says one dealer. At a three-day Southern show he has seen buyers spend the first day reviewing the merchandise, the second day examining the dealer (including the issue of whether he was of good Christian stock), and the third day finally getting down to price. Such behavior is heresy at Brimfield. Brimfield remains a market for the driven. Many of the people, whether buyers or sellers, know each other well. They follow the same network of shows and auctions throughout the year. The distinction is that dealers often save their best for Brimfield. "Brimfield is not great for prices, but the thing about Brimfield is that you can find things you might not find anywhere else," says one major antiques dealer. "There are no amateurs at Brimfield."

Schiff moves rapidly during the rush, buying a small Griswold No. 6 griddle while passing on what appears to be a small glue pot, a mechanical grinder, a waffle iron, and a cider press—all of cast iron. He also does not buy a rusty, four-foot-diameter flat metal object that a dealer swears was used as a huge skillet in a lumberjack camp in the backwoods of Maine.

He finds a muffin pan he likes except for the $100 price tag.

"Why do you want that price?" he asks the dealer.

"Because it's rare," replies the dealer, a stocky man in his forties.

"It's rare because I want it, isn't that what you mean?"

"No, Joel," he replies, with a touch of irritation in his voice. "I've been selling cast iron since I was young and I would sell Griswolds for anywhere from seven fifty to eleven dollars. But in all my years I have never seen anything like this." The dealer is referring to the Griswold Manufacturing Company, which for a century made America's best cast-iron cookware. He points to the name Griswold in the middle of the pan and the initials PPP SEP 1870.

"But you don't go by that," responds Schiff. "You can't go by the name. You go by what the shape is, and the design."

"Joel, I did my part. I found it."

Despite the exchange, Schiff almost buys the muffin tin for $90 until he finds two small cracks. He passes on it.

The second field on this Wednesday opens at nine when Heart-O-The-Mart opens its gates. Joe and Rachel prop paintings up against their tent but hardly sell anything that they have brought from home. At noon a different kind of rush begins on Jeanne Hertan's field. She and her manager, David Lamberto, allow the two hundred dealers to park and set up and they invite all buyers onto the field. However, they prohibit the dealers from removing any wares or displaying them until noon. The result is a controlled frenzy that feeds Brimfield's image as wild and wacky.

The starting signal is always the same. Hertan, dressed in a white cowgirl outfit complete with shiny white boots and a ten-gallon hat, takes her place on the porch of her ranch house. At noon, she rings a metal bell hanging on the porch. The response is a sharp metallic clang. The crowd erupts into movement. Truck doors open, tent flaps are pulled back, boxes hoisted. Movements become a blur, a tableau of energy, as dealers hurry to unload everything from brass bed stands to shiny nickel buttons.

On this day a large crowd gathers around four panel trucks parked in the field to the south of Hertan's house. As soon as he hears the bell, a man in charge signals several of the young, stocky men waiting by the truck. They climb up to the open doors, and soon objects, packed in newspaper and brown paper, tumble to the ground. Other workers unwrap them, but not as fast as customers, who grab some of the tossed objects and begin forming their own piles of merchandise. The hundreds of wrapped objects are revealed to be metal pails, wrought-iron plant holders, watering cans, baskets, and worn wooden flower boxes. It is hard to tell who is moving faster, the men unloading the truck or the buyers picking stuff off the ground.

A young man watches in amazement. "This has to be the most ridiculous way of doing things," he says to no one in particular. "It's crazy."

For twenty minutes the cascade of objects keeps pouring out. The man directing the workers examines the crowd and concludes that many have lost their touch of frenzy. "In ten minutes, everything doubles in price," he yells. "You had better come and get it now."

"He's kidding, isn't he?" someone asks.

A few minutes later a rescue van arrives. Its siren screams, causing a few people to jump. But it does not seem to have the same effect on others as it inches slowly down one of the narrow lanes crowded with people and a growing number of antiques. Almost everyone is so busy by this point, hawking or gawking, that they are oblivious to the slow-moving truck. Fortunately, the patient only passed out briefly. By the time the paramedics arrive, he is sitting up.

Elsewhere on the field some buyers search in frustration for the doll lady, June Secrist. Medical problems have forced her to miss this May show. Secrist's booth is famous for throngs of women who grab at teddy bears, homey dolls, and other stuffed toys, all clothing made from vintage fabric, as they come out of the boxes.

Crowds gather around other tents. Some greedily grab objects, while others take one quick look and move disdainfully away. Some wear t-shirts with phrases such as "I collect old clocks" or "Swords Wanted." Others try to catch the attention of attendants still piling gear out of the truck.

"Fireworks paraphernalia?" another man asks. "Do you have anything that involves fireworks?"

"Any busted typewriters here?" asks yet another.

Field operators take different strategies when it comes to the rush. Some like to keep the crowds out until the last moment. The concept of fencing the fields and charging an admission began in the late 1970s. While the going rate is $5, scalpers sometimes charge up to $25 a ticket. The distinction is that the scalpers have acquired dealer passes, the especially prized tickets distributed early to those who are setting up. Early admission is prized because buyers can pick through the merchandise before the crowds arrive. The dealer tickets are so prized that one year someone printed counterfeits and tried to sell them. He was arrested. Two fields, Hertan's and May's, try to circumvent that problem by ordering dealers not to take anything out of their vehicles until the gates open. "It gives everyone a fair shot," explains Dick May. Not everyone likes it. "The truth is, when the gates open, there is absolutely not a thing to buy," one buyer reports. It is also not easy to enforce. Dick May recalls a year when one dealer opened early, and everyone followed. "There wasn't anything I could do about it," he says. He vowed that that would not happen again. Now he hires extra security, including former police officers, who patrol the grounds on golf carts. "Some people do get itchy and want to open, but generally we can control the dealers," he says. "Of course, you could not control the dealer who told someone, 'I have a Civil War sword right here in the truck,' and he had them stand right there until he opened the truck."

Gordon Reid's old field has retained its reputation as the premiere field at Brimfield. But the rush there will have to wait for Friday. Reid's two daughters continue to open the field only two days for each show, Friday and Saturday. Jill, Judy, and their husbands continue to maintain that there is no need for more than a two-day show. "Jacques and the girls have always had something of a chip on their shoulders in dealing with the other fields," says Beall. "Despite all the years, they still have never really accepted any of the other fields, and they continue to wish they would go away."

Buyers have been known to become so frantic to get in that some even try to scale the fence early. Judy Mathieu says one of those climbers fell one day and broke his leg. "He told me at one point he was going to sue us," says Jacques Mathieu, Judy's husband. "I said, 'Well, that's going to be pretty difficult because before you leave here, I'm going to have you arrested for trespassing.' He kind of quieted down after that." A portion of the property is protected by only a creek, and one year it became obvious that one young man really wanted to get an early start by leaping across it. "He would break from the line and come down and look at the creek," says Judy Mathieu. "Then he would go back, and break from the line again and look at the creek. Finally he came down, then backed off, and ran for the creek and leaped." Jacques Mathieu likes to keep the weeds up high along the creek to disguise just how wide that little creek can be. *Splash* went the intruder. Adds Judy: "By this point I was going down there with a couple of the guys and we helped fish him out. We told him he was going to have to go back outside. So he headed for the bridge, but I said no, not that way, the way you came. So he trampled through the creek, getting wet all over again. Meanwhile everyone is clapping and jeering the entire time this is all happening."

CHAPTER 4

Joe and Rachel

By the time the rush is fading at Hertan's field early Wednesday afternoon, Joe Laskowski makes a surprising realization. He is not going to find a single painting here. He is disappointed. Rachel is also taken aback. Joe has been on such a buying binge for two days, she did not see the end coming. Joe has purchased twenty and sold ten, making money every time. Joe is so willing to take risks that something usually develops. Rachel has not yet adjusted to Joe's quick and, in her view, near-reckless pace. She prefers a safer route, but that approach, at least over the last two days, will not pay the bills. She has bought only one painting, and she wound up returning it. Earlier in the day she had purchased a still life for $400. But when she took it out of the frame and looked at it more carefully, she began to suspect that it was a painted-over print. She showed it to several friends who are art dealers, Chris Smith, Mike Pacitti, Fran Smith, and others. Opinions were mixed. Rachel's uneasiness grew. She did not want to take the risk. She returned the painting/print, and the seller did not argue too much, although he wasn't happy. He refunded her money.

Rachel is beginning to wonder why she is at Brimfield. "I'm at the point where I don't care if I ever do another Brimfield," she says, sighing. She is standing beside a mill pond as serene as one of the Impressionist landscape paintings of her native eastern Pennsylvania that she favors. The water glistens in the sunlight and fades to the far shore where a single Colonial farmhouse rises up on a grassy green slope. The stillness of the scene is broken only by the chirping of songbirds and the occasional car that passes on the distant road atop the pond's embankment.

Joe and Rachel are still getting to know each other, still exploring a relationship both believe holds promise. They met a year ago. With Rachel just coming out of an understanding with another man, Joe wasn't even sure they should date. But they did, and one thing led to another. By fall they were hunting for a house they could buy together. They searched the towns west of Philadelphia, where Rachel had grown up, and their price limit had been $160,000, maybe $170,000. The Realtor asked if they had a dream house. Rachel knew she would love an older farmhouse, with some acreage, near a lake or creek, and if there were space, a separate apartment for her father, Willard "Bidge" McKay. They also needed room for her rottweiler, Ryzo. Named after a survivor of the atomic bombs dropped on Japan at the end of World War II—he escaped radiation poisoning by jumping into a pool for twenty minutes—Ryzo definitely needed to be able to roam.

So when the real estate agent found the two-hundred-year-old farmhouse with a separate building for her father, on

nineteen and a half acres along Perkiomen Creek, it was difficult to resist. Not only had the house aged well over the last
two centuries, but it also came with provenance. Henry
Mitchell, a famous sculptor, was a previous owner. According
to local lore, Mitchell also owned an old mill just downstream
and he often partied there with the well-heeled Annenbergs.
Carl Zigrosser, a famous print collector and author, had been
a neighbor. (Later Joe and Rachel would find a book by Zigrosser that contained pictures of their house.) The down-
stairs and the living room were lined with shelves ready for
Joe's collection of art books. The house had been on the market only one week and it was already under contract. The
price under that deal was $265,000. That was $100,000 more
than what Joe and Rachel wanted to pay, but the property also
had more potential. The rental apartment on the land, where
Rachel's father could live, significantly increased their ability
to pay the mortgage. They were so convinced that this was an
ideal property and a good deal that they bid $10,000 above the
asking price of $265,000. At first, it did not look as though they
were going to get it. Then the other bidder withdrew his offer.
Rachel was excited about acquiring the property. The main
house has one-foot-thick flagstone walls in the oldest part of
the structure and is long and narrow, with views of the creek
from every room. The Perkiomen looks more like a small
river; it has to be 150 feet across and it flows within ten feet of
the house. On sunny mornings, it dapples like an Impressionist landscape. About fifteen of the nineteen and a half acres
are underwater and they include an island in the middle of
the stream. Rachel has seen a bald eagle near the island.

Joe and Rachel are ready to close on the house, but details keep surfacing. It seems that every time Rachel's cell

phone rings, it is the Realtor. First it was the issue of the septic system. Then the well. Then questions arose about the town's sewer line that passes through their property. She is already worried about paying the mortgage. These calls are only adding to her anxiety.

The sale of art is usually steeped in money, class, and prestige. Paintings are sold in galleries, often sterile rooms with high ceilings, white walls, and hot bright lamps that shine beacons on each framed work. As a painting's or an artist's reputation rises, a work moves to such financial capitals as Zurich, London, or New York, where it goes on sale at prestigious auction houses. That means a Van Gogh, which never sold for more than forty Belgian francs during the artist's lifetime, can go for $20 million, $40 million, or even $90 million.

That is not the world that Joe and Rachel inhabit. They search at the bottom of the art market. A few months ago, Joe was at a local auction where an older Oriental rug had come up for sale. No one bid on it. There was good reason: the rug was worse than threadbare. Finally, Joe bid $15. A friend asked if that was a sympathy bid.

"No, I really like the rug," Joe replied.

But when he brought it home Rachel was unimpressed. "It was really gone," she says. "It just couldn't go down in the house."

They did find one section of it that was not too deteriorated, and they cut it off, thinking they could use it to make pillows. They threw the rest out in the trash. Several weeks later they were at another auction and a rug came up for sale. The pattern looked familiar. They noticed the rug was missing one corner—the one they had cut out.

Rachel grew up with antiques. She has learned the trade from her father, who began by restoring old cars and later moved to restoring and selling antiques. Bidge McKay was incredibly handy at whatever he tackled, and like many antiques dealers he loathed a nine-to-five job. Urbane and gregarious, he could also sell when necessary. He was always around the house, while Rachel's mother was the full-time breadwinner, a lawyer for Prudential in nearby Fort Washington. Growing up, Rachel thought nothing of it. The house was filled with antiques. Sometimes pieces of furniture would disappear, often after visitors came into the house to inspect them. Her own start in the antiques business began when she was about ten years old, when her father asked her to watch the booth while he went out buying. There was one item not marked, snowshoes. Concerned, Rachel asked how she should price them. Her father said he had paid $10, wanted $15, and anything over that she could keep. While he was gone, a customer came in and asked about the snowshoes. Rachel asked $25 and the buyer agreed to that price. Her father made $5 on a $10 investment. Rachel made $10 on a zero-dollar investment. A promising beginning.

It was not always an easy childhood. One afternoon during a high-school track practice a friend and teammate told Rachel he had a gun and was going to kill himself. While she did not believe him, suicide was not unheard of among adolescents; a senior had killed himself the year before. Soon thereafter, Bidge McKay, who was on the volunteer ambulance department, was one of the first to respond to a call from Rachel's friend's home. The young man had successfully carried out his threat. Rachel began to feel abandoned. The previous summer, one of her best friends had

suddenly died in her sleep after sustaining a brain hemor-
rhage. Also, her older sister had left for boarding school. At
nearly the same time, another student in the school killed
himself. Rachel's world was unraveling. She was hospital-
ized for three weeks. After she finished her sophomore year,
her parents and she decided she would be better off not returning to the local high school, and Rachel chose Westtown, a Quaker boarding school. It was a choice she later
regretted. Some of her youth-group friends had attended
Westtown, but Rachel found the school too confining, and
she was upset that not very many of the students shared the
Quaker philosophies she learned growing up. Within two
months she ran away. "I had an epiphany," she says. "I realized that anything is better than killing yourself, so why
not just do something crazy? I didn't have to do what was
expected of me—I could run away, I could take a trip across
country." She came home after two weeks that were mostly
spent with friends in Princeton. Later, she spent a week in
Florida with her father, sorting through what she should do.
At the end of the week, she told him she was not going back
to either school. Instead, she took two part-time jobs and
earned her Graduate Equivalency Degree six months before
she would have graduated. She left immediately for Antioch College in Ohio.

College was a relief after such a troubling adolescence.
She took painting classes, had the opportunity to undertake
several internships, and majored in creative writing. After
her graduation it took about six months of traveling and
then working as a landscaper back in her college town before she concluded she was not going to make a career in creative writing. She went to work alongside her father, who by

then was handling antiques at Alderfer Auction Company in nearby Hatfield, Pennyslvania. She had already worked there part-time one year, photographing and preparing catalogs. Now she was assigned to inventory consignments. She reported on each item brought in, describing it as completely as possible.

Rachel had the greatest difficulty evaluating antique rugs and the easiest time assessing paintings. It was difficult enough to sort out furniture and decorative items, but rugs were just impossible to catalog. She had always loved art, which was why she had taken painting classes in college. Art also seemed easier to quantify. Usually the artist was listed, and it was easy to look up the painting or a comparable work by that artist. Still, she noticed that other, more experienced dealers could just take a look at certain elements of a painting, the frame, the back of the canvas, the pigment, and make out much more than she could.

"How do you do that?" she asked art dealers who came into Alderfer's to bid on a work.

"You just know," they would reply. "You just learn. You learn to judge a painting on its merit."

In time she did, but it was three to five years before she was comfortable with her judgment. By then she had left Alderfer's after her parents divorced. She had become uncomfortable working with her father, feeling somehow that she was being disloyal to her mother. Shortly after that, circumstances brought her to Radford, Virginia, where she worked part-time for the Ken Farmer Auction Company, and then to New Jersey, where she began to work in Mike McClintock's Lambertville art gallery. McClintock was a self-made dealer who had built a thriving art business. He was not always easy to work with, and Rachel worked in his gallery only for six months. Too often, she felt, he had assigned her menial tasks. She spent too much time dismantling frames and sweeping the floor. McClintock likes Rachel. That's why he had hired her and why he continues to buy from and sell to her. "Rachel liked to learn," he says, "and I liked to teach." Over the years he was impressed by how much she picked up. Yet he worried sometimes that she was still a little too tentative, a little too afraid to trust her own instincts. In the summer of 1993 or 1994, and in succeeding years, he offered to pay Rachel $100 a day to set up and sell art for him at Brimfield. Rachel does not remember much about that first trip to Brimfield, except that she was very busy. She had limited opportunities to get out on the fields, although she did find two paintings. One was a landscape that she bought for $200 and was unable to sell. She eventually put it up for auction and got back only $150. The other was a watercolor and she paid $900 for it.

In the summer of 1997, Rachel decided to work for herself with the support of the seemingly endless supply of art and other treasures discovered by Jim Meyer, an expert picker and friend of her father's. Meyer was both a dealer and an art restorer. He worked three days a week in his mother-in-law's beer distribution business and the rest of his time in antiques, especially old master prints and Pennsylvania paintings. He was helpful in passing on tips for understanding a particular painting, and he aided Rachel's self-employment by giving paintings and odd things to her that she could sell on eBay. One of Meyer's specialties was frakturs, Pennsylvania Dutch birth and baptismal documents from the early nineteenth century. When he began

collecting frakturs, which are large, ornate documents written in Dutch with colorful drawings of trees, flowers, and
birds, they could be acquired for $10 or $20 apiece. By the
mid-1990s he was getting more than $3,000 apiece for them.
Meyer urged Rachel to buy and sell what she liked and what
was important to her.

Art dealers are competitors, but they watch out for each
other. Rachel and McClintock are still tied together every
time they return to Brimfield. They have made an arrangement so that Rachel rents a space at Heart-O-The-Mart and
McClintock reimburses her. In exchange, she sells some of
McClintock's paintings and gives him two of the cherished
dealer passes needed to get on the field early. Other art dealers have similar arrangements. Fran Smith, who has been
coming to Brimfield for twenty years, rents some space at
his prime location in the front of Heart-O-The-Mart to two
other dealers, Chris Smith (who is not related) and Mike
Pacitti. When the three are scouting for paintings on the
fields, they call whoever is staffing the booth to see if a particular artist is in *Who's Who* or *Davenport*. All these dealers
come from the same geographic axis of eastern Pennsylvania and New Jersey; they often see each other at auctions;
they buy the same type of art. Their backgrounds, however,
are quite different. Fran Smith, who is over seventy, worked
for a utility company and then as an autograph dealer before he taught himself the art business the hard way, by
going to auctions and seeing what sold and for how much.
Chris Smith is forty years younger, majored in art in college,
and thought he wanted to work in a museum until he
learned that was far more boring than dealing art. Mike
Pacitti, who bridges the age gap between the two, had been

a contractor until heart bypass surgery convinced him to pursue his true love, art. Pacitti is also quite an accomplished artist and loves both painting and art restoration.

While Rachel and Joe are buying a wide variety of art, they consider their specialty to be American Impressionists. Joe favors artists from the Ashcan School, a group that early in the twentieth century painted gritty urban scenes. Rachel especially likes Pennsylvania art, an inclination that may be tied to her roots, since the McKays have been in the state for 250 years. Or perhaps it is the style of the artists. She is especially drawn to the New Hope School of Bucks County. She also specializes in the Philadelphia Ten, a group of women artists who exhibited from 1917 to 1945. The women are not as well known as the Bucks County artists, but that is all right because their paintings are far cheaper. Rachel has been buying and selling art for more than ten years, but she is still cautious in what she buys. She is good at spotting bargains and living cheaply, and over the years she has not only bought and sold paintings but also two houses upstream in the Perkiomen watershed on the Unami Creek and in New Hampshire. It was the sale of those houses that helped get the down payment on the newly purchased house. For a short time, until the mortgage closed, Rachel actually had some money in the bank and felt more like a normal, middle-class citizen than she ever had before. It was a good feeling, having pocket change and a touch of financial security.

Rachel also has to be careful with money because she has something of an exasperating weakness. She likes many of the paintings she buys. She likes them too much. As in any business, art or antiques have to be viewed as commodities if a dealer is going to be successful. When one becomes emotionally involved or attached, then it becomes difficult to assess value. The problem is that Rachel has heard too many stories from dealers such as Meyer and her father about how much some dealers would have been worth, if only they had kept more of their prizes for themselves. "Every dealer has a few of those stories," says Rachel. As Rachel buys a few Bucks County works and more from the Philadelphia Ten, she finds herself holding on to them longer and longer. Or deciding they will be part of the permanent Rachel McKay collection. There is plenty of room on the walls of the farmhouse to hang the best works, and Ryzo is there to protect them.

Joe really is not as worried as Rachel about finances. Yes, he does take chances on paintings such as the Alechinsky. It is not a big risk. He is sure that he can get his $200 back, that someone else will be just as willing to gamble in the hopes that the painting is an original. Besides, who would paint a fake Alechinsky? Not a lot of living rooms sport a surrealist, let alone an Alechinsky.

Why should Joe worry about risks when it is a miracle he is even alive? He was a miracle baby, born three months premature to parents who were already in their forties. His parents, Bernard and Kathryn, had had a healthy daughter and then over the next seventeen years Kathryn miscarried seven times. Born on Christmas Day in Pennsylvania Hospital in Philadelphia, Joe weighed two pounds three ounces and spent the next two months and two days in the hospital. Even then, he weighed only five pounds and everyone had to wear a mask when he arrived home to protect him from germs.

He had a normal childhood growing up in Delaware. But as an adult he struggled at times, never quite settling down at either school or work. One day he began ticking off all his schools and employers from over the years. He went to so many schools that he was in his mid-twenties before he got his bachelor's degree from Lenoir-Rhyne, a tiny North Carolina liberal arts college. Later he tried real estate school, paralegal school, and a master's program in educational design. Over the next ten years he was a bank employee, photo studio manager, newspaper editor and, later, news photographer, advertising salesman, collections agent, wedding photographer, manager of a leather-goods store, graphic designer, advertising salesman again, and art museum communications director. There might have been other jobs, Joe just could not remember.

Joe never frets. Over the years he has developed a confidence in his ability to see quality in a range of objects, especially in art. He bought his first painting when he was twenty at an auction near home. He knew absolutely nothing about art, but he liked this landscape. Eventually he gave it to his sister and the painting is still in the family. After that he started going to flea markets, house sales, buying only what he liked, which were mostly etchings. It was a part-time hobby that kept him busy when he was in school or working.

The turning point, the realization that he could make money off his hobby of buying art and other antiques, came one day when a cousin invited Joe to come to an art consignment shop and examine a particular etching. The cousin said he did not know who had done it, but Joe immediately thought he knew. He bought it for $150.

Joe was surprised no one had recognized the etching, because he was sure it was by James Whistler. Called *The Pi-*

azetta, it is one of twelve etchings of Venetian scenes that Whistler completed in 1879 for what was called his first Venice set. *The Piazetta* shows a square opening to St. Mark's. It is especially striking because it leaves out such details as the upper parts of the columns of St. Mark's. But, when Joe took it to a Philadelphia art gallery, the dealers there dismissed the etching's importance. They argued that it was part of a line of the least valuable of the etchings, a fifth-state print. (After the initial production of etchings, Whistler had gone back and revised it. Later states are rarely as valuable as first states.) They offered him $325. Even though the gallery had a strong reputation for prints, Joe decided to get a second opinion. At first the dealers at the second gallery were also unimpressed. They also had difficulty recognizing the print and felt it had to be a later state. They agreed to do some research, and it was a few weeks before Joe heard back from them. The etching was not a state at all; it was a very early proof before Whistler made any of the states. Joe sold the etching for $11,000, moved to Washington, D.C., and enrolled in George Washington University's art appraisal program. Now his self-schooling in art was aided by teachers who could teach him to evaluate a painting by its frame, its paper or canvas, and its oils. The courses were designed to certify antiques appraisers, so Joe also learned about other antiques, furniture, and pottery, as well as the ethics and laws associated with assessing, buying, and selling antiques. "The program was really helpful," he says. "It sort of tied up everything I had learned in the last ten years."

He worked with a dealer for a while, then took a part-time job with United Parcel Service so that he could hunt for art on his own. He likes to work alone. Even when he and Rachel arrive at a field, they usually divide up. Obviously they can cover more ground that way, but Joe really prefers to sift through paintings alone. A therapist told him that this is likely a response to his earliest days, a response to being left in the hospital after his birth. While the nurses undoubtedly took good care of him during this time, at the end of their eight-hour shifts, they all left him in the hospital. The therapist suggested that this had bred Joe's desire to be as independent as possible, to take a long time to trust people or to warm up to relationships, in art or in life. Rachel has her own reason for going solo on the fields: She does not have the patience to wait while Joe looks at every little thing. After he met Rachel, he was inspired to finally work at what he loves, discovering art, full-time.

Joe's perception of art is slightly different from that of most other dealers because he is color-blind. He cannot make out certain shades of reds and greens. Yet he has never considered this a handicap, and his biggest problem so far is that sometimes he cannot make out an artist's signature if it was painted in red. He stopped worrying years ago about his abilities to judge art, and he can recall when as a dealer he learned not to second-guess his judgment. A few years earlier he had gone for the weekend to a Catholic retreat. The retreat was outside Philadelphia and Joe and the others arrived on a Friday. "We spent the night there and then the next morning after prayers we were free to do what we wanted," he explains. "Most people stayed on the grounds and meditated but I got in my car and went out looking for paintings. They didn't say we couldn't leave and we were right off the Main Line of Philadelphia." He found an estate sale nearby. Much of everything in the house, even its design, was from the Arts and Crafts Movement. Almost everything was being sold. He came across a painting by a Spanish artist, Gonzalo Bilbao Martínez. It was for sale for $250. "I must have stood in front of that painting for two hours trying to decide whether to buy it. Two hundred and fifty dollars was a lot of money for me at the time, and I wasn't sure. I kept asking everyone who passed, 'What do you think? What do you think?' Finally another guy said he was going to buy the painting and that's when I made the decision to go ahead and buy it. I sold that painting for twelve thousand."

The rushes are over for the day. After more than thirty-six hours of frenetic activity, even Brimfield slows down at times, and Wednesday afternoon is one of them. People do get tired. After lunch, Rachel wants to deliver McClintock's unsold paintings back to his tent at Sheltons. Later, she is hoping to get over to Fran Smith's tent and talk to Mike Pacitti, the big, gentle giant of a man who is encouraging her to take up painting again. They talk art together, discussing such technical points as form, tone, texture, and color. Pacitti recommends that she read John Sloan's *Gist of Art*, a seventy-year-old classic that sets down the lessons of the recognized artist. Sloan was a member of the Ashcan School and he taught for years at the Art Students' League in New York.

Joe wants to go back to some of the fields they only passed through yesterday. He knows there has to be more art out there that everyone has missed. He relishes being a picker, being able to spend virtually all his time searching for art. It is a wonderful life, and despite the setback of not finding anything at Hertan's, Brimfield has been everything everyone promised. Flipping art here is fun. But he knows that the only way to truly make money, the only way to move up in the art world, is to go retail, to own a gallery. He has dreamed about it for years, and now that he is dealing full-time, it is closer. But not yet within reach. It will not be anytime soon, unless he or Rachel can discover something big. Rachel told him that years ago her father made a big hit, a big score, and it helped change their lives. He wonders if it can happen again.

CHAPTER 5

The Dealers

When Rachel gets to Mike McClintock's tent later on Wednesday afternoon, he is in the back, telling stories. McClintock always has good stories, especially the one about how he bought his first painting. He was looking over the wares of a dealer who had a shop on the Jersey coast when he came across a portrait that he liked. He knew immediately not to show any interest. "I knew that if I said I wanted to buy it, he would make it difficult for me and drive up the price, or maybe not sell it at all," says McClintock. "So I did not ask about the portrait, but I asked about the frame. He wanted fifteen dollars for it. I knew I had to haggle, even though it would be impossible for him to lower the price, but if I didn't he might not sell the frame at all. After we had talked about it, and he said, 'Is this for the painting too?' I said, 'You want money for that portrait too? It's not worth anything at all, I'm just going to give it to my daughter so she can turn it around and paint on it.' And he said, 'Here, just take the whole thing for fifteen dollars.'"

McClintock suspected that the portrait had been painted

by an artist named Louise Nevelson, who had studied under several artists, including Theresa Bernstein, a Philadelphia Ten painter. McClintock was working with a partner, George, who took the painting to a dealer to price. George reported back that the dealer said it was probably worth about $1,600 and that he had accepted the offer. They split the money. McClintock says he was more than satisfied. Years later he was thumbing through a directory at a show and he looked up the Nevelson and discovered that the dealer had sold it for $4,000. It wasn't a half hour later that he saw the dealer. He complimented the dealer on the sale. The dealer said that the directory was in error, that $4,000 was only the buy-in price, a level the painting never reached at the auction. The dealer said it was too bad, he wished McClintock and George had remained a partner rather than just quickly cashing out on the deal.

McClintock was confused. George had never told him that they had options, that they could have teamed up with the dealer and together try to sell the Nevelson.

The dealer told him that the painting had sold at auction for $20,000.

McClintock laughs ruefully. "I got a good lesson in the art business."

The two men talked for awhile longer. The dealer decided that he owed McClintock as a result of the misunderstanding. He also determined that George should be taught a lesson for not explaining the options to McClintock. "Here's what I'm going to do," the dealer said. "I'm going to give something to George that he will pass on to you. But when you open it, you have to open it in front of George."

Months later at a show George delivered the package to

McClintock. As agreed, he opened it in front of George. Inside was a watercolor by George Catlin, a nineteenth-century artist who has become famous for his portraits of Native American Indians. An attached note said, "Here's your profit on the Nevelson." The watercolor was worth $10,000.

How did George react?

His mouth dropped open, he muttered, "You son of a bitch," and he walked away.

Brimfield is the antiques mecca of America not just because of the stuff on its fields but because of the people it draws. Foremost in that category are the dealers. Dealers can be eccentric, crafty, entrepreneurial, secretive, maddening, unusual, knowledgeable, broad-based, roaming, and downright entertaining.

Consider nicknames. Monikers are common, perhaps because it is easier to identify somebody by what they deal or buy than it is to remember their name. That is one way to find the Violin Man, the Typewriter Keys Guy, Cast Iron Joel, or the Doll Lady. Other pseudonyms are a little bit more complex, such as Primitive Man, who likes early American eccentric pieces; Rusty Mike, who deals in tools; or Cadillac Jack, borrowed from a fictional character in a Larry McMurtry novel about a wandering antiques dealer. Others take pseudonyms for the love of the name: Bottle John, Shark Tooth Charlie, African Bob, Flintlock, Big Chuck, Mark the Shark, Santa Claus, The Bear, Trader Bill, Farquar, Whitey, Bulldog, Art Shark, Buffalo, Moose, Moon, Easy Walt, Quarter Roy, Bubba, Red, Solly, Butch, Biff, Woody, Brownie, Frenchie, Binky, Skip, Mimi, Lone Ranger, and Salty Dog.

Rachel has begun calling Joe "Encyclopedia Joe" because of his amazing ability to recall artists from memory.

Brimfield regulars look for certain people. One is Joel Schiff, the collector of cast-iron cookware. Another is Walter Parker, who always wears a top hat and wanders the fields, waiting, knowing that someone will want to buy the hat right off his head for a tidy profit. There are dealers who have had their share of success, such as Gary Sohmers with the long gray ponytail and his Wex Rex booth that sells vintage movie posters, old-time videos, and other cultural kitsch treasures of the late twentieth century. Do people take a second look at Sohmers because he is as frenetic as a humming-bird on steroids or because they have seen him so often on the television show *Antiques Roadshow*? Brimfield can also produce dealers who offer higher-end products, such as Robert Lloyd, who sells American and British silver and has a shop in midtown Manhattan. Lloyd sells silver starting at $25, and at some shows he brings in items that can go for up to $60,000. But he comes to Brimfield just as much to have fun, and that is obvious from the bocce set under his tent and the television by the table in the rear, where at night Lloyd and other dealers break out the cards and sometimes feast on lobster. There is also Santa Claus, who, with his long white beard and flowing hair, needs only the red suit. Actually, Richard Conley has the suit; he wears it as a department store Santa every holiday season when antiques trading slows. "The rest of the year I try to do as little as possible," he says. But for all his laid-back, old-time hippie demeanor, Conley has a detailed knowledge of antiques, not only furniture but also art, pottery, and other fine works. Back home in Orange, Massachusetts, he has a warehouse of furnishings.

The Key Guy is both notorious and comical. An older man, he is famous for making the rounds of the fields trying to sell antique keys to dealers. Rarely do they want them. But for some the Key Guy is so persistent that they pay him a few bucks to take his keys and help him on his way. All transactions have to be in cash and the Key Guy insists upon a written receipt in which the buyer has to record the serial numbers of each bill. No one is sure why. One year the Key Guy made such a nuisance of himself that he was kicked off the J&J field. He appeared the next year much the same except that on his head was an outlandish, incredibly obvious, garish red wig. When dealers asked him what was with the wig, he became alarmed and put his index finger up to his mouth. "Shhh, don't tell anyone," he would tell the questioner. "I'm incognito."

If there is one common trait among Brimfield dealers, far more prevalent than eccentricity, it is intelligence. Even if they wear ragged blue jeans or stained sweatshirts, their intellect and breadth of knowledge should not be underestimated. As one dealer said immodestly, "We may be the biggest assembly of underachieved geniuses in the world." Brimfield promoter Don Moriarty once overheard two men talking nearby. "They were two big burly guys, they weren't dressed all that well, and they needed a shave, but one of them was one of my dealers," says Moriarty. "He was holding a picture and I couldn't quite hear what he was saying until he got excited and said could you believe that another dealer had only offered him sixty-five thousand dollars for this. Well, I was not trying to listen, but I could not contain myself and I looked at the picture. It was of a carousel horse. You never know what you are going to find here."

Mike McClintock never thought he would be an art dealer. He grew up in a working-class family in eastern

Pennsylvania. His father was a television repairman, and young Mike McClintock often struggled in school. Only years later would he learn that when he failed to follow directions, forgot things, or made careless mistakes, it was not because he was dumb. He had a learning disorder, ADHD, or attention deficit/hyperactivity disorder. Following high school, he married, moved to the New Jersey coast, and also became a TV repairman. "If you were to tell me then that I was going to go into the arts and antiques business, I would have told you that you were nuts," says McClintock.

He had always been a collector; he was interested in history, especially military, and weaponry, guns, and swords, particularly from the Civil War. Even when he got into the TV repair business in the late 1960s, it was becoming increasingly clear that the industry had no future for repair technicians. During the slow winter months on the deserted Jersey coast McClintock found himself working less and less. He began going to flea markets to pursue his hobby, and one day at the Lahaska Flea Market in eastern Pennsylvania he sold a Colt revolver to a collector for $350. "Later, I was getting a cup of coffee when I came across a dealer who had an identical gun that he was selling for a hundred dollars," he says. "I started to say to this guy that you are selling this too cheap, that I just sold a gun like that for three fifty, but before I could say it he shut me up by saying, 'Either buy the gun, kid, or get out of here.' So I bought it for a hundred dollars, and went back to the collector, and sold it to him for three fifty. That was a profit of two hundred and fifty dollars, which was more than I was making at the time working fifty hours a week."

It took only a few years before McClintock was dealing a

range of collectibles, antiques, and eventually art. He found he had two attributes that helped him to succeed.

The first was a man named Frank Henderson, who was a friend of the family when McClintock was growing up. Henderson was a diabetic and he used to come to the McClintock house daily to get an insulin injection from Mike's mother, who was a nurse. Henderson lived in a palatial estate at the top of the hill in town. He was an old-line blue blood whose family money had been earned off the trade of nineteenth-century clipper ships. A bachelor, he was content to live off that wealth. Young Mike McClintock called Henderson "Pop-Pop." "When I wanted to shoot my BB gun, I would go to Pop-Pop and we would go out in the field and he would use Canton china right off the Yankee clipper ships for target practice. If I had to kneel down on the ground he would get out an Oriental rug so that I wouldn't get muddy. On Thanksgiving my mom would ask me to go up and see Pop-Pop about getting a platter for the turkey. He lived on a hill, and I had a wagon, and he piled it with platters. I would start going down that hill, picking up speed as I went, and when I made the first curve a couple would go flying, and on the next curve a couple of more would go flying." Fortunately the larger ones survived. Despite Henderson's seemingly cavalier attitude toward heirlooms, he took McClintock to museums and exposed him to artwork that others of his age and background never got a chance to see. McClintock believes that helped him later. "I seemed to have a second sense about certain objects," he said.

McClintock found that his other advantage, probably developed to compensate for his ADHD, was a very good memory. He began to build a library of art books. His memory seemed greater when he was examining paintings. "For many years, I could remember every deal I made. I could remember who bought it and for how much. When I find something, my instinct is to buy immediately. Then I go do the research. I cannot read quickly, but my huge library does help me learn about what I have bought. You can't remember the name of every artist. But you need to act on the ones that express emotion. You'll make money most of the time that you buy. I paid tuition for five daughters to go to college, but it was nothing compared to what I paid to learn this trade over the years."

McClintock sets up an attractive tent at a great location at Sheltons field. His tent faces the road and people come in and out all the time, although on this afternoon few seem to be buying. Rachel finds that business is also slow down the road at Fran Smith's tent. Actually, it is Fran's along with Mike Pacitti and Chris Smith, but Fran Smith's paintings dominate.

There may not be another tent like Fran Smith's at Brimfield. Located prominently on Route 20, he sells striking and elegant eighteenth- and nineteenth-century paintings with ornate frames. They hang from the tent walls, are mounted on stands, or are displayed on tables covered with bright blue cloths. Finding Fran Smith's tent at Brimfield is the equivalent of being treated to a ballet performance at the circus, of being offered truffles at a doughnut shop, or of wearing a tuxedo to a baseball game. It doesn't look as though it should work. Even he admits that he is surprised he has lasted all these years at Brimfield.

Fran Smith is finding it harder and harder to find good art. "The problem is that there are just not enough of these paintings, and they are in high demand. No one really collected this type of American art until thirty years ago. They all wanted European art. Now, that's all changed." It has not completely discouraged him, however, because ultimately he loves the hunt, the search for good art. "Years ago as a boy I had a Geiger counter, and I loved to search for uranium. It's the same today, only it's paintings. I like to buy more than anything else in the world. It's the searching and the discovery, it's the treasure hunt."

He uses Brimfield as a forum to sell. He likes shows, even though he has a gallery that is run by his daughter. He had a shop back in Pennsylvania when he had the autograph business, but he never really liked sitting around in it, so he sold it. That's when he began going to shows. At one time he was selling at up to forty shows a year. The first time he came to Brimfield, nearly twenty years ago, he was put in the back of the field at Heart-O-The-Mart. The field was raw and as the day went on, Smith found a fine dust covering his paintings. It was either hot or it was cold, but the people were what fascinated him, especially his neighbors. One was a former priest who sold primitive antique furniture. As the day progressed, the priest would drink, becoming increasingly inebriated and prone to reciting long passages of Shakespeare in a loud bellow. Another dealer was a woman who sold vintage jewelry. She would wrap necklaces and other pieces into huge mounds of tangled glitter and then leave the booth. Customers would come and find themselves spending so much time unraveling the mounds that they felt bound to buy. The dealer would return, take their cash, dump more jewelry she had found on the fields, weave it into another ball, and leave. That cycle kept repeating itself for days. Both of these dealers are now long gone, and Smith's booth has grown and moved to the front of the field. Yet Brimfield remains attractive. "I really like it," he says.

For Fran Smith, and for that matter Pacitti and Chris Smith, the week is just beginning. They opened this morning and they will be here through Sunday because Fran in particular likes to sell to the retail market that comes in on the weekend. There is a rumor that Martha Stewart may be in town this weekend. It was Fran Smith who convinced Pacitti and Chris Smith to join him at Brimfield. Sales are important to them. Pacitti hopes to make up for their costs by selling at least $15,000, although $20,000 would be better. Still, Pacitti and Chris Smith come to Brimfield to buy.

"You can find anything here," says Chris Smith.

Rachel has been talking to Pacitti about art, although it is less about what they are buying and selling and more about what they are both painting. For years Pacitti liked art but rarely did anything about it. A big, burly shy man with a beard, he was too busy doing construction. He worked long hours, both running his own company and supervising projects for others. The money was great, but the hours were brutal; often he did not see much of his wife and kids. Finally, he began to cut back, and he had time not only for his family but also for other pursuits. He began to paint and then to hang around galleries. He got to know some of the owners, and there was a painting at one gallery in Mullica Hill, New Jersey, near where he lived, that he really liked. But it was just too expensive. One day Pacitti had an idea— he asked the owner if he could make a copy of the painting. The owner was dubious, but he allowed Pacitti to bring in his paints and a canvas. As Pacitti worked, the owner was amazed at how he was capturing the scene. One day, as

Pacitti was finishing, the owner brought up a painting that had a small chip in it and asked if Pacitti could paint over it. "And that's how I got into the art-restoration business," says Pacitti.

After that, he began to take his painting more seriously. He worked construction during the day and then often went to a gallery at night and restored paintings. It was not easy, especially because he really needed natural light to do a good job. As he learned from other artists through his restorations, his own paintings became better. Restoring a painting meant he truly had to study and learn from it. "A dealer would give me a painting and he would say, 'Be careful with this, it's worth about thirty thousand dollars.' After you worked on it for awhile, you would say, 'Yeah, I can see why.' As I worked on them, I got inside the artist and understood the way he did certain techniques. I got a greater appreciation for what he was doing." He was selling everything he produced. Then, in 1995, everything changed.

The gallery owner he was working for died. Both he and Chris Smith, who had been working for the same dealer, no longer had jobs. Chris Smith had started by literally sweeping the store and had moved up to where he was selling and helping with restorations. At the same time Pacitti seemed to be getting tired more quickly and often. His doctor ran some tests and told him he needed heart bypass surgery.

"It changed my outlook on life," he says.

Pacitti left construction work for good, giving up a good and steady paycheck for an uncertain future. He and Chris Smith decided to open a shop together in Mullica Hill. At first, it was a struggle but soon the restoration business picked up. It was easier to breathe again.

He also discovered that his art and his outlook on art were changing. Now, with a change in career and the opening of the gallery, he is selling the paintings in his collection. It isn't that he needs the money from them. Rather, he realizes that while he admires these Hudson River artists, the works he has collected are clearly not their best work. They paled in comparison once he began to study the greatest works of these Hudson River artists. Now, to keep for himself, he is buying only art from contemporary artists, often people he knows and whom he sometimes visits and paints with. Their art, in comparison to the Hudson River paintings he collected, is better and cheaper and he likes it more. "I prefer plein air landscapes, realistic landscapes, and not studio designs," he explains. "I like the spontaneity that you can see from observing life." The scenes he is painting have no buildings or other features that tie them to a particular time.

The paintings Rachel is creating are colorful, bright Impressionists. While her art is very different in style, she understands what Pacitti is saying about his decision to sell his Hudson River painters. "The more and more you learn art, the less you listen to people who tell you what you are supposed to appreciate," she says. "It becomes easier to buy quality, no matter what the name attached to it. It's better to buy quality art from an unknown painter than it is to buy mediocre art from a named artist."

Pacitti has urged Rachel to find what she really likes and to go after it. "I love what I do now," he says. "You figure, whatever time I have left, I want to do my way. That's what I'm doing. I love art. It's a lot of fun."

CHAPTER 6

Scores

RACHEL WAS ONLY eleven years old when her father and his friend Jim Meyer made their big score. It happened in the fall of 1982 at the Perkiomen Flea Market near their Pennsylvania home. McKay and Meyer had an understanding that when they were together and found something, they would both share the expenses and the profits. It was around dawn, already deep into the business day at Perkiomen, when a dealer from northwest Philadelphia pulled his truck into a vacant space. His tardiness was not surprising to McKay and Meyer; they knew him to be a little lazy and slightly arrogant. Even years later McKay refuses to provide the dealer's name, calling him only Joe. As Joe began to unload, a crowd gathered. One customer saw a painting the dealer was lifting out of the truck.

"What do you want for it, Joe?" asked the potential buyer.

"A buck and a half," the dealer replied.

In flea market parlance that meant $150. The customer looked more closely at the painting. It depicted a brilliant white magnolia bloom set against a dark background. The potential buyer, in a remark he would regret the rest of his life, said, "Oh, who wants a dumb Victorian flower?"

McKay waited until he was sure that the other potential buyer was not interested and then asked the dealer if he could take a closer look. "He handed it over and I looked at it," says McKay, "and the painting was absolutely perfect. It was so perfect I had to touch the canvas to make sure it was an oil painting and not a lithograph."

By now McKay was reaching for his wallet.

"Just buy it," urged Meyer.

The two men had another understanding—when they found a good buy, they did not beat the seller down over price. "You don't want them to come back and complain about anything you did," explains McKay, "and they can't if you take them at their asking price."

Meyer had another reason to buy. He had spotted the signature, Martin Johnson Heade. Heade was a popular artist of the Hudson River School who had fallen out of favor and was only beginning to make a remarkable comeback. More than twenty years later Heade's popularity has risen to the point where the U.S. Postal Service issued a stamp featuring one of the artist's floral images.

Long after the deal, McKay learned through a friend that Joe, the dealer who had sold him the Heade, had bought the painting through a connection with a church parish. A priest had told Joe that a woman had died and the family was selling many of her possessions. The son-in-law had hated the woman and he had put several of her paintings, including the Heade, in the attic with piles of junk and surplus items. Joe sifted through what was up there and paid $50 for the painting. McKay also found out that Joe had tried to sell the painting to a doctor who collected art. But when Joe called on a Friday night, the doctor was reluctant to leave his house. The doctor wanted to know more. Joe reported that the painting was by someone named Head, dropping the *e* at the end of the name.

"Do you mean Heade?" asked the doctor, pronouncing it so that it rhymed with "kneed."

"I saw the signature," said Joe, "and it's like I said it is."

In that case, the doctor was not interested.

Now that they had the painting, McKay and Meyer discussed what to do with it. Sotheby's seemed the obvious choice. The auction house, along with its prime competitor, Christie's, has controlled much of the fine art business for more than two hundred years. McKay called Sotheby's. "I was connected to the American art section and I explained that I was Willard McKay and I was interested in selling a Martin Johnson Heade."

"Well, who are you?" asked the Sotheby's official in a haughty tone.

"I'm Willard McKay."

"What do you know about Martin Johnson Heade?"

"I know I just bought one at a flea market and it has his signature."

The Sotheby official paused. "Well," she said with reluctance, "if you send us a photograph of it we will take a look at it."

McKay and Meyer decided they were not interested in Sotheby's. McKay then called Christie's and the response was far different. Within two days they were at the New York auction house. Christie's officials were nearly as excited about the find as the two dealers. They estimated it would sell for $40,000, a sizable amount in 1982, and they featured the painting on the cover of the auction catalog. It sold for $66,000. That was 65 percent above the estimate and more than four hundred times what McKay and Meyer had paid for the painting.

Neither Meyer nor McKay had ever seen that kind of money before. Rachel said she remembered the excitement that ran through her house for weeks before and after the auction. Some of the money paid for new Apple 2E computers for Rachel and her sister. Both families put most of the money aside to pay for their children's college education. Willard McKay said he's never regretted that decision to sell, even though today the painting is worth a million dollars.

Every dealer dreams of the big score. It's the ultimate quest, the raison d'être, the absolute essence of why they are at every dusty flea market and grimy estate sale. Making a score is the final examination, the complete testing of the years of work they have put into understanding everything from ancient needlepoint to modern hulks of rusting machinery. Every year there are stories of big scores. Around the time of this year's May Brimfield, reports surface about how a man in Los Angeles had found a painting wrapped in a blanket at a garage sale. The owner said it had been sitting in her garage for sixty years. He paid $5 for it and hung it in his kitchen. Two years later he researched the painting *Ripening Pears* and discovered that the artist, Joseph Decker, was famous. He sold it to the National Gallery of Art for a million dollars. One would think such dumb luck would infuriate knowledgeable dealers. Instead, it seems to goad them. At least that is the case with Joe and Rachel. There is just too much of value out there, value that has been lost and is waiting to be rediscovered. "It is really what keeps me going, that there is so much lost art out there," Joe says. "That is what makes each day fun, the idea of waking up, and going out, and having the thrill of finding something that no one else has found." Joe says that if all of the lost art in the world suddenly was discovered, he is not sure he would be interested in dealing art anymore.

Of all of the great scores that have occurred, one stands out. It occurred in 1989, and it was so phenomenal, so unexpected, that dealers still talk about it. It happened at a flea market in Adamstown, Pennsylvania. Or so everyone has been led to believe. Even years afterward the discovery remains cloaked in mystery.

"Some people say it was a setup," says Marilyn Gehman, who with her husband runs the Shupp's Grove summer market at Adamstown. "The thinking is that the man who said he found it was an employee of a museum. It was just a way to bring this valuable piece out on the market, without attracting attention."

Brian Block wants to believe that the story is true and that it happened at his Adamstown market, Renningers. "The bottom line is that I do not know for sure," he admits. "But this is a topic that comes up at least once a month out here. It's a believable story. It's the ultimate find. Not only is it a document that was bought for four dollars and that sold for more than a million dollars, but it's a piece of history, of American history."

Actually the document, a rare original copy of the Declaration of Independence printed on July 4, 1776, was sold for $8.14 million. But that's getting ahead of the story.

Adamstown is perched in the rolling hills of eastern Pennsylvania, fifty miles west of Philadelphia, just off the Pennsylvania Turnpike. It calls itself "Antique Alley" and "Antiques Capital USA" and in many ways it is like Brimfield. Title it the "Indoor Brimfield." It features miles of shops, primarily co-ops and consignment shops, where small dealers and collectors place and attempt to sell their finds, small and large, as well as several places such as Renningers, Shupp's Grove, and Stoudtburg that have outdoor markets.

In the summer of 1989, a man described as a stock analyst from the Philadelphia area, an occasional map collector, came to one of these outdoor markets. That identification and much of what is known comes primarily from David Redden of Sotheby's, who met the collector. The map collector has never been identified. He supposedly arrived fairly early in the morning. (Both Stoudtburg and Renningers are "flashlight markets," where dealers arrive and sell in the summer as early as three in the morning. Most of the bargains are gone before dawn and dealers pack up and leave by noon.) While shopping, the collector found a painting that was torn and in poor condition. He told Redden that the painting was "a dismal dark country scene with a signature he could not make out." While not impressed with the painting, he admired the frame, which was gilded and ornately carved. He paid four dollars for the painting and frame.

Sometime later he took the painting apart. The frame was beyond repair and the collector eventually threw away both it and the painting. But after he pulled it apart he found, between the painting and the back panel, a copy of the Declaration of Independence. It was folded several times. He knew enough to check the document's authenticity. He brought it to the Library Company of Philadelphia, which has experts in eighteenth-century documents because of its extensive collection. That repository is a legacy of the library's founders—fifty subscribers, including Benjamin Franklin, who each invested forty shillings to begin the institution in 1731. Officials at the Library Company were impressed by the document found in Adamstown. They suggested that the owner contact an auction company.

He called Sotheby's and he apparently did not get the same kind of reaction as had Willard McKay. Instead, he was connected to Redden. In 1991, when the two talked, Redden was a rising star at Sotheby's; his cachet has only been enhanced since. Color Redden an entrepreneur willing to take risks. It was Redden who, in 1993, after several trips to Moscow, convinced the Russians to auction relics of their space exploration, from space suits to capsules. He arranged for Sotheby's to auction a *Tyrannosaurus rex* skeleton that sold for $8.4 million. He also pushed the posh auction house at the turn of the new century to go head-to-head with eBay by selling on the Internet.

When the map collector called, Redden asked if the copy of the Declaration of Independence contained all the signatures. Normally callers said yes, it did. This caller said it did not and Redden was encouraged. The caller reported that the document only had two names, printed in block letters, John Hancock, who was president of the congress in 1776, and Charles Thompson, the secretary. Redden asked if the document was eight by eleven inches. Again, most callers replied in the affirmative, but broadsides normally measure at least fifteen by eighteen inches and this one was fifteen by nineteen. After talking some more, Redden was convinced that this call was different from the hundreds he had fielded in the past. He was so intrigued that he and an associate, Selby Kiffer, took a train to Philadelphia to see the document.

What the two men hoped to see in Philadelphia was a Dunlap Broadside, a rare and extremely valuable copy of the Declaration that was printed by John Dunlap on the night of July 4, 1776. Working off a copy handwritten by Thomas Jefferson, with changes scribbled in at the suggestion of Franklin and John Adams, Dunlap and his printers set the type that night. Only a few copies remain.

From the moment the owner unfolded the document, Redden and Kiffer began to get excited. True, one would not expect to see a valuable eighteenth-century document stored, let alone folded, this way. The print type and the paper looked right. Even more surprising was the condition: It was amazingly good. As they examined the document, both in Philadelphia and later back in New York, the Sotheby's officials drew on extensive scholarship on the Declaration of Independence.

The most detailed analysis was conducted in May 1975 when Frederick Goff, an expert in early printed books and documents, accomplished an extraordinary feat. Goff convinced such libraries as Harvard, Yale, and the New York Public, historical societies in Maryland, Massachusetts, and New York, and other institutions to loan him their copies of the Dunlap Broadside. Goff obtained seventeen copies. Working in the Preservation Research and Testing Laboratory of the Library of Congress in Washington, Goff and his assistants removed the copies from their cases or mountings. Using a light box, cameras, and other equipment, the researchers studied the documents and came to several conclusions.

First, they confirmed what others had already surmised, that the broadside cleverly hid a number of problems that had surfaced in the proof as a result of Jefferson's handwritten draft. Jefferson had begun writing the draft that would become the Declaration on June 11, 1776, and his text was presented to the Continental Congress on June 28. Then, for three days he and other delegates, wearing formal coats and wigs, worked inside the Pennsylvania State House to revise and approve the document. They sweated in the sultry heat and swatted at horse flies as they debated and amended his draft. Each time an amendment passed, Jefferson used a quill pen to scribble in the changes. When Congress finally approved the document on July 4, it directed Jefferson and four others to get it to Dunlap. Congress was eager to have the Declaration read throughout the colonies. Considering the number of changes recorded by Jefferson, the typesetter did a remarkable job in reading the document and setting the type. Jefferson had included a number of marks to show where a speaker would pause as he was reading the document. The typesetter had translated those marks into quotation marks. Dunlap, or whoever read the proof, ordered that the quotation marks be pulled. That created the most noticeable feature of the Dunlap Broadside. The printers were in a hurry by this point, so, to save time, blank spaces were substituted for the quotation marks.

Goff also found that very good paper, probably imported from England and carrying a variety of watermarks, had been used. He concluded that the printers rushed as they made copies. He found that the press was slightly askew as copies were made and that some copies were folded horizontally across the center before the ink from the upper portion was dry. He also determined that there were at least two separate press runs that night, because in some versions the *P* of Philadelphia was located directly beneath the comma following Charles Thompson's name. In others, the type had been set so that the *P* lined up under the *n* of Thompson's name.

Redden and Kiffer were aware of these characteristics and saw that they corresponded with the copy now before them. The folds in the document appeared to have been there for some time, but they had not harmed the integrity of the broadside. "I imagine that every Dunlap Broadside was folded at some point; it was so big that it needed to be in order to be sent elsewhere," says Redden.

After examining the document, they were finally ready to give their assessment to the owner. They told him it appeared to be a rare copy of the Declaration that had been printed on July 4. They tried not to be too excited. They said it might be worth millions.

"He couldn't speak," says Redden, recalling the scene. The owner "was completely overcome for several minutes. It was like what you might see on *Antiques Roadshow*, but without the benefit of the cameras."

Redden was confident of the document's value because it is so richly woven into American history. Its value was also extremely high because so few copies of the Dunlap still exist and this one was in such good condition. Dunlap may have printed between one hundred and two hundred copies the night of July 4. They were distributed by horseback, coach, and ship up and down the colonies. Many were discarded after they were read. Posted copies were destroyed by British troops when they occupied new territory. Only twenty-four, now twenty-five, known copies remain and most are safely guarded in the vaults of institutions. Some are in poor condition. The more famous version of the Declaration that most of us are familiar with, the one now stored in the National Archives, is a version that was prepared on parchment by Dunlap between July 5 and 19. It was signed by delegates beginning August 2.

The newly discovered Dunlap Broadside was scheduled for auction in New York on July 13, 1991. Despite its importance and rarity, it was unclear how much it would fetch. In the previous twenty years, four Dunlaps had come up for auction. One had gone for only $92,000. But a copy auctioned eighteen months earlier by Sotheby's had sold for $1.6 million. The Adamstown version was in better condition than the one last auctioned. Sotheby's placed a preliminary estimate of $800,000 to $1.2 million on the Adamstown Dunlap. When Redden opened the bidding, the Dunlap drew offers from several buyers. Then the bidding grew stronger. When he finally brought the gavel down, it had been bought for $2.42 million, a new world record for a document. The winner was an Atlanta businessman, Donald J. Scheer, whose company, Visual Equities, bought art primarily as an investment strategy. The Dunlap was the first historical document the publicly traded company had purchased. In a press conference following the auction, Scheer said all the right things about the document's historical value and symbolism.

Questions arose almost immediately after the auction. "It's a great story that some believe and others say can't be true," wrote the *Maine Antique Digest*, one of the antiques industry's most venerable and respected publications. Suspicions were raised partly because the copy was in such good condition. Dealers in ephemera questioned how a document in such an abused frame could have survived more than two hundred years in such good condition. Some questioned whether it had been stolen from another collection. The document's credibility was also hurt by the map collector's decision not to identify himself. "Once he got a lawyer, he really kept quiet," says Block, the Renningers manager. A Sotheby's official says that over the years some of the world's most powerful news organizations repeatedly have offered exclusive interviews and deals to get the owner to come forward. He has always refused. The seller watched the auction from a glass-enclosed booth at Sotheby's and then slipped quietly away.

Suspicions have their role: Thefts of historic documents have occurred and sometimes have not been discovered for decades. In 2000, Christie's sold a 1776 copy of the Declaration for $140,000 that had been printed by the *South Carolina and American General Gazette*. Someone at the Charleston Library Society read a news story about the sale and wondered about the society's onetime copy, which the society could prove it had possessed as recently as 1871. But no one knew what had happened to the document. By the time all the library's documents were microfilmed in the 1950s, the copy had vanished. The society could show that the stains recorded on the copy inventoried in 1871 seemed to match the document Christie's had auctioned.

The dispute kept several lawyers busy until a deal was struck to return the copy to South Carolina so that it could be publicly displayed.

Documents also get lost, even documents as valuable as a Dunlap Broadside. In 1968 a Philadelphia auction company was sifting through the contents of a 132-year-old bookstore, Leary's, in Philadelphia, that was going out of business. While employees were cataloging the inventory they discovered an unknown copy of the Dunlap. In 1985 a member of a historical society in Exeter, New Hampshire, was going through old documents in the dusty attic of the organization's early eighteenth-century historic house when he found yet another unknown copy of the Dunlap Broadside.

Nine years after Scheer and Visual Equities bought the Dunlap, they put it up for resale at Sotheby's. By this point Redden had helped launch Sotheby's Internet auction site. He needed dramatic documents to sell on the new electronic forum. The Dunlap was perfect. Since its previous sale, no other copies had been found, so online bidding began at $4 million. Bidding started at 9:01 A.M. and was sluggish for hours, even stopping for a while, until 4:30, when it picked up with a flourish. The bids were going back and forth so rapidly that the auction went well past its 5 P.M. scheduled close. It finally ended at 5:37:59 P.M. The winning bid of $7.4 million (plus commission, for a total of $8.14 million) was made by longtime television producer Norman Lear. At a press conference the next day Lear announced that he had not bought the document as a collector or an investor but intended the purchase as a philanthropic gesture so that he could share the Declaration with the rest of the country. He followed through on that pledge, creating the Declaration of

Independence Road Trip, during which the copy was displayed at museums, city halls, and even at the Super Bowl. Newspapers at each stop wrote about the document's arrival and related how a collector had bought it as part of a picture frame for four dollars and sold it for millions.

The mystery of who bought the copy in Adamstown has begun to be supplanted by the mystery of who sold it. In 1991 the *New Era*, a newspaper in Lancaster, Pennsylvania, tried and failed to find anyone in Adamstown who would admit to selling the picture. Some suggested it might have been sold at a local auction, but the auctioneer denied it. Since then, at least five dealers have volunteered that they were the seller. Some, while providing entertaining stories, have sought anonymity. Others have been more boastful.

"I'm the dummy who sold the Declaration of Independence," says John Brautigam. A former prison guard who sometimes collects and sells antiques, Brautigam says he found a beat-up old frame at a house sale in Devon, about a mile off Philadelphia's Main Line. He paid two dollars for it and he could still remember the house where he bought it. He remembers the owners telling him that most of the stuff they were selling had been owned by one of their parents.

"I wanted to put a print in it, but when I took the frame apart I found something inside folded up," recalls Brautigam. "I took it out and unfolded it and it was a copy of the Declaration of Independence. It looked like a reproduction to me. I told my wife, 'I'll save it and give it to one of the kids.' And she said, 'They've got enough of that stuff, just put it back in there.' So I did."

A few weeks later, while setting up outside on a summer day at Renningers, he remembered selling it to a tall man with dark hair, who was well dressed. Brautigam thought he sold it for six dollars, but he was willing to say it might have been four. It was not until later, when the news stories came out about the discovery, that he realized what he had sold. He says he would not be so certain, except that he remembered the folds, which were identical to the pictures of the folds in the document sold by Sotheby's. He showed them to his wife and she said, "Yeah, that's the one."

Brautigam has no way to prove the document was once his, has never contacted Sotheby's, and he has thought about writing Lear to relate his story. Sometimes his friends kid him about selling the document. "It's not really a laughing matter," he says. "It was just a stupid thing. But it was just one of those things that was not to be."

Two other Renningers dealers claimed for years that they were the real sellers. Hugh Thomas, a dealer from the Lancaster area, told others at the Adamstown flea market, including manager Brian Block, that he found the painting along with other items from an estate near Lancaster. Thomas said he was storing the items in an old chicken coop when a buyer approached him. Thomas said he sold a number of things to the buyer. "Hugh was adamant that he was the seller and he tried to do everything he could to prove it," said Block. "One of the things that he said first made him suspicious was the person he thinks he sold it to had been a regular up until the time of the discovery. From that point on, Hugh said he never saw him again. That made him suspicious. There is some validity to the story, considering that at one point Lancaster was the capital of the country and the British were bearing down on it. It makes sense that somebody would hide a document like that." One huge flaw in the story is that the purchase supposedly occurred in Adams-town, not at a chicken coop. Also, when Thomas sold at Ren-ningers, he usually sold indoors.

The other Renningers dealer was Louise from New York. She maintained that the broadside must have been hidden in a trove of material she cleaned out in the late 1980s from a small museum on Long Island that had just closed. "I al-ways believed that Louise might have sold it," said Block. "It was just the way she presented her story. She wasn't working hard to get it back or get any money, she just wanted people to believe that she had sold it. It was such a sad tale."

None of these dealers could ever prove they sold the doc-ument. Even if they could, they were owed nothing. The best they could ever anticipate would have been the prover-bial fifteen minutes of fame and perhaps a fee from the mys-terious buyer so that they would shut up. This may explain why the Philadelphia map collector never has come for-ward. It is also a reminder that a score has two sides, and for every winner there is a corresponding loser.

Several months before the May Brimfield show, just as Joe Laskowski's relationship was growing with Rachel, he thought he had found a Dunlap. He was scanning the offer-ings at an auction in Chesterbrook, Pennsylvania, when he saw a framed copy of the Declaration. He was surprised to find it, especially when he noticed that it did not have all the signatures at the bottom. Instead, just like the Dunlap, it had the names of Hancock and Thompson in printed block let-ters. It was good size, at least fifteen inches by twenty inches, and it was on what appeared to be older paper stock. He tried not to get excited, especially when he noticed another dealer was paying nearly as much attention as he was. Chuck Beale, whom Joe knew slightly, specialized in eighteenth-century antiques, from furniture, silver, and art to documents. The more Joe watched Beale, the more he was convinced that Beale could be a competitor when the document came up for auction. Finally, he decided to approach Beale and make a proposal. Rather than bid against each other, and drive up the price, they could work together as partners to buy the piece.

Beale was slightly surprised by the proposal. He had looked at the document and quickly dismissed it. "The chances of it being real are pretty slim," Beale told Joe. Still, it was possible that someone could have made a mistake. They worked together and bought the framed copy of the Declaration of Independence for $80.

Millions of copies of the Declaration of Independence have been printed and there are numerous copies of the Dunlap version. A fifteen-by-twenty-inch version can be bought at the Liberty Bell Museum gift shop in Philadelphia for $2.50. Some facsimiles can be valuable, however. The most sought after are the copies printed in 1776 by various Colonial newspapers. At least twenty-four newspapers published their own version of the Dunlap Broadside, and some versions have sold for as much as $300,000. More recently a Chicago printer published a very good facsimile of the copy found in Leary's bookstore. That version included the name of the printer on one side, but when the name was clipped off, the copy was good enough to even fool some dealers into thinking they had a Dunlap.

To find out what they had bought, Joe and Beale took it first to Independence Hall, then to the American Philosophical

Company, and finally to the Library Company. It looked very much like the copy on display at Independence Hall and no one could say it was not authentic. Joe was getting excited. "We thought it was the real thing," he says. "We were extremely excited about it. We thought we would be famous."

Still, no one could authenticate it until they reached the Library Company. Here, the experts took it out of the frame and asked if they could hold it for a while. Several weeks later, they called with the news.

"It is the finest facsimile ever made," they told Beale. He remembers them also telling him that it had been made during the twentieth century by that Chicago printer from the copy found in Leary's. The paper stock was very close to what would have been used in the eighteenth century, but the best clue was that the watermarks were different. They valued the document at perhaps $800 and wondered if the owners were willing to donate it to the Library Company's collection. The two partners agreed to give it away.

"With something like this, you always come away with something," says Beale. "You learn something about the decorative arts or ephemera that you did not know before. In this case we got to see an original Declaration and we learned things that people simply don't know. As long as you don't have to pay too much for the education, it's always worth it. It gets you ready so that next time, if the opportunity is there, you will find the real thing."

CHAPTER 7

The Love of Art

ON THURSDAY MORNING the crowd has been gathering for more than an hour before the nine o'clock opening of Dick May's field. There are reports that Route 20 is backed up seven miles to Sturbridge. As the crowd congregating on each side of the highway grows, people begin to edge increasingly onto the tarmac. A squad of Brimfield police works to keep the traffic moving, but it is not easy. A yellow school bus rolls by carrying kids making faces at the crowd. "Go home, fleas," one yells through the window. Five minutes before nine, the crowd on the opposite side of the street begins surging across, as inevitable as tidewater through an open sluice gate. The traffic comes to a standstill. One officer grows increasingly frantic.

"Folks, you are impeding traffic," he says. "Move. MOVE now. MOVE westward NOW."

No one budges. Other cops look amused as they watch their colleague.

He glances at them for help. They laugh. What can they do?

Finally, at 8:57, the gates open. The crowd pours through.

Each entrant hands the five-buck entry fee to a guard as he or she passes. Rachel and Joe are quickly through. Her adrenalin is pumping. This has always been her best field. She always finds art at May's. She feels that her failure to find anything over the past three days is about to change.

It does. A dealer is still pulling stock from his trucks when Rachel finds the Wachter paintings. Charles Wachter, a New York-based artist from the mid-twentieth century, is not well known. In recent years his art has sold for $300 to $700 apiece, according to the *Davenport* art guide. The dealer has fourteen paintings, plus a photo of Wachter. A man asks about a couple of the paintings and the dealer quotes $300 for one and $200 for the other. The man puts the paintings down and pokes around the booth. Rachel takes a closer look at the paintings now that the man has apparently passed. Several of the landscapes are quite good; one depicts a sail-boat with a yellow sunset backlight; others are of street scenes. They show signs of age, many caked with a thin layer of grime. As Rachel examines them, she knows that's not a big problem. She can probably ask Jim Meyer to do the restoration work, or Mike Pacitti. Rachel asks how much the dealer wants for all of them. The dealer says $1,400, which is $100 each. Rachel agrees. As she writes the check, she is pleased. She already knows of a buyer who will take one, and she thinks she can get $700. The dealer begins to put the Wachter paintings in the back of the truck to hold for Rachel. Realization dawns on the man who first asked about the paintings, as he learns that Rachel has bought them all. He scowls, grumbles, and walks away.

Then, just like that, she keeps buying. She finds a paint-ing of a boy leaning over a fountain, drinking water, by a known illustrator, George Cullman. It is not great art. But it will sell on the Internet, and especially with the name Cullman attached to it. She buys it. At another booth she finds a landscape signed M. L. Coolidge for $200. Mabel Coolidge is an artist from Worcester, Massachusetts. While she is listed, there is not very much on her, and Rachel has never heard of her. Still, the landscape is well done. It appeals to Rachel, so she purchases it. Next, she finds a black-and-white photo by someone named R. L. Coffin. She knows she is gambling now, for she really does not have time to do as much research as she wants because the rush is going to be over soon on her best field. She is intrigued by the Coffin photo, which has a label with the name Amherst Country Club. She buys it too.

Finally, as the rush is dissipating, she abandons the caution which has prevailed all week. She finds a very large landscape, a snowy winter scene, by Knut Helder. Here is an artist with a name. Rachel knows that Helder was based in New Orleans in the first half of the twentieth century and that he did a range of Louisiana landscapes, from canals to bayous to shrimp boats. This painting, with its scene of fallen snow, is a little unusual for Helder, but Rachel's eye tells her it is genuine. There is one problem: The painting is larger than what she prefers, at least three feet high and close to five feet long. Rachel sells almost entirely on the Internet, and shipping big pieces like this can be a challenge. She asks the dealer what he wants. He says $3,000. Rachel is surprised; she expected a higher price. It is the end of the rush and he must want to unload it. She knows that Helders usually begin at $4,000 and only climb. They dicker and agree to $2,500.

On Thursday evening Joe and Rachel sit tired and cold in a friend's trailer parked in a back field at Hertan's. The market stretches out so far that by evening everyone is exhausted. Not only did Rachel have a good day at May's, but Joe found a John Joseph Enneking painting for only $2,100. Enneking is a well-known American artist. Joe is certain he can double his money.

"This has been a great show," he tells Rachel. "We bought a lot of paintings, far more than we ever could have found at auctions for the prices we paid."

Rachel reminds Joe that they also spent a lot of money at a time when they are going deep into debt buying a house. Rachel knows Joe has a good eye; he continues to amaze her with his knowledge. Sometimes, though, she wonders if he gets overconfident. Still, he's a natural art dealer. He does not seem to worry about some of the things she does. She has a tendency to dwell on uncomfortable issues, not just finances but ethics. "Sometimes I do wonder about the moral issues," she says now. "We work to get a better price, but when we do that it hurts someone else who is making less money off a painting. So you do think about those kinds of issues at times. But at the same time we are the major rescuers of art. We find art that has been abandoned or lost, we restore it, and we find new homes for it."

Joe and Rachel have a love of art. It can be seen not only in what they buy and sell but in what they collect. They buy many types of paintings but they especially like to deal in American Impressionists. So far at this show they have not found any of the artists they most admire. These are the paintings that are a delight to find but can be painful to sell, even when a healthy profit is attached.

Joe has developed an affinity for the art of the Ashcan School, a group of painters who flourished in the first two decades of the twentieth century. Critics applied the derisive label "Ashcan" because the paintings focused on gritty views of streets, alleys, and bars filled with common immigrants, laborers, and shopkeepers. Yet while their subject matter was considered radical for their time, the Ashcan painters' style was deemed so conservative by the 1920s that they fell out of favor.

Joe and Rachel both also like the Pennsylvania Impressionists, who go by such names as the New Hope School and the Bucks County artists. There must be at least forty artists labeled Bucks County, famed for their early-twentieth-century landscapes. Edward Redfield was called the dean of the Pennsylvania Impressionists, renowned in his day for his winter landscapes. He was famous for hiking through the farm fields of Bucks County, standing knee-deep in a snowstorm, his canvas strapped to a tree, as he captured the scene, as he put it, "at one go." Painters, maintained Redfield, needed to see, hear, smell, feel, and even taste what they depicted. The energy on his canvases proved his ability to impart those senses to a painting.

There is a reason why Joe and Rachel are not finding Ashcan or Bucks County paintings here at Brimfield. Like many works, the Ashcan and Bucks County paintings were once forgotten and unfashionable. But they have been rediscovered and their prices have soared.

Viewpoints toward art can be so fickle. In 1947 Redfield had fallen out of favor, too conservative and dated for the art world. That was when he began burning many of his paintings. No one knows how many paintings Redfield destroyed over the next decade in a series of bonfires that caused thick acrid black smoke to rise over Bucks County. In 1957 he told a reporter, "I burned 700 to 800 canvases in the last five years. It's a relief to see them go. They are battles lost."

Redfield was rediscovered when a large collection of New Hope School paintings was placed on the market in 1979. Today many Bucks County paintings fetch six figures. A Redfield painting of the Brooklyn Bridge recently sold at Christie's for $966,000. Joe or Rachel would love to find an Ashcan or Bucks County painting, but they know it is a long shot.

That is why Rachel in the late 1990s began buying the art of the Philadelphia Ten. Not too many people are familiar with the names in this school, coined after the annual exhibits that the artists held in Philadelphia between 1917 and 1945. Perhaps their art never rose in price and has been lost in obscurity because they fell victim to changing fashions. But there have long been nagging suspicions, first raised by some of the artists themselves, that there is another reason for the anonymity of the Philadelphia Ten. The artists are all women in an art community long dominated by men.

Rachel had never heard of the Philadelphia Ten until 1998, when an exhibit was organized to recognize the women. Select paintings were exhibited in Philadelphia and later in Florida, Massachusetts, and Texas, and a book about the artists was published. It was Jim Meyer, her dad's old sidekick, who first suggested that she collect and deal their art. She was quickly attracted to the artists and their work. "I like them because of their history and because of the bright, strong colors they used. Compared to other Impressionists' paintings, they are still inexpensive. Their paintings had been forgotten, which is confusing, because there is no reason why they should have been ignored. And finally, these are paintings by women artists, and I'm a woman, and I want to promote art produced by other women."

Eleven women participated in the first exhibit in 1917. The "ten" in the name is something of a misnomer. Not only did it fail to accurately reflect the count in the first year but membership fluctuated in subsequent years. Ultimately thirty women participated at various times, over the twenty-eight-year span of exhibitions. The 1917 exhibit featured 247 paintings, primarily still lifes, landscapes, and a few portraits.

The Philadelphia Ten was a diverse group of young artists trained in Philadelphia art schools by New Hope School practitioners. Mary-Russell Ferrell Colton contributed paintings from the American Southwest, where she eventually moved. She developed an undercoating to her paintings to bring out the vivid colors of the Arizona landscape. When necessary, she waited days for the light and the mood to be just right. Later, with her husband, she founded the Museum of Northern Arizona to preserve the artistic culture of the Southwest. She was especially influential in preserving native Hopi artwork. Cora Brooks specialized in still lifes, especially large, vivid, colorful floral arrangements, the flowers often picked from her Maine garden. Brooks was just gaining critical acclaim—she had a solo exhibit in Washington in 1929—when she died unexpectedly of pneumonia at age forty-four. One of the most prolific was M. Elizabeth Price, who painted highly decorative panels featuring delphiniums, poppies, peonies, and hollyhocks, often with gold or silver leaf backgrounds. Harriett Whitney

Frishmuth, a sculptor who studied under Rodin in Paris, successfully produced lean, highly polished, and sensual figures. Maude Drein Bryant, married to artist Everett Bryant, worked out of their home and Brookside Studio along the Perkiomen Creek, upstream from Joe and Rachel's house. Art critics said that her still lifes were clearly influenced by Cézanne and Van Gogh.

Denise Colton, the granddaughter of Mary-Russell Ferrell Colton, lived near her grandparents in Flagstaff while she was growing up. She says that her grandmother was very independent. "My grandmother lost her father when she was only about fourteen, to cancer, and it was not easy for her. It was a friend of the family who helped get her through art school, and the thought was that her art would be her livelihood. It was seen as a way for her to be able to fend for herself. She always felt that she was something of a misfit, that she did not fit in with others. Most of these women were very independent. How much guts did it take for all of these women to do what they did? It had to have taken an enormous amount of courage."

Such formal exhibits as the ones held by the Philadelphia Ten were not unheard of in their day. The National Association of Women Painters and Sculptors had been founded in 1889 and had been having annual exhibitions in New York and hosting traveling shows around the country. But they were still unusual in 1917 when women in the United States were on the cusp of finally getting the right to vote.

Colton does not remember her grandmother ever complaining that women artists were not appreciated as much as male artists. Yet for some it was an issue. Art critics reviewing the annual shows often praised the artists with a touch of condescension. Not much was expected from women artists in those days. A critic commenting on the 1929 show observed that women artists usually concentrated on "sentimental pieces depicting some aspect of infantile or maternal life, or still-life pictures that showed a predominance of floral decorativeness." The critic was surprised to find that there were no "mother pictures" but "rugged outdoor pictures of landscapes and seascapes."

Philadelphia Ten artist Theresa Bernstein was outspoken on the issue. Bernstein told a story about the lack of respect given women artists in her day. She often signed her paintings "T. Bernstein" to disguise her gender. One day in 1919, after she had a solo show in New York, three men who were members of the National Academy of Design arrived at her doorstep in Manhattan. Bernstein answered the door and they stood there until one of them said, "We like your father's work very much."

"Oh, he'll be pleased," she replied.

"We'd like him to join the Salmagundi Club," they said.

"Oh, he'll be pleased to hear that," said Bernstein.

They left. Bernstein's father was never an artist. Only later did the visitors learn that T. Bernstein was Theresa Bernstein, the young woman they had taken for the artist's daughter. She never received a formal invitation to join the Salmagundi Club.

A critic in 1917 described her as "a woman painter who paints like a man," and Bernstein was often frustrated by the overt discrimination of the male-oriented art world. She noted that her works were accepted for exhibition by the National Academy of Design thirty times, but the male-dominated organization never invited her to be a member and rarely invited any women artists to join. "One has to understand that there are limitations not in one's expression, but in one's status," Bernstein said. "The onus is there even when it is not elucidated or emphasized." She also complained that "my work has been cut up and stolen and had things thrown at it—ink, mud. Maybe they didn't want me to be known."

Expressions of frustration are counterbalanced by those of others who say that Bernstein was a woman of her time, content as a wife taking a secondary role in her marriage. Married to artist William Meyerowitz, Bernstein spent much of her time promoting her husband's career, at least according to some accounts. "She was perpetually overlooked," Jan Siedler Ramirez, a curator for the Museum of the City of New York, told the *New York Times* when a special exhibit was being planned in honor of Bernstein. "She knew all of the important painters but she chose to be a wife, and to make her husband's life as comfortable as possible," said Ramirez. "She was just a modest person."

Of all of the Philadelphia Ten artists, Bernstein's story may be the most compelling. Like many of her colleagues in the Philadelphia Ten, she was raised in the Philadelphia area by well-to-do parents and she graduated from the Philadelphia School of Design for Women. Unlike some others, her father sustained financial setbacks shortly after she began her career, which meant she was dependent on her art for her livelihood.

Bernstein moved to New York after finishing art school. By the time she met Meyerowitz in 1917, her work had already been exhibited. While he was familiar with her paintings, he had believed her to be well along in her career and in years. He was acquiring art to hang in settlement houses when he knocked on her door. When she answered and identified herself, he replied: "I thought you were an old lady." They married three years later.

She could sell art—she sold ten pieces in a day after a solo exhibit opened in 1919—yet money could still be tight at times. In her biography of Meyerowitz, one of seven books she authored, she described how they always prepared their own canvases, buying a large roll of linen, putting it on the refectory table of their home, and using it as a tablecloth. She had to warn guests not to spill food on the tablecloth. Over time the couple would cut off pieces for paintings. One day a friend remarked, "I can't understand why this tablecloth keeps shrinking all the time."

They lived in New York, summered in Gloucester, Massachusetts, and had a wide assortment of friends including Edward Hopper and Georgia O'Keeffe, John and Lionel Barrymore, George and Ira Gershwin, Heywood Broun and David Sarnoff. Bernstein and Meyerowitz both taught art and they were also active in a number of social causes.

Over the years Bernstein's art reflected her concern for the poor, the downtrodden, and the ignored, especially women and sometimes minorities. She painted from the early years of the century to the 1960s and beyond. She painted New Yorkers celebrating the Armistice on Fifth Avenue, women waiting at an employment agency, a group frolicking on the beach, a scene at the opera, a jazz band, and a group of hippies lounging in New York's Central Park. Bernstein said she liked to paint scenes such as beaches because they were full of life and activity. In a 1980 interview in *American Artist*, Meyerowitz said: "My wife's strong point is her love for and interest in people. She's a genre painter in the real sense of the word—her work has to do with people. When she does beach scenes, she includes mothers, children, dogs, everything. She loves compositions with lots of people; and she's a master of the big idea, expressed through big powerful forms."

For a while her work was associated with the Ashcan School. Her brush marks were firm, her colors vibrant, and the scenes were often gritty and realistic. One painting created in 1917, *Waiting Room—Employment Office*, is especially compelling. Bernstein later explained that she had been powerfully struck by the scene she saw when she went looking for domestic help; holding as many details as possible in her mind, she had begun the work immediately upon getting home. The painting shows a group of women waiting, one knitting, another by the telephone, one reading a newspaper, and another off to the side. Some are clearly immigrants; the last one is alone and black. Each is vulnerable to forces she cannot control.

Bernstein exhibited with the Philadelphia Ten until 1931. She left the group, expressing dissatisfaction about recent reviews and about how her paintings were being exhibited. Some suggest she may have dissociated from the Ten because her paintings were moving further from the Impressionist landscapes and still lifes of the others. By the 1930s, she was focusing more on subjects and scenes, including paintings and portraits of such jazz greats as Louis Armstrong, Jelly Roll Morton, Fats Waller, Cab Calloway, Duke Ellington, and Billie Holiday. She continued to paint entertainers into the 1950s, producing a striking rendition of Judy Garland. During the Great Depression, Meyerowitz and

Bernstein survived primarily by obtaining more than 150 portrait commissions. Still, times could be tough. In her biography of Meyerowitz, Bernstein remembered how he had been painting horses when a buyer called seeking two paintings, one for each side of a fireplace. The buyer was coming right away. Meyerowitz could find only one painting. It had a number of horses in it so he cut the painting in half—to Bernstein's horror—and touched it up. She described the next scene: "When the buyer arrived, he chirped, 'I knew you would find me some paintings.' "

Other Philadelphia Ten artists also experienced emotional and financial hardships. Rachel has the letters that Bryant kept during her lifetime, including one dated December 9, 1934, from her husband, who was living in California. Everett Bryant reported that he had been to four relief agencies seeking to apply for a new government-funded art program, probably the WPA. "All of the people turned me down flat," he wrote. In another letter only dated February 24, he told his wife to sell any of his paintings that she could. "I have only sold one painting here in six years and it was for $25." And in another letter he reported that it was raining and water was coming through the ceiling. "I applied to the state for old age pension," he wrote. "Advised that son should help."

Rachel acquired the letters from a book dealer who had bought the estate of Maude Bryant's son. He found Rachel through her website, which touts her role as a dealer of Philadelphia Ten art. Her reputation has produced other offers and contacts with family members of some of the artists, including Denise Colton. The two women met in Paris, where Colton now lives, and Colton was immediately impressed with Rachel's skill as an art dealer. "Rachel has an intensity that leads her to help sniff out and find things," says Colton. "She has a genuine interest in art and the history of art and the artists of other times. It is something that is very real. I think that is why she finds things, because she has that intensity." At the time Rachel had found a Mary-Russell Ferrell Colton painting at auction. "I was just amazed that Rachel could recognize it," says Colton.

Rachel has acquired a couple dozen Philadelphia Ten paintings, but she has only been able to keep about half that many. She admires the women for what they did and assumes that someday other women will agree and buy the paintings of the Philadelphia Ten. But so far recognition and art prices have risen slowly and future prospects are not clear.

The art world has long maintained that its evaluations are based solely on merit. Yet over the years women artists have never attained the same standing as men. While a few women, such as Bernstein, complained, widespread recognition of the extent of the disparity did not occur until the 1960s. Since then, some contemporary women artists have seemed to be doing better than women of previous generations. There have also been attempts to resurrect and raise the reputation of earlier women artists. Still, a significant gap remains. A writer who recently reviewed the auction offerings of contemporary artists at Christie's, Sotheby's, and other major galleries found that there were eight times more works being offered by men than by women.

A few years ago Rachel offered a painting by a Philadelphia Ten artist, Eleanor Abrams, to a prominent Pennsylvania dealer for $13,000 and he laughed in her face. Yet she has seen prices rising and she wonders what she could get now for the

piece. A Cora Brooks recently sold for $45,000 and one by an-
other Philadelphia Ten artist, Fern Coppedge, sold at auction
for $80,000. Two of Rachel's favorite artists are Cora Brooks
and Elizabeth Price. Both of these painters specialized in still
lifes, which was a common theme for many of the Philadelphia Ten painters. Yet still lifes today remain unpopular with
many buyers of art, perhaps because many buyers are men.

Of all the Philadelphia Ten painters, Bernstein's work
today may be the most prized. Her paintings have sold for
as much as $100,000. Fame came because she simply out-
lived her critics; indeed, she lived until she was 111. The
story of the feisty old painter who tried to outwit critics by
the way she signed her paintings gained reknown.

Her *New York Times* obituary in 2002 quoted Jan Ramirez,
who had organized the exhibition of Bernstein's work at the
Museum of the City of New York. "She was just a great
painter, period," said Ramirez. The obituary also noted that
her paintings were in the permanent collections of the Met-
ropolitan Museum of Art, the Library of Congress, the
Smithsonian Institution, and the Chicago Art Institute. Yet
questions persisted about the merit of her work.

An exhibit at the Boca Raton Museum of Art in Florida
around the same time drew a harsh review from the *Palm
Beach Post*. "Bernstein had an interesting life. Alas, that
doesn't make her pictures interesting," wrote the reviewer.
"She painted with a good deal of sweetness, but unfortu-
nately, not a lot of sizzle. Judging by these pictures, the truth
is there's a reason for her obscurity."

All this talk of art makes Rachel curious about how much
money they have spent during the week at Brimfield. It is

getting late in the trailer, as Rachel reviews the registers of their two checkbooks. Together, they have bought $10,000 in art. That worries her. They were all good buys, but the financial pressures just keep coming. All week she has been on the cell phone with the Realtor about last-minute issues involving the new house. Other dealers have told her she is crazy for buying a house. "People like us can't afford to have mortgages," one told her. "You either have to spend the money on art or on a house, you can't afford to do both." Rachel did not want to believe that, she had insisted that she could do both. They had to get home and they had to start selling some of this art.

Rachel and Joe review their plans for tomorrow. They will go to J&J in the morning and then leave in the afternoon. Joe has complained all week about the cold, hard ground in the tent, and Rachel has finally agreed they can spend Friday night in a motel, although it seems like a waste of money. They will stop at Elephant's Trunk, a well-known weekend flea market in Connecticut, on the way home.

Some say it is dangerous to love art as much as Joe and Rachel do, that the couple are mixing emotion with business. Fran Smith never collects art, preferring to find and sell quickly, unless he can hold on to a piece in the hope that its value will rise sharply. Neither Joe nor Rachel entirely accepts the concept that they should not collect what they deal. "I get emotional about everything I buy," says Joe. "You just have to divest yourself of that emotion and move on." Adds Rachel: "The point is you have it for a while, and then you move on."

That's what Mike Pacitti did with his Hudson River paintings. It sounds so easy, but for Pacitti it took heart bypass surgery for him to make the realization. Joe is certain he can sell whatever he needs to, no matter how strong his attachment. Rachel is a little less certain. She has difficulty even thinking about selling any of her remaining Philadelphia Ten paintings. The more she learns about the women, the more she appreciates their art. Still, if the day comes, she thinks she can sell what she needs to. She wonders how much it will hurt.

CHAPTER 8

Ties That Bind

By Friday, the mood sweeping across Brimfield is buoyant. J&J opens at 6 A.M. and the crowds are the biggest of the week. It is becoming obvious that no one needs to worry too much about Brimfield's future. Forget eBay, forget the economy, forget the market doldrums. The crowds and the money are here, at least this week. One antiques trade journal will subsequently confirm that excitement with an upbeat story carrying the headline: "Brimfield is Back—Antique Shows Recover after a Three-Year Lull."

The diversity of merchandise is greater than ever. Fields brim with the unusual and exotic: life-size figures of Jimmy Carter, Ronald Reagan, and the first George Bush; an eight-foot-tall replica of the Statue of Liberty fashioned into an outdoor ornamental lamp; a seven-foot-tall stuffed parrot with a brilliant red chest; an elephant's leg hollowed out and perfect for a planter; a fifteen-foot-tall snowshoe; a rotating barber pole; a large mural of a New England clipper ship tied up to a wharf and sitting next to a giant ice cream sundae as tall as the highest mast; and a large sign with orange letters on a white background advertising Nigger Head brand oysters.

Some items are selling repeatedly. Merchandise flips and flips again when times are good. Today at one J&J booth an unusual metal sculpture/lamp that stands five feet high and sprouts limbs is for sale. It is a metallic lemon tree, with a wrought-iron trunk and branches, metal leaves painted green, and oval yellow bulbs for the fruit that light up. On Tuesday, a Florida dealer sold it for $400 to a couple who said they were from Pennsylvania and were going to put it into the conservatory of their home. A New York City dealer now is asking $800 for it. Joe is startled to discover that the California painting he bought on Tuesday for $125 and sold the next day for $250 now has a price tag of $850 on May's field. "But the price is negotiable," the dealer tells one inquirer.

Elsewhere on the field a Pennsylvania dealer is trying to sell a model of a Spanish galleon. But this is no regular model; eight feet long and four feet high, it is a Hollywood prop that may have been used in B movies of the 1920s, '30s, and '40s. At least that is what the dealer was told when he bought it last year for $5,000. He has no proof, no provenance, and his efforts to sell the ship for up to $11,000 at other shows have failed. Now the dealer is asking $5,500, and inquirers get the feeling that the price is soft.

The question of the week is whether the ten-foot-tall Bob's Big Boy will sell. A shabby leftover icon of the restaurant chain, its paint is peeling, it is missing an arm, and some say that elsewhere these plastic statues are just melted down and thrown away. Yet it towers over Main Street, attracts attention every day, and is beloved by owner Jerry

Pasternak. A big man with a Falstaffian bellow of a voice, Pasternak has other big boy toys in his tent, including gasoline-powered model airplanes that fly and a one-ton, two-foot-long black metal replica of a locomotive. He likes the Bob's statue so much that last winter he displayed it in his front yard to snub his Newburyport, Massachusetts, neighbors. "We live in Yuppieville with all of the doctors and lawyers in town, in the historic district with all of the fancy houses," he explains. "So you can imagine how popular this was in this neighborhood. But when I finally put it in the pickup and moved it, people were calling and saying, 'What happened to the Big Boy? Was it stolen? Did you sell it?'" When he drove around town showing it off, "everyone was laughing and waving and freaking out. And then you should have seen people when we drove down here on the Mass Pike."

As much as he's attached to the Big Boy, Pasternak can part with him for $3,500.

Buyer interest has risen and waned all week. Finally, Greg Renshaw buys the Big Boy for $2,000. Renshaw may not have Pasternak's girth, but in other respects they could be twins. He has a gift for the same easy, glib talk as Pasternak, and he shares the same attachment to big boy toys. Back at his warehouse in Putnam, Connecticut, he owns everything from nineteenth-century polished oak bars and stained-glass windows to nine vintage cars, including a 1960 Jag and a '57 Mercedes. He's been accusing town officials of not doing enough to promote Putnam's burgeoning antiques boutiques. He thinks he might hoist the paint-blistered Big Boy to the top of his antiques warehouse/shop to tweak the town's petty bureaucrats.

Brimfield draws disparate people with separate interests and then finds ways to unite them. Over time those connections can deepen and develop into bonds. That is why Brimfield is not only a market but a community.

The concept of community is raised during meetings with eBay. Don Moriarty and Tim May both meet with the eBay representative. He makes his pitch, that eBay needs Brimfield and that Brimfield needs eBay. If Brimfield promoters agree to provide a booth where eBay can meet with dealers, the online auction company will offer space on its site where Brimfield can promote itself. In theory, it sounds great, but neither May nor Moriarty is impressed. Moriarty is concerned that the eBay representative is young, new to the company, and has little authority. Moriarty says that if the company can bring something back in writing, a legal obligation, then perhaps they can make a deal. But he wonders if this new young executive will be gone by the time the corporate lawyers can agree on a draft. Joel Schiff also meets with the young man from eBay. He tells him that eBay needs to be on the fields. "You need to build a community and you can't do that online," says Schiff. "With a physical market, people meet each other, they trust each other, they have more faith in the basis of prices than when they don't know each other." Schiff knows Brimfield needs eBay here. The relationship can benefit both of them.

J&J marks the end of the Brimfield rushes, and by Friday afternoon business gives way to more social pastimes. Those who were competitors just a few hours ago now relax together. Meals, card games, parties, and other gatherings break out. Some people are going over to the First Congregational Church for its annual church supper. It may be the last one. The church has a new minister, and members of the congregation are getting tired of the fund-raiser. Many of the dealers and collectors have been coming here for years; they have formed attachments with their neighbors, formed cliques and become friends. Many will not see each other again until July, or even September. As with all communities, this one is not immune to love or death, celebration or pain.

On Friday night a crowd of nearly two hundred gathers at the Quaker Acres field around the canvas tent of Tate Conkey. It has a distinctive metal awning in the front, and inside it has been cleared of vintage chairs, tables, chests, and other antiques. A New Hampshire bluegrass band, the Mill City Ramblers, is entertaining the crowd. Conkey regularly hosts a Friday night Brimfield party. This one, however, is exceptional. The band stops playing as Conkey's longtime girlfriend Meaghan arrives in a wedding dress. The crowd stands and spectators stare. She shivers, either from nerves or the cold. A woman in the crowd removes her antique fur wrap and places it around Meaghan's shoulders. The violinist begins playing the wedding march. The bride strolls to the rear of the tent. She takes the hand of the groom. The ceremony with justice of the peace Beverly Krzynowek is brief. Afterward the band plays, dealers dance, steaks are grilled, and the wedding cake is cut. Then, faster than one can say congratulations, Tate and Meaghan Conkey are gone. While it is only eleven, they have an auction to run tomorrow.

As word about the Brimfield wedding spreads, veterans remember the last one. Walter Parker and Dyan Larson were married on a Friday at dawn by J&J's gate before a crowd of hundreds waiting to rush the field. The bride, who sold vintage clothing, wore an antique dress and sneakers. The groom had a beaver top hat, a 1920s-era tux with tails, t-shirt, shorts, and sneakers also. A hand-cranked phonograph played a 78-rpm record of the wedding march. Even justice of the peace and town clerk Pamela Beall donned a vintage dress and a tri-cornered hat secured with a black velvet ribbon. The couple chose that time and place to be first on the field, and that's how it worked out. The ceremony was just ending when the three of them, on cue, yelled "Yahoo, shop till you drop!" The starter's gun fired. The gates opened. The crowd surged forward led by the Parkers with a red wagon in tow proudly displaying a "Just Married" sign. The Parkers bought an antique picture frame to hang their wedding picture, a carved ivory head for him, and an antique clock for her. While they rested at the J&J food court, a professional singer, Merle Boas, sang to them. He began with "Isn't It Romantic" and ended with "You Stepped Out of a Dream." On the fields again Ken Woodbury played a waltz on one of the Victrola phonographs he sells, and the couple danced in the dusty aisles. A crowd gathered and applauded. They were celebrities for the day. Two days later a woman running an antiques shop on Cape Cod recognized them. "I was just at your wedding," she told them. They still run into people who remember the wedding.

The other side of life sometimes visits the antiques market. Judy and Jacques Mathieu now live in the house owned by her parents, Gordon and Madelyn Reid. Their driveway, which leads to the J&J field, has a chain barrier and "no trespassing" signs. A few years ago Judy saw a couple who had parked at the base of the driveway walking along the creek. Judy thought they were rather presumptuous to come onto her property, so she walked down and asked what they were doing. The young woman replied that her father-in-law had died the year before. He had loved the famous antiques market field. He wanted his ashes to be spread here, near the creek. She asked if that was all right.

Judy Mathieu was dumbfounded. "I told them to go ahead and do whatever they felt was necessary." She walked back to the house and watched as the couple wandered farther down the creek. It was obvious they were saying a prayer. When they were done and they appeared to be leaving, Judy went down again. She said: "I hope everything is all right with your family." They talked for a few minutes. By the time the couple left all three of them had tears in their eyes.

Judy still sees them occasionally at the shows. "Last year I saw the woman again," says Judy, "and she said her mother-in-law also wants her ashes buried here whenever she dies."

Ties can unite not only individuals but also a crowd of strangers. A few years ago, also at J&J, a vehicle accidentally struck a young girl. Brimfield paramedics summoned an emergency helicopter to airlift the girl to a hospital. Rumors were already spreading through the crowd. The arrival of the chopper as it swooped in and then away from Brimfield set off a new round of gossip. To quell the rising speculation, an announcement over the J&J sound system explained that the hurt girl was going to the hospital. The crowd's reaction was spontaneous. Dealers began raising money to help the girl and her family. Interest was high. Periodically additional announcements were made. First came the news that the girl was being examined at the hospital. Next came word that she would have to undergo an operation. Then she was in the operating room. The sound-system speakers are scattered across the field. Each time the speakers came alive, all activity and commerce ceased. Finally, the last announcement: the girl was out of the operating room, everything had gone well. Applause and whoops of joy sounded up and down the dusty lanes, across the canvas tents, and well beyond.

By Saturday Joe and Rachel and many other dealers are gone. Officially Brimfield has two more days, but the community that has been here since Monday is breaking up, to be replaced by newcomers. Dealers know that with the rushes over the best deals are gone. The remnants are left for the amateurs, the weekend shoppers. Many dealers hate the weekend at Brimfield—they loathe the stupid questions and the clumsy attempts to bargain. Many would rather clear out than face that ordeal. Those who leave are replaced by a new breed of dealer. Many sell surplus merchandise, reproductions, and anything low-cost.

Howard Roberts wonders how Saturday will go. For him, it has not been a very good show. He did sell the mounted sailfish and the traffic light, but not a whole lot more. He and another dealer, Frank, often sell to a clientele they have dubbed the sorority sisters. These are the comfortable, middle-aged, wealthy, and rarely employed ex-college roommates or country club golfers who fly in to Brimfield early in the week to have a flea-market adventure. They are identified by their heavy gold bracelets, dark glasses, and Southern drawls. They can be a deliverance during a slow show. The crowds are big for this show but not with sorority sisters. Now the weekenders are coming, the couples who have left the kids behind with the grandparents in their over-mortgaged homes, and he expects the worst. Sure enough, a fellow wants to pay $45 for the $75 fishing pole. Then someone offers $200 for a brass candelabra going for $385. Another says the best he can do is $400 for a pond boat from the 1920s with an asking price of $900.

A woman comes in and asks how much for a coffee server. By this time Roberts is getting tired of their foolish antics.

"Four hundred and fifty dollars."

"Would you take two hundred?"

Howard scowls. He waits, debates with himself on whether to say anything, and finally can't help himself. "Just as a point of reference, I paid three hundred and eighty-five dollars for that piece. It is silver plate, English, from the 1880s."

"It is very beautiful," she replies, trying to look neutral.

Still, it is a beautiful day and Roberts eventually decides that he can't take these people too seriously. He finds a captain's hat that says Cunard. It is from the *Queen Mary*. When he first spotted the hat in a vacant house he was cleaning out, he hoped it would say White Star Line, which owned the *Titanic*. Anything associated with the *Titanic* carries significant value. He dons the cap and stands without expression. No one notices him, or laughs. He spies the ticket booth used at Wednesday's opening rush. He considers how close he wants to get to that booth. Last Wednesday a man was emptying an old metal vase filled with packing material into a trash can next to the ticket booth.

"I've got to empty this to make sure there is not another mouse in it," he had explained to a ticket taker who stood only a few feet from the trash can. She watched, first with curiosity and then, after his explanation, with alarm. He ignored her expression.

"Oh, thank you for doing that right here and telling me," she said sarcastically.

He shrugged, again oblivious to the irony in her voice.

"We find them in houses all the time," he said.

That exchange was days ago. Roberts mounts the ticket booth.

"Get your tickets now for the ship," he yells. "Ship tickets going now."

A few people laugh.

An outboard on a trailer slowly goes by.

"Get your tickets, the boat is leaving now," Roberts says, pointing to the passing boat.

For all practical purposes, the May Brimfield show is over.

July

Good as it is to inherit a library, it is better to collect one.

AUGUSTINE BURRELL

The buyer has need of a hundred eyes, the seller but one.

SEVENTEENTH-CENTURY PROVERB

CHAPTER 9

The Town

THE HOT, SULTRY sun is only beginning to falter in the sky on this July afternoon as several knots of men begin gathering in front of Brimfield's ornate town hall. The Victorian structure has been restored recently to its original colors, beige on the clapboard facings and a plum on the fanciful gingerbread trim. A spectacle is unfurling by the time television news vans arrive a few minutes later. The group gathered are hoisting placards and forming a processional on the sidewalk. The signs say "Support Your Local Police," "Brimfield Selectmen spending your Tax $ on their Lawyers," and "Not on your protection." Down the street the thousands of tents and booths have been set up for the July show, which officially begins tomorrow. Tonight, the pageantry begins not with a rush but with a picket line.

The picketers are Brimfield police officers, or were until they were fired three days ago. The Brimfield board of selectmen, three elected part-time officials responsible for running the modest municipal government, fired every police officer, full and part-time, except for the acting chief. The decision, coming on the eve of the biggest antiques fair in the country, is national news. It has also split the citizens of Brimfield. It is not just that some of these cops have lived in the community all their lives or that they have been trying to form a union since being canned. The decision is exposing a division that has festered for decades. On one side are those who support the people everyone who lives here calls "the fleas." These residents make their money off the market and argue that commerce brings both capital and goodwill to Brimfield. On the other side are those who want the fleas gone, who consider them a nuisance that harms more than it helps. In the thick of the dispute, the pivotal character who may be more torn than anyone else, is the chairman of the board of selectmen, Robert Cheney.

Joe and Rachel have not heard the news of the dismissal and are surprised to see the men picketing when they arrive in town. "There is always an accident at Brimfield, where they have to bring in the rescue and clear the traffic," says Rachel. "If that happens this time, what will they do?" Joe tries to honk to show his support, but he is so excited and hurried that he can't find the car's horn.

Inside town hall, Cheney is explaining that the decision is not as dire as it might appear. "There is a lot of misinformation out there," he tells reporters who have gathered. "Lots of people, even people who live here in town, do not realize that this is a part-time police department. I had a woman who lives in the town who called from the Cape, and she said, 'Oh, this is terrible, I'm going to have to cut my vacation short and come home.' I asked her, 'Why are you going to do that?' 'Because there are no police,' she told me. So I said, 'Do you realize that these guys only patrol six hours a day?' "

Cheney expects that the Massachusetts state police will continue to patrol the town as always. He also anticipates that the town's one remaining officer, acting police chief Robert Boucher, can hire temporary officers from other towns. However, Massachusetts is very much a union state; other officers are refusing to come to Brimfield, refusing to get involved in what they perceive as a union dispute.

The conflict began months ago when the former police chief, Jack Jovian, resigned just before the May show over a staffing dispute with the board of selectmen. Jovian had been a popular chief and several officers would have benefited from his plan to reorganize. No one, including the chief, was supposed to work more than twenty hours a week except during the three shows. That was when they earned the overtime that made the job financially attractive. The rest of the year they worked private security or for other small police departments. Many yearned for full-time police work. After Jovian left, some worried about job security, while others wanted to stage a protest during the May show. Instead, they met with the union with the toughest, most nononsense approach, the Teamsters. Fourteen members of the department had signed union cards when the selectmen acted on July 3 on a legal technicality. Police officers had annual contracts that were renewed each July 1. The board voted not to renew any of them, except for the chief's.

Cheney denies that the union efforts affected the board's decision. "We're in the middle of the hiring of a new police chief, and we feel that the new chief, whoever he or she is, should have a role in the process of reviewing who should be on this force," he says. "I've done a fair amount of soul searching since this began. It would be far easier for the board to post a meeting and simply to reappoint these guys. It would be the easiest thing for this board. But we have decided to take the tough stand and we will take the heat for the week." Privately, he has other reasons. There have been complaints about several of the officers, concerns that some were stopping young women on dark streets for no apparent reason. He wants the new chief to check out those reports, to see if they are true. He also questions whether it makes sense for a town of 3,300 to hire eighteen cops. No other town of this size has so many, and Brimfield does only in order to have extra staff for the flea market.

The issue always seems to return to the flea market. Local chamber of commerce studies indicate that the shows produce millions of dollars for the local economy. The flea market benefits everyone from hotel keepers and restaurant owners to the high school kids who help out for a few hours on one of the fields. "I know of families who have sent children to college off the money they have raised each year from parking cars," said Pam Beall, the town clerk, who often gets exasperated by the complaints about the market. She says the market preserves open space in town and allows the same families to stay on the land generation after generation.

The First Congregational Church is one beneficiary. Each year the church ladies sell hundreds of blueberry, apple, and cherry pies at a stand, while the men collect ten dollars for every car that parks on the church property. "We'll never have a loan on the church again," says Anne Dutka, a church elder. But even the church has been reassessing the flea market. As expected, members have cancelled the Friday night church dinner for the July show. It isn't that they haven't been making money from baking chicken or ham with all the fixings, said Dutka, only that members are tired or on vacation. Maybe they will do it again, but the new minister is exploring other ideas, such as selling bottled water on hot summer days.

Many residents question how much they truly benefit. David Lamberto and Don Moriarty both attended a special meeting of the town's financial committee and board of selectmen recently, because someone had made a bookkeeping error, and it looked as though the town was spending $100,000 more on police and other services than it was taking in. It took hours of bickering before the error was discovered. Residents know that for three weeks of the year they will need to find a way around Route 20, that the town library will be closed, and that they had better lock their windows tight. Even Beall, who generally does not mind the show, came home one day years ago to find a young boy ransacking her house. He admitted he was looking for things he could sell at the antiques market. At the time she was still a reporter with the local newspaper and her research found that the burglary rate definitely rose during the shows. Maybe that is why, when the yellow school buses sometimes grind to a halt in the stop-and-go-traffic on Route 20, students press their tongues to the windows and yell, "Go home, fleas."

Publicly, Cheney tries to support the Brimfield shows. When asked by strangers about the markets, he admits that "some people do complain about them." Then he adds, "Overall, everyone enjoys it." But his support goes only so far. Before his election, the town had developed a plan to spend about a million dollars in state money to improve Route 20. The road would be repaved, sidewalks installed, trees planted, and elegant streetlights erected. The road can be dangerous during the three weeks of the show. The two-lane highway is narrow, and huge crowds walk in either dust or mud and they often encroach onto the road. Close encounters between pedestrians and automobiles are common. After Cheney's election, he questioned the need for spending money on land that Brimfield residents rarely use. While the money would come from the state, the town would be responsible for future maintenance. Cheney disliked the financial responsibilities and the aesthetics of the plan. "If I wanted to live in a town that looked like Cambridge, I'd live in Cambridge," he snorts.

The truth is he really has little use for the shows, despite his reputation as someone who knows more about antiques—or at least antique clocks—than just about anyone at the Brimfield market. A third-generation clockmaker, Cheney is a clock consultant at the historic Sturbridge Museum, the author of a paper debunking commonly accepted views about the history of American clockmakers, and he owns a clock he hopes to sell for a half million dollars. Perhaps his knowledge is the problem in his relationship with Brimfield.

Cheney has risen to the comfortable and polished realms of museums and big-pocket collectors. It's quite a step up from more than a century ago when his grandfather, Clarence Cheney of Worcester, began his avocation as a clockmaker by trekking into homes to wind clocks once a week. By the time his father, Bradford, took over the business after World War II, electric clocks were already beginning to replace traditional wind-up pieces. His solution was to become Worcester's public clockmaker, responsible for maintaining and repairing clocks in public buildings, schools, and all those high colonial towers, steeples, and cupolas that are a New England heritage. Cheney began working in his father's shop at seven years old, sweeping the floor. Eventually he could repair an old banjo clock under his father's supervision. By the time Robert Cheney graduated from college in 1974 with a degree in political science, he knew he wanted to go into the profession. At the same time, he knew he was not going to climb those tall, swaying clock towers that smelled musty inside and were caked with ancient pigeon droppings. His family heritage in horology gave him enough confidence to enter the elite world of high-level restoration and museum conservation of historic timepieces.

He moved from dowdy Worcester to historic and charming Brimfield, restoring the two-hundred-year-old Major Abner Morgan house with its nine working chimneys. He set up his shop on the second floor and repaired older, rarer clocks. He became an expert in early American clockmakers. He has worked hard to understand the requirements of these rare and high-priced timepieces and to know the best experts in the field. "There are different rules of engagement in museum pieces," he says. "You do not just automatically repair a museum piece. It has to be studied and determined what is the best solution for it. Sometimes you may hurt the value by restoring it. It might be best just to leave it the way it is." He must be making the right calls since he has worked with more than thirty museums. Rich collectors hire him to inspect and buy rare and valuable timepieces. In 2000, he spent a year at the Concord Museum in Concord, Massachusetts, researching eighteenth-century American clockmaking. In an article in the highly prestigious *The Magazine Antiques*, he challenged many of the conventional theories on early clockmaking, arguing that early American clockmakers were far more dependent on British parts than historians had theorized in the past. Not everyone agreed and some were dismayed that Cheney had criticized the legendary clockmaker Simon Willard. But over time he felt that his views were prevailing.

The ticking of the pendulums of historic clocks extends beyond his shop into many rooms of the rambling house he shares with his partner, Denise Johnson, her two children, and his son from a previous marriage. In a parlor is a 1790 tall clock by Andrew Fairbairn of Edinburgh that Cheney bought the year before at the September Brimfield show. When he bought it, the dial was bent, it needed resilvering, and its mechanical works were broken. Now it keeps perfect time. An even bigger gamble sits in the hall by the front staircase. There, its pendulum ticking solemnly, stands a tall clock made by Gawen Brown in Boston around 1749. The handsome case features a Japanned coating. Japanning was an attempt by Western cabinetmakers to mimic lacquering techniques that had begun in China as early as 1200 BC. Europeans and the few Americans interested in lacquering did not have access, as the Japanese did, to the sap of a sumac or lacquer tree. Instead, Western cabinet finishers used a complicated recipe of spirits, gums, and oils to varnish. This clock did not have that surface when Cheney bought it for $130,000. Instead, it had a garish red coat of paint, probably applied around 1890, to conform with the Victorian style of the time. When he purchased it, he was convinced that the Japanned coat was underneath and that, if so, the clock was extremely rare. While a number of English clocks were Japanned, very few American clocks were finished in this style. After the auction, he had the clock x-rayed. His hunch was correct: The x-rays clearly showed a coating that could only be Japanning. It took two years to painstakingly remove the outer coats. Revealing the Japanning had been "a huge relief," says Cheney. If the clock had not had a Japanning coat, could he have gotten his money back? Not necessarily, he says. Trading at his level, one cannot afford to make those kinds of mistakes. "If I would have been wrong, that would not have been good," he says. Cheney now plans to sell the clock privately. He hopes it will fetch $500,000. It will be a nice reward. The antique clock business has been slow the last couple of years. It was so bad a year ago that Cheney seriously considered making a career change.

Cheney only occasionally goes on the Brimfield fields. When he does, he walks rapidly, stopping only when he spies a clock, and he almost always rejects it and moves on. Other clock dealers hail him and he will stop and talk business. The odds of finding a good clock are just not there. Sometimes he wonders why others find the Brimfield market so attractive. One friend often stayed at Cheney's house during the show. He would complain that he just could not afford to buy merchandise at the same level as Cheney. But Cheney closely watched what his friend was buying. He noticed that the friend might spend close to $25,000 each trip. Multiply that by the three shows and it equaled what Cheney would spend on just one clock. His friend, Cheney concluded, was afraid of making big decisions, of taking big risks. If he continued on this course, he was doomed to the mediocrity that littered the fields.

Cheney has taken the big risk by dismissing the police, and by Wednesday his confidence is growing. There have been no problems, although he's a little worried about tomorrow. That's when May's field opens. Normally a dozen police are assigned to work Thursday morning to handle the traffic and pedestrians. So far the crowds have been down, perhaps because of weather that has been alternating between hot and sultry, and rainy. Maybe news of the police situation is discouraging people from coming. Either way, it is making Cheney look good. The field promoters, despite the small crowds, are grudgingly backing the town. Dealers are finding it is easier without cops enforcing the no-parking restrictions along the side of the road. A young resident mentions the situation with the cops to Rachel, telling her that the cops were getting too important for their own good, that they deserve what they are getting.

Former police officers do not know what to do. They have begun circulating flyers and posting signs calling for stronger action against the board. One sign propped on a car says, "How do you spell relief? RECALL." Everyone knows it is a hollow threat. Cheney's plan is working.

Thursday at three in the morning, Robert Boucher's phone rings. The acting chief groggily picks up the receiver. A man on the other end of the line bluntly warns him to watch out if he is on the road later this morning. The line clicks dead.

Later in the morning Boucher is still thinking of that call as he directs traffic around May's field. He is alone, but traffic is down again. He hopes it will stay that way. If someone wants to barricade Route 20, this would be the day to do it. He does not think that will happen. Fifteen minutes before his scheduled nine o'clock start, Dick May opens the gates. The small crowd surges in.

Cheney, who has been watching from the side of the street, is delighted. He's been working eighteen-hour days, but it's worth it. He is gaining control of the flea market, making it more manageable, more profitable for the town. Budget numbers are still being compiled, but it looks as though the town will spend only about $7,000 for overtime and other expenses. A year ago the cost was $19,000. "We have had overwhelming support," he tells an inquirer. "I've had calls from people I did not even realize lived in this town, who wanted to say we did the right thing. People are behind us one hundred percent. People are saying we finally solved the traffic problem in town—we got rid of the police department."

Then a cloud appears. Mark and Lee Gillespie, brothers from Alexandria, Virginia, are returning to their tent on this Thursday morning. They are dealers of high-quality silver and this is their third time at Brimfield. They long resisted coming here because they felt that their silver was priced too high for the Brimfield market. Some of the pieces, from flatware to tea sets, are of museum quality. Friends kept telling them they were wrong about Brimfield, that the market was broader than they thought. So last September they tried it. They sold twice what they anticipated. Brimfield also gives them the opportunity to search for more antiques, and for the last half hour they have been checking other fields.

Now they notice that the flaps of their tent are not as secure as they had been when they left for their motel last night. It must have been windy, thinks Mark Gillespie. They enter the tent and realize wind was not the intruder. Display cases are pushed over. It takes only a few moments to confirm that thieves got in during the night. The brothers begin to tally what is missing, but at first it is an overwhelming and impossible task. Among the missing items is an eighteenth-century Argyle tea pot, their rarest and most valuable piece.

They call the Brimfield police, but are told there are no officers, and if they want to file a complaint they need to come to the office. Mark Gillespie hikes the half mile to the police station, a dreary room only slightly larger than a closet, with artificial wooden paneling, buried in the cellar of the old town hall. There, the one clerk cannot find a blank police report. She takes some information and promises to get back to them. Instead, Mark Gillespie calls the Massachusetts state police, who promise to send a detective immediately.

The news spreads during the day, especially after the detective spends more than two hours with the Gillespies, writing a report and taking pictures. The Gillespies tally the loss at $100,000. Reporters have heard about the theft and find the Gillespies angry about the decision to fire the police department. "What we have is not only a town that has eliminated every member of the police department, but then it goes and advertises, through the media, essentially inviting every criminal on the East Coast to come to Brimfield where there are no police," says Lee Gillespie. "Any public servant who gets rid of the police department just before an antiques show like this has a hole in his head. Think about what they did. By getting rid of the police the way they did, they put the risks on their shoulders. If I lived in this community, I would not feel safe right now. It was just plain stupid to do something that risky."

Cheney is not about to let this theft spoil his day or his victory over the police. He has no sympathy for the two crime victims. Instead, he says the Gillespies are to blame. He tells reporters that "anybody who leaves $100,000 of silver unattended overnight, I think they should have their heads examined."

CHAPTER 10

The Collector

JOEL SCHIFF IS perched on the edge of the open side door of a Navigator van, carefully studying a large cast-iron pot. It is about two feet long and one foot wide, with three legs each about six inches high. On the side is the date 1785 and inscribed is the word "iohaniflack." "It's a wild piece," says Schiff. "I'm trying to find out how much wear there is on it." He turns it over. The bottom is black with carbon. He nods and says, "It certainly looks like it is the right age."

Still, Schiff worries that the piece is a fake, and that's a significant concern because the dealer is asking $1,400. The handles do not seem worn enough and there are marks that could have been left from a casting procedure that was not used until the nineteenth century. Another collector passes by and Schiff shows him what he has found.

"What do you think, Paul?" Schiff finally asks.

"I don't know, Joel. It makes me a little bit nervous," Paul replies.

"What do you mean?"

Paul points to where the handle touches the lid. "There should be a lot more wear there," he says.

Schiff nods. As he does, he wonders if Paul's criticism is valid or self-serving. Is he denigrating the pot so that Schiff will not buy the piece, possibly opening the way to acquire it himself? They look some more and then Paul leaves. Afterward, Schiff continues his examination, clearly torn.

This would be his first and probably only major purchase at the show. Schiff drove up from New York to Brimfield on a Saturday, stopping at a modest flea market in nearby Palmer. It was awful, nothing but junk for sale. On Sunday he drove thirty miles from Brimfield to Putnam, Connecticut, an aging mill town like hundreds of others in New England struggling to discover a revival. For Putnam it is antiques, shop after shop after shop of consignments. A friend had told Schiff about a particular piece, and while he could not find it, he was impressed by the number and variety of antiques shops.

As Schiff was getting back into his van, two pimply-faced youths stopped him. They told him how much they admired his van. Once white, it is decorated in graffiti. Schiff lives in New York City, where anything white is an open invitation to the city's graffiti artists. The work the youths were admiring came from one particular artist who called himself the best graffiti artist in New York. Schiff thanked the admirers and said that while he agreed that some of the scrawls were quite good, others he wished he could get rid of. The kids said they would love to have a chance to work on his van someday.

"Well, how about right now?" asked Schiff, who had nothing else planned.

The kids looked surprised but they quickly warmed to the idea. They directed Schiff to a body shop in a dead part of town. A biker dude, the owner or manager, supervised for a while, clearly worried. Eventually he left the kids to their work because it was clear that they knew what they were doing. Later, other aging bikers, guys in their forties, fifties, and sixties, wandered in from the bar next door. Graffitti was not quite their thing. However, the kids were carrying out an antiestablishment act of some kind, and that was cool. The kids spent five hours and used countless cans of paint. They retained the best designs while adding new features in the gaps. It was an ever-evolving process. Schiff drove back to Brimfield.

Joel Schiff is considered a little different, though not because of the van or his pirate-parrot outfit that goes along with his hobbling on one leg. No, there are a lot of colorful characters at Brimfield; one almost cannot have an identity here without taking on a touch of eccentricity, and Schiff fits right in. It also isn't his obsession with collecting cast-iron cookware that makes him different. That pastime seems exceedingly pedestrian in comparison to collecting such oddities as the wrappers around Chinese firecrackers, tea bags, wooden nickels, coat hangers, smiley faces, air sickness bags, RCA Nippers, menus, and nude-woman lamps. It is not even his drive, his intensity to get out in the fields—he is no different from hundreds of others in that respect.

What makes Schiff stand out is that he is a pure collector. He buys, but he does not sell. Most dealers start collecting, and when they accumulate an excessive supply they begin selling, partly out of necessity. Selling also produces cash to buy ever more expensive, rarer items. Schiff is not opposed to selling or dealing, he just is not interested. Once in a great while he will sell something, but he prefers to trade. The problem is, hardly anyone has anything he needs, so stacks of extras just keep piling up in his apartment.

Brimfield cannot survive without collectors and collectors-turned-dealers. Fortunately for Brimfield, the trait, if not universal, is certainly dominant. While certain animals—magpies, pack rats, and monkeys—are notorious for collecting, the characteristic is even more ingrained in humans. Collections of pebbles have been found in caves in France populated eighty thousand years ago. Cave paintings, sculptures, and ornaments were common thirty thousand years ago. History shows a relationship between power and collections. In Rome two thousand years ago the emperors held the great collections, in the Middle Ages it was the church, and a century ago it was the American robber barons. Morgan, Hearst, Mellon, Rockefeller, Carnegie, and Frick looted great collections, amassing piles of art, pottery, glass, furniture, stamps, and coins. But the Industrial Age they created also produced a middle class that has brought a degree of egalitarianism to the pastime.

Diversity has also led to varying views of what is valuable and worth saving. Today, the list of collectors and collector organizations would be as long as this book. Collectors devote countless hours not just to their collections but to writing and exchanging ideas in newsletters, annual meetings, Internet discussion groups, and price guides. Fred Dole, who for years now has been helping out at J&J, says he was working at the information desk at the field one day when a woman came up and began asking him about toilet paper. He thought she was complaining that one of the temporary toilets had run out. "No, you don't understand," she said. "I collect antique toilet paper. I wonder where I can get some." Dole says, "That pretty much says more about the world of collecting than anything else."

Why do we collect? Experts, from self-styled collecting gurus to psychologists, say it can be for the beauty of the object, its current or future monetary value, or for nostalgia, as a remembrance of a time past. Or, say the Freudians, it is "a redirection of surplus libido onto inanimate objects."

Schiff is not a wealthy collector, although he devotes most of his energy and resources to his collection. He grew up as an Army brat, moving from military base to military base as his father pursued his career. He lost his leg in a childhood accident, when he fell into a creek one day and his leg became trapped under a rock. He was lucky to escape. Now living in New York, he has worked driving a cab and doing other jobs, but mostly he has just lived off his leg. That's the way he describes it, living off the huge settlement his parents had invested after the accident. His collecting began more than thirty years ago.

In the late 1960s Schiff was living on an old barge that had been owned by the Pennsylvania Railroad before the company went broke. A river rat named Casey helped Schiff and others buy a string of barges that lined the New Jersey side of the Hudson across from New York. Schiff paid $2,000 for his barge. For a while he paid a dockage fee, but then ownership changed. Local authorities wanted to get rid of the colony of barge owners; soon they were squatters, unwelcome residents of a city that could not figure out how to banish them. It was an interesting community.

"There was a lab tech, soap opera actors, an auxiliary

policeman, and there was Henny," recalls Schiff. "Henny had provided a refuge to people for more than thirty years. If your marriage broke up, if you were down on your luck, if you were just slightly on the wrong side of the law, and it had to be just a little bit and not a lot, Henny would take you in, no questions asked. He would share his home with you, share his food, not asking anything in return and not questioning how long you needed to stay. Eventually most people did get back on their feet, and that's when it was payback for Henny. If they were in the restaurant business, as many of them were, they would bring him food, sacks of food, which he would share with others. Or if they were in the haberdashery business, they would bring him clothes. Whatever they had, they would share with Henny just like he had shared with them."

Henny lived in a barge at the end of the causeway. Once a machinist, he rarely worked and he was often into his cups at the gin mills. When that happened, sometimes he would literally crawl his way home on his hands and knees. Sometimes he would be so drunk that he would fall into the drink. At high tide that wasn't particularly dire, because the water would often come within an inch of the causeway decking, and, says Schiff, "People would hear him and they would come running and pull him out. But when it was low tide, that drop could be as much as twelve feet down into water that was so foul as to be almost indescribable."

One day Schiff was using a torch to burn off paint in one of the bathrooms on his barge. A spark landed on nearby foam insulation. It flamed quickly and the fire moved up and climbed to the roof of the deck, which was covered with flammable tar paper and lathing. Schiff fought unsuccessfully to extinguish the fire. Eventually he realized he was not going to be able to douse it, or even contain it. The barges were tied in tandem, one to another, creating the possibility that the fire could leap from Schiff's to others. He called the fire department. In the past he and the other barge owners had offered to pay for fire service. The city had ignored the squatters on their request. When firefighters arrived, they quickly sized up the situation. First they made sure everyone was off all the barges. Then they monitored the fire, keeping it from destroying the causeway but allowing the blaze to leap from barge to barge The authorities no longer had to resolve their squatter dilemma. Only two barges were able to untangle their tethers and flee. The remaining barges, including Schiff's, were destroyed.

Henny continued to live on the river, although his barge and most of his possessions were destroyed by the fire. He found a place to live in a scow tied up nearby. Everyone said Henny was lucky, until the day a few months later when he came home drunk and fell, yet once again, into the river. This time there was no one to hear his cries or pull him out. He wasn't found until days later.

Afterward, Henny's friends held a wake. Many talked of a man who had always been there when they needed help. His ashes were scattered on the river. Friends were invited to take a remembrance of Henny. Schiff found in the scow two pieces of cast iron, a saucepan and a broiler, which had survived the fire. He marveled at Henny's two relics. At its height the fire had burned at white-hot temperatures, fed by ancient yellow pine planking, lathing, and tar paper that had marinated in petroleum for a century. It was a miracle that the pots had survived. "It seemed to me that the fire could not destroy the cast iron," says Schiff. "Even though I am an atheist, it seemed as if this was almost the hand of God shining down. It also seemed to me that this material was something that could make a difference." It was as close to immortality as Schiff was going to find.

A year later Schiff was in an antiques shop in Sturbridge, looking for more cast iron. He was intrigued by a technology first discovered in China nearly two millennia ago, one that transformed social history, beginning in the seventeenth century, by making the task of cooking meals and sustaining a family far easier. It was at Sturbridge that he learned about Brimfield, ten miles to the west. Like everyone else, he was amazed. He began to ask dealers if they had any cast iron. "I would be asking people if they had cast-iron cookware and they looked at me like I was crazy," he recalls. "The problem with cast iron was that in most situations people could get only one or two dollars for each piece, and it just wasn't worth it for them to bring the goods. For the first fifteen years, even when I guaranteed I would buy everything they would bring, I still had difficulty convincing dealers to bring things." Part of the dilemma may have been that cast iron was so plentiful that it became invisible to dealers searching for antiques to sell. Cast iron had been such a staple until the 1940s, when finally it was supplanted by aluminum and stainless steel.

That attitude changed in the mid-1980s. Schiff pins the date to 1984, when the first price guide was published. It was not a very good one. But it told collectors and dealers who had cast-iron pieces not only what they had but also what they might be able to get for it. Collectors already knew that some of the best cast-iron pieces had been made by the Griswold Manufacturing Company. From the end of the Civil War until 1957 the firm had produced hundreds of different pieces, from skillets to pots to muffin cups, from a shop at 12th and Raspberry Streets in Erie, Pennsylvania. Collectors created the Griswold and Cast Iron Cookware Association (GCICA). The organization provided support through everything from holding annual conferences to selling distinctive yellow-colored t-shirts with the group's emblem, which features its initials. (A curious dealer asked Schiff, who often wears a GCICA t-shirt, how many he owns. "Not as many as you or I would like," he replied.)

The organization had its share of petty fights and miniscandals, from the insistence of some members that the world of cast iron is centered in Erie to attempts by dissidents to stuff the ballot boxes during officer elections. That eventually led to a rival organization, the Wagner and Griswold Society (WAGS). With the two organizations boasting more than a thousand members between them, cast-iron prices began to climb. A Griswold muffin pan could go for $25 and a skillet for $30 while a Griswold No. 1 would fetch $3,500. A few rarer items were selling for anywhere from $6,000 to $9,000.

Schiff belongs to both organizations and tries to remain clear of most of the politics. He views anyone else who buys cast-iron cookware as the "noble competition." He explains: "I'm always telling people it is important to know that the competitor is not your enemy. If you form a good relationship, over time you will make deals with other people, you will be able to help each other out." He worries that it is not his fellow collectors but the tens of thousands of designers out there who are a greater threat, finding a rare piece and selling it to a client interested in tacking it to the fireplace to complete "the country look" design for his or her living room.

Schiff's apartment in New York is a two-story walk-up with one difference—space is exceedingly tight because of an overwhelming volume of cast iron. Cookware hangs everywhere, except in the bathroom, where Schiff worries the moisture could make the pieces rust. "Well, my ex had this totally unreasonable demand that nothing should come into the bedroom, which I thought made no sense at all," explains Schiff. "And then she said, 'Either it goes or I go,' so I brought in another hundred pieces in case it was not clear. We have a good relationship now that she is not in the house." The kitchen contains a black cast-iron stove on one side, a white porcelain sink on the other. From the ceiling hang cast-iron pans, pots, and molds, and directly over the stove is a large four-foot-diameter ship's wheel from an ice ship that once plied the Hudson. A grappling line stands on the wall about waist high. Visitors sidle into the living room, which contains a small daybed, literally the only place to sit. On the opposite wall, against an unfinished brick wall, shelves hold more molds, waffle irons, and a large metal "Griswold" sign. By the daybed stands an amateur miniature photo studio. The back bedroom contains a platform bed with walls lined with shelves with even more cast iron. A small alcove holds some books, and yet more iron.

One of Schiff's favorite pieces is a Japanese teapot with detailing on the body resembling the strokes one sees in brush paintings. It begins on one side with a tree whose branches are in full bloom and as the pot is moved clockwise the branches become increasingly sparse, a movement from summer to winter. "This is an artistic calligraphy," says Schiff. "I think what is being said here is, tacitly, that in addition to the art of life residing in the brush painting and calligraphy, we who do iron are no less artistic. This is more than a piece of craft. It is also a piece of art. It has the same spirit as is in brush painting. That's why I like it so much." Other favored pieces include tiny toy tea pots, a Russian water pot, bean pots, a Spoors square-bottom tea pot, an English water kettle, an Azerbaijan coffee roaster, cookie/biscuit muffin molds, acorn penis pans (originally called acorn pans but Schiff added the middle name because of their shape), corn cob pans, corn dog makers, a cornbread maker, three-cup molds (totally impractical and clearly designed by a man who did not cook, says Schiff, because who would go to all the trouble of making batter for only three muffin cups?), a Chinese incense burner, long-handled, short-handled, and flexible-handled waffle irons, communion waffle irons, square-mold waffle irons, wavy-mold waffle irons, waffle irons with the design of a cross, an anchor, fish, waves, scales, and a lily, and cast-iron molds in the shape of a rabbit, a fish, a lobster, and a pig's head. He also collects thousands of antique postcards that depict scenes featuring one or more pieces of cast-iron cookware. Schiff says he has only a third of his collection in the apartment; the rest is in storage elsewhere. How many pieces does he have? Replies Schiff: "I stopped counting five years ago when I had five thousand pieces."

Some collectors overindulge. A nineteenth-century British nobleman, Thomas Phillips, sought to acquire one copy of every book in the world. Phillips was said to have allowed his wife and children to live in squalor, but he left a collection so vast that Sotheby's held more than sixty auctions. Newspaper tycoon William Randolph Hearst bought so many treasures that he had difficulty finding places for them or finding them after he had found places for them. According to one biographer, Hearst, beginning in the 1920s, created his own holding company to buy art and stored it in garages and warehouses in New York, Los Angeles, San Francisco, and at his mansion in San Simeon. At one point the inventory was managed by thirty employees and included 10,700 crates of goods and tens of thousands of books.

Two brothers, Langley and Homer Collyer, of New York City, in 1947 showed just how dangerous collecting can be. Police received an anonymous phone call informing them that a man had died at the Collyers' Fifth Avenue brownstone. Police had to force the door open and shovel through mounds of trash before they eventually found Langley Collyer, dead in his bed. They assumed that his brother, Homer, had made the call, but they could not find Homer. They spent nineteen days emptying the house of the reeking piles of garbage and trash, the vestiges of a lifetime of collecting. That's when they found Homer Collyer, in the same room as his brother. The best guess was that Homer was digging his way toward his brother when huge piles of refuse toppled onto him, pinning him to the floor.

Obsession can be scary. Bill Heuring, a New York dealer who reconditions and sells antique cash registers, says he has seen collectors spend their savings and lose their wives and children over their quests to buy just one more piece. Marilyn Gehman, who runs a market in Adamstown, Pennsylvania, says she often sees people who appear to be living out of their cars, who use the market's restroom and showers. "We see a lot of homeless people, people who are homeless because they have an addiction, similar to what one has for alcohol or drugs, for collecting," she says. "Many of the people are very intelligent. They can speak two or three languages, they have multiple college degrees, yet they are living out of their cars and they are fixated with buying antiques and collectibles."

Schiff's collecting is restrained by his economics, and he tries to balance what he can do on his income. He says that his income is directed to three areas: food, transportation, and cast iron. Schiff has a long-term plan for the collection: he wants to turn it over to a museum. Such aspirations are not unusual. Entire museums have been structured around collections. J. P. Morgan's collection of Egyptian art, Chinese porcelain, and early manuscripts is displayed in the tycoon's former palatial mansion in New York. A museum in Old Lyme, Connecticut, was created by another collector who specialized in nuts, nutcrackers, and anything else related to nuts.

Schiff has long wanted his collection to be part of a museum of the kitchen or hearth. His vision for the museum is centered on not just the objects but what they have meant for society. "People look at objects such as jewelry as to the thing itself," he explains. "It becomes a suspended object, something to be approved of, to admire, solely for its beauty or for the nature of what it is. That, and also for its investment value. I don't look at things that way. I like to look at objects, especially what I have been collecting, as texts, as anthropology, as something that tells us something of life. What I think these objects do is that they tell many stories."

He is convinced that the story of the hearth goes to the heart of understanding social history, especially the role women have played. The development of the cast-iron stove, to a considerable extent, first emancipated women from both the drudgery and dangers of working over open kitchen fires. As early as 1640, cast iron was being forged in Saugus, Massachusetts, although it would be more than another century before stoves arrived. Cookware's arrival preceded the other great development in the home, indoor plumbing, by another century. Cast-iron appliances also became indispensable. For example, George Washington's mother bequeathed her cast iron in her will, and the members of Lewis and Clark's expedition found that a cast-iron Dutch oven was one of their most essential tools. Over time, cast-iron appliances led to the mass production of food products, moving the country toward greater urbanization and greater freedom for women. Schiff does not aim to create a stand-alone museum but perhaps to have his collection mixed with others in an interactive museum. Patrons might not only learn but even use his pieces to cook food they would then eat. He even would like to use his life insurance policy and whatever is left of his assets after he dies to help the museum's endowment. The only problem is that he has yet to find anyone interested enough. He's talked to a number of regional museums, universities, and culinary schools, but so far he has found no takers.

These days Schiff spends long hours online and at shows searching to buy something new. It rarely happens anymore. When it does, he is surprised, puzzled, and a little fearful. That's the situation with the $1,400 pot he has found here at Brimfield.

"It's quite a spectacular piece," he says, after his friend Paul has left. "It's definitely one of a kind."

Schiff wants the pot to be authentic, but he wishes he could do a strike test to determine the type of metal. He is also worried that the 7 in the date does not look the way the numeral did in Europe in the 1780s. He knows he has to make a decision. Finally, he approaches the owner, Mario Pollo of Woodstock, New York. Pollo tells Schiff he just bought the pot a few hours earlier from a dealer who said it used to be in a museum in Vienna.

"I bought it and I really did not want to sell it," says Pollo. "But someone said I had to at least let Joel see it."

Schiff makes a decision. He dickers, but buys it for $1,300. As he writes the check he asks Pollo to hold it until next week when he can transfer money into the account. With his fixed income, that's a lot of money. He really has no choice. Joel Schiff is on a quest to build the most complete collection of cast-iron cookware that he can. He just can't stop now.

CHAPTER 11

High Risks

FOR ONCE JOE and Rachel are hunting together when they find the European and American Impressionist paintings. Prices are incredibly low—as little as $2,000.

The dealers selling the paintings are eating lunch.

"Let us know if you want a closer look," says the older of the two dealers. He has a thick Eastern European accent.

By now Joe and Rachel have recognized the booth from the last show. Joe likes to take risks, but what these dealers were offering in May was too risky even for him. Has anything changed? He decides to probe further. Joe points to a landscape, a European street scene. What can the dealer tell him about it?

"It's a Showfield," the dealer says. "He's a German painter."

Joe wonders if the dealer means Schofield, who was an American painter. Joe asks if he can look more carefully and the dealer pulls it from a protective wrapper. Joe closely examines the canvas and then turns it over. A label on the back says Walter Schofield, 1867–1944, $12,000–$30,000.

Joe asks if the dealer meant to say Schofield instead of Showfield, but the dealer is adamant in making the *h* sound in Showfield. Joe does not bother showing the dealer the label on the back. Joe knows that the artist he is familiar with, Schofield, was a Bucks County artist. The dealer insists this artist is German.

"Not American?" asks Joe.

"No, German."

"How much?" asks Joe.

"Two thousand dollars."

"Can you guarantee it?"

The dealer acts as if he hasn't heard Joe. He turns his attention to Rachel, who has picked up another painting. Joe asks again, can the dealer guarantee that the painting is authentic? The dealer looks at him quizzically. Joe tries for a third time.

"Can you guarantee this?"

Quietly, the dealer shakes his head, and replies, "No, I can't guarantee it."

Joe puts it down. Perhaps this is a matter of cultural miscommunication, either intentional or unintentional. Joe knows that despite what the dealer said, the painting implies that it is by Schofield. And it is clearly not. It is the wrong pallet, the wrong type of scene for the Bucks County artist, and the price is ridiculously low. Schofield sells for $100,000 or more, and he was definitely not German.

Joe and Rachel remember this booth so well because after the last time they were here, they had debated with another dealer who had been impressed by several of the paintings.

"They look right," the dealer argued. "They look very good."

Everything about the paintings looked wrong to both Joe

and to Rachel, even the signatures. They also wondered why this other dealer was so high on the paintings. One of the tricks of dealer art is to know one's competitors. Some can be trusted. The reasons others are less reliable vary. Some might accidentally misrepresent a picture or just plain be wrong. Others, not many, but a few, might be inclined to intentional misrepresentation. One known scam is for dealers to work together but to pretend to be strangers. While one sells, the other takes on the guise of a customer, talking up a piece each time someone comes by, giving the piece credibility through his seeming impartiality and adding pressure on the real customer to buy it.

Joe and Rachel move on. Like other buyers and dealers, they are a little disappointed by the July show. The amount of everything—the crowds, the dealers, and the art—is less than in May. There are still opportunities, but not as many. One day Joe buys several paintings, carries them to a table where he is about to have lunch, and sells two of them before he bites into his sandwich. The buyer spotted Joe leaving the field and trailed him to the lunch spot. Joe doubles his money on both paintings. Still, that's the exception at this show.

At Joe's suggestion, they are not camping at their booth at Heart-O-The-Mart but are instead staying at a motel in Holyoke, which is twenty miles away, for $60 a night. The closer hotels are more than $100 a night. One evening Rachel tries to take a bath, but the water is yellow. She notes that prostitutes seem to be hanging around the parking lot at all hours of the night.

They have both heard about the Gillespies' silver heist. Everyone has by now. The consensus on the fields is that it must be an insurance scam. How else could anyone lose $100,000 of merchandise? Some field owners, who want dealers and customers to know that they must fend for themselves, are even more suspicious. David Lamberto, who runs Jeanne Hertan's field, says, "I wonder if it was a plant by the police who were fired. You have to be awfully stupid to leave that much silver out and leave the booth for the night. It has a false ring to me."

There is a hole in the insurance scam theory. The Gillespies do not have insurance. Neither do Joe and Rachel, or many other dealers at Brimfield. Insurance for itinerant dealers can be prohibitively expensive. It also can be difficult to inventory or document an item's value, especially when it changes price and ownership so rapidly. Insurance companies are wary about venues like antiques markets.

Brimfield, for all its romance as a place where treasure can be found among America's discarded junk, has a tawdry, sordid side. It's another reason why Robert Cheney does not care to step onto the fields. He does not trust what some merchants are selling. It is unusual to find dealers who will stand behind their wares or offer refunds if a buyer is dissatisfied. The policy across the fields is strictly caveat emptor, buyer beware. "There is high risk out there in those fields," art dealer Fran Smith likes to warn. One Brimfield legend tells of how a dealer one day picked up some rocks in the field and tried to hawk them as "moon rocks." According to the tale, he found more than one gullible buyer. Few dealers sympathize with ignorant buyers. They expect people to do their research, just as they once did. Anyone stupid enough to buy a fake, whether it's a painting by Showfield or a moon rock, deserves to be fleeced.

The "outlaw" nature of Brimfield is enhanced by its setting in such a rural area. Even when Brimfield had a local police department, it was better at patrolling traffic than at investigating crime. A former police chief once estimated that larceny around Brimfield can increase by as much as two thousand percent just before the shows begin. He did not say how often stolen items are recovered. Sometimes it winds up being the crime victim's responsibility to solve the case. A few years ago a reporter for a nearby newspaper, the *Sturbridge News*, systematically traced how stolen items ended up at Brimfield. One was a stained-glass window that was stolen on a Monday from a home that was being renovated in Springfield, twenty-five miles to the west. The homeowner wondered if the theft was linked to Brimfield, which was opening the next day. She went to the show with a friend. She searched for only a couple of hours before she found the window for sale for $650. Police confiscated it and questioned the dealer, who said that a man riding a bicycle had brought it to his shop the week before. The dealer claimed to have paid cash for the window and did not write down the bicyclist's name. Police were not buying the story, but they were not sure they had enough evidence to arrest the dealer. The Springfield resident did get her window back. Such tales are well-known among police departments throughout central Massachusetts, many of which consider Brimfield a giant pawnshop.

Local police previously excelled at taking reports when bad checks were passed at the market. In the early 1980s a Brimfield police chief estimated that the show had generated a hundred bad checks from a number of sources over the previous three years. Once a buyer came to Brimfield dressed well and riding in a chauffeured limousine. Some dealers were impressed enough by the look of the buyer to trust him and to take his checks. They all bounced. One time police traced at least $50,000 in bad checks ranging from $300 to $3,500 written to dealers based throughout the eastern half of the United States. Anyone stuck with bad paper knows prospects are remote that they will get their money or the item back.

The theft at the Gillespies' booth is part of a wave of more serious crime. "One of the scariest things that is taking place is the series of high-end robberies," observes Lois Shelton. In May a theft occurred at the booth of another silver merchant, Robert Lloyd of New York City. On Saturday night of the show Lloyd locked his cases, which contained British and American silver flatware and hollowware primarily from the sixteenth and seventeenth centuries. He left a young man to sleep in the booth overnight. "Fortunately he did not wake up, because I don't know what would have happened to him," said Lloyd. The thieves took more than four hundred pieces of silver. The total loss was considerable. Lloyd was lucky in one respect—he did have insurance.

The previous year, on a different field, someone had parked a truck by a booth during the night and nearly emptied the booth. People saw it happen, thinking that the dealer was packing and leaving early. It was all hauled away in banana boxes. Even when a dealer secures the merchandise there is no guarantee that it is safe. Two years earlier, a dealer from Delaware, Sandra McQuillan, lost $20,000 of gold jewelry. It had not been easy for the thief to get to the jewelry because it was locked in a show case that was bolted to a display table and covered with textiles and then a tarp. But the crook had taken his time one night, carefully selecting the best material. McQuillan could sympathize with the Gillespies, because she too lacked insurance and she had found the police less than helpful. "I spent a long time with the investigating officer, and he insisted on having me try and remember every single detail," she recalls. But later she had difficulty obtaining a copy of the police report. Her name had been misspelled and much of the jewelry was identified only as "miscellaneous." There was also one confusing entry—the report said "suspect is not a Puerto Rican." McQuillan had never said anything about Puerto Ricans.

Few police, even in major urban departments, have the expertise to investigate the theft of antiques or art. Instead the task normally falls to such organizations as the FBI, Scotland Yard, and Interpol. Even their resources, however, are limited when it comes to catching art thieves or recovering property. Interpol reports that the theft of antiques and art is one of the greatest sources of property crime in the world and only 5 to 10 percent is ever recovered. In the United States most such thefts occur during burglaries of homes. The Art Loss Register, an international organization begun in 1991 to monitor stolen art, lists more than 150,000 paintings, sculptures, and other artworks that have been stolen. About 10,000 new items are listed each year.

Forgeries and fakes are just as great a problem. Some experts have suggested that up to 30 or 40 percent of the art and antiques sold not only at antiques markets, such as Brimfield, but also at reputable dealers, auction houses, and displayed in private homes, collections, and museums, are frauds. Others dispute those figures, but the bottom line is that no one can be certain about the degree of counterfeiting in art and antiques.

Sometimes forgeries have a direct link to thefts. The most famous art heist of all time, the removal of the *Mona Lisa* from the Louvre in 1911, was inspired by art forgers. A ring of forgers had already created several fakes of da Vinci's masterpieces when they concluded that the fakes would be far easier to sell if potential buyers knew that the real painting had been stolen from the Paris museum. After the shocking news of the theft, authorities immediately feared that the *Mona Lisa* would be shipped out of France. Borders were closed and ocean liners were stripped and searched. But, according to some accounts, the crime ring had already shipped their copies to the United States, where they easily found buyers. Even after the original was recovered in Italy two and half years later, rumors persisted for decades that the authentic painting was still at large.

At Brimfield, police usually consider that what is offered or sold on the fields is a private, civil matter, as opposed to a public, criminal case. While there are criminal fraud statutes on the books, very few complaints are ever made. "One of the problems is that [a criminal complaint about an antique] puts the police as the expert over the word of others in the antiques world," said one high-ranking Brimfield police official. "Police do not have that kind of expertise, no one has the type of expertise to be able to say what of all the objects on these fields is authentic and what is not. Plus, it is not a captive audience, people have choices, they can make up their own minds on whether to buy something."

Many dealers seem comfortable with the caveat emptor attitude. They are used to taking care of themselves. After the burglary at the Gillespies', dealers have begun talking more among themselves about taking precautions. Some make sure they have dogs in their vehicles where they store their goods at night. Others are vowing to sleep with their goods. Some are packing guns. People are warned not to enter a closed tent if they know what is good for them. It may very well be bravado, but the idea of vigilante justice is never far off. There is an often-told story about a group of dealers dining one evening at Francesco's in Brimfield, when they recognized a man who walked in. He had been a good customer at the last show, too good. When they got home, they discovered he had passed bad checks. One thing led to another. That night, according to the story, the stranger barely survived after nearly being lynched by the angry dealers.

Joe and Rachel trust in their judgment as experts in art. For Joe, the key is becoming as familiar as possible with artists and their work. He has spent years haunting bookstores, buying catalogs of previous art shows and books on artists, devouring them at home. It helps with the especially suspicious paintings, such as those being sold by the Eastern European dealer. If a painting like the Pierre Alechinsky he bought in May turned out to be a fake, then he is out only the $200 he paid for it. Joe and Rachel also try to get to know the dealers, what they sell, and who will stand behind their sales. They are wary of four or five dealers now at Brimfield, either because they have questions about their merchandise or they have learned that these dealers have faced civil and sometimes criminal complaints. It is rare for an art dealer to go to jail, but it does occasionally happen.

Unsigned paintings are perhaps the biggest challenge for any art dealer. Joe says there are just too many possibilities in trying to confirm the artist. And signatures can mysteriously show up on paintings. Once Joe bought an unsigned watercolor for $10 that he and Rachel were sure had been painted by an established artist, it was so good. It depicted a Victorian house, in a Mediterranean style. They never could establish where it came from and they eventually sold it at auction for $15. A few weeks later the watercolor came up for auction again, but this time it miraculously had a signature. The last time Joe saw it, the watercolor was on eBay with a bid of $990. That trend seems to be on the rise.

Mike McClintock has repeatedly told Rachel of a similar episode when he resisted the impulse, urged by many of his colleagues, to tamper with a painting. McClintock was at a show when he came across a still life that seemed exceptional. It depicted a table holding a mug and some pipes in what appeared to be a classical trompe l'oeil, a popular technique of the late nineteenth century that conveys a sense of three dimensions in a two-dimensional painting. McClintock bought it on the spot for $275. His research led him to believe that John F. Peto had painted it. Peto favored informal arrangements of objects such as pipes, mugs, and newspapers. Peto's style later influenced Pablo Picasso and other artists. After a promising start, Peto moved to New Jersey, where his career declined. He often sold or gave still lifes to friends, local merchants, and tourists. Shortly before Peto died in 1907, a dealer bought many of his works and later attributed them to a better-known artist who painted in a similar style, William Harnett. It was not until 1949 that Peto was rediscovered, and his work, which had been fetching large sums under Harnett's name, was rightfully attributed to him. Another reason Peto had not been recognized was that he often did not sign his paintings. That was McClintock's problem. In fact, the painting had only initials and they were not Peto's and they made very little sense. A number of friends urged McClintock to paint over the initials or to change them. After all, it was clearly a Peto, so what was the harm? McClintock resisted and instead wrote to a prominent Peto scholar. Nearly two years passed before the art professor could see the painting, and when he did he had only one question for McClintock: how does it feel to own a painting worth $30,000? The initials actually helped the expert verify that the painting was a Peto. The professor explained that many of the paintings Peto produced for friends included the initials of the future owner. In this case the initials were of a well-known friend. McClintock later sold the painting, with the verification that it was a Peto, for $16,000, a little less than the expert had predicted yet considerably above McClintock's investment of $275.

Joe and Rachel, along with most dealers, especially dread discovering that they possess a stolen painting or antique. Technically, anyone who has a stolen object can be prosecuted. That rarely happens when the dealer who possesses it gives the object back to the original owner. It gets more complicated when the object has passed through several dealers. Once, Rachel brokered a painting by the Pennsylvania Impressionist Daniel Garber from a Boston dealer. Later she learned it had passed from a Philadelphia dealer to Chicago to Boston and then on to her. The Philadelphia dealer who had originated the transaction had never paid the person who had consigned it to him. In this situation, the legal issue was between the Philadelphia dealer and the person who had consigned him the Garber.

In some respects, dealing in art is slightly easier than in other areas. Unless one is selling a print or a copy, the issue is whether the work is the original or a copy. The rules are looser for other antiques and collectibles, where reproductions often stand next to originals. Some objects for sale at Brimfield are clearly reproductions. Often they are wrapped in Asian newspapers or are a combination of old and new, such as the dolls that June Secrist sells at Hertan's field that women fight with each other to buy. The rag dolls are new but are dressed with vintage cloth. In other situations the materials are aged to look antique. Usually dealers are quick to admit they are offering a reproduction, at least when asked. Then again, some dealers selling reproductions maintain they are selling originals.

Not too far from where the Eastern European dealers are selling their paintings, another dealer is selling Chinese artifacts. The dealer has the pottery, vases, bowls, fossils, and architectural panels in the front of the booth, near the American antique dolls and bottles. He says the Chinese wares are all from the fourteenth to the sixteenth centuries. Some pieces still have dirt on them. The dealer tells questioners that individual pieces go from $100. None carry certifications of authenticity, but the dealer's Chinese friend, who sold him his entire inventory before he returned to China, assured him that everything is genuine. "Some of it is likely coming from the Three Gorges Dam region or from Shanghai where there is a lot of new construction going on," he says. "The Chinese do not have time or the interest to stop and take care of this stuff. There is just too much of it." He is pretty certain his friend bribed Chinese officials to get the material out of the country. He brags to one onlooker that he has already made $23,000 from selling the stuff, and he stresses that once he has recouped his investment, he is going to stop selling these pieces at wholesale prices. He has plans to convert several of the vases into lamps. "People are going to have to pay more for this real soon," he says.

What the dealer is selling might truly be an incredible bargain. The problem is that for years the market has been flooded with Chinese pieces that are either fakes or reproductions. Many of the pieces are so good that they can fool experts, and some museums across the world have displayed fakes along with authentic pieces.

The field owners would appear to have the power to police the fields of counterfeits and reproductions. Already they keep new, surplus goods such as socks or flashlights, off the fields. Some promoters insist that dealers sell only antiques, and they quiz prospective dealers before allowing them on their field. Others make no differentiation between allowing reproductions and authentic items, as long as they look antique. But even those who try to limit merchandise say the task is daunting. Don Moriarty has been running Heart-O-The-Mart for twenty-five years and he still tries, but he sometimes has difficulty distinguishing between an antique and a reproduction. "We try and tell dealers when they start with us that reproductions are not allowed," he says. "And sometimes they say back to us, 'Why not? You've already got reproductions on your field.'"

Howard Roberts always wondered why other show promoters did not insist on refusing reproductions, until one year when he was in Atlantic City. The Atlantic City show was one of the few venues around the country that was strict about banning reproductions. It even had a group of inspectors. One inspector told Roberts he could not display a particular chair for sale, because it was a reproduction.

Roberts disagreed; he had paid good money for the chair and he was convinced it was authentic. But the inspector won, and Roberts realized that in such subjective debates, where he did not have clear-cut proof, he would always lose this argument. Roberts never again questioned why reproductions showed up at other fields. Dealers often complain that reproductions undercut the market for true antiques, making the genuine article more difficult to sell. But they can also experience the perverse satisfaction of seeing the gullible taken in by their own greed.

For this July show, Roberts has a far more superior, higher-quality display of antiques than he had in May. He especially likes the engraved 1801 Philadelphia Water Company walking stick and the silver tea set that lists its owners back to 1806, when it was first presented as a wedding gift. The prize item is a leopard fur coat. "Everyone is talking about it," he tells his wife, Linda, hours after they open. And why not? When has anyone seen such a perfect fur, complete with the preserved head?

He wants $2,400 for the fur, but there is a problem. Customers walk into the booth, rave about the fur, and then warn him that leopards are endangered. There are laws against selling the furs of such animals. He could go to jail for selling it. To Roberts, that makes no sense. It is clear from the records he has that the fur coat has to be at least fifty years old. Laws about endangered species could not be more than thirty years old, at best. Yet people keep warning him to be careful, that he might be breaking the law.

Indeed, others have gotten into trouble. A Georgia lawyer owned an Indian headdress that had once been Geronimo's. It was worth a fortune, but it contained golden eagle feathers, and golden eagles were an endangered species. Federal laws say that it is illegal for anyone to sell anything related to an endangered species, even if it was acquired years before the law took effect. The lawyer's grandfather had obtained the headdress from Geronimo back in 1907. The lawyer, Leighton Deming, tried for years to sell the headdress, and in 1999 he thought he had a buyer who was willing to pay a million dollars. Shortly after Deming arrived at a Philadelphia hotel in preparation for completing the sale, armed men stormed the room. They weren't crooks—they were FBI agents who had arranged an elaborate sting. Deming was arrested and booked for trying to sell the eagle headdress. He eventually pleaded to a misdemeanor and in return gave up the headdress to the federal government.

While Brimfield may be wide open on most of what is sold on the fields, federal and state wildlife officials are especially vigilant, raiding dealers and confiscating a wide range of furs, stuffed animals, and the like. In the past year officials have confiscated stuffed owls, hawks, a bobcat, a bear cub, a coyote, a mounted baboon, bear hides, a crocodile hide, and sperm whale teeth. No one has been arrested recently, but they have been warned that they could face fines of up to $100,000 or two years in jail. "People who are really into antiques are aware of the restrictions," a federal agent says after one of the raids. "It would be better if the antiques industry would just police themselves." The news surprises Roberts, and many other dealers he talks to. Sandra Cleava, a spokeswoman for the U.S. Fish and Wildlife Service in Arlington, Virginia, later confirms that the law makes no provisions for antiques. Someone acquiring many of the great wildlife trophies that Theodore Roosevelt bagged a century ago, the stuffed heads and furs of rare and exotic species, would have great difficulty selling them today, she says.

Roberts reluctantly puts the leopard fur away. He wonders how he can dispose of it. There are ways that it can be done. Another dealer on the fields is known to sometimes display objects such as this, and when he is asked about them, he assures the questioner that the piece is not for sale. It would be illegal to sell it, he says. If it were for sale, it would cost $3,000, or $5,000, or even $10,000, depending on the item. That is one way, but it is risky and legally questionable. The safest solution is for Roberts to take the fur back to Pennsylvania. As long as he keeps the fur in Pennsylvania, where he found it, and does not cross state lines when he sells it, and any buyer does not cross state lines, the federal government will probably be unable to act. Most states also are unlikely to arrest him for selling the antique fur. He could also give it away. Or keep it.

For now, Roberts will hold on to the fur. He found it along with the engraved walking stick and silver tea service at a house he has been asked to clean out. It is located just off Philadelphia's Main Line, once the address of Philadelphia's elite. During a quick visit a few weeks ago he was surprised by the condition of the house. It was filthy. At first, he could not believe there was anything of value there. Then he got to the attic and was amazed by what he found. This is what Roberts relishes, a house of both mystery and wealth. Such a house is rarely encountered. When this show is over, he's going back and he's going to find all its secrets. He can't wait.

CHAPTER 12

Raiding Attics

PHILADELPHIA WEATHER FORECASTERS say it is only going to get hotter today and perhaps for the rest of the week. Yet Howard Roberts's crew of Eddie, Michael, and the new guy are all wearing trousers, long-sleeve shirts, and hats at Roberts's urging. Now he hands each of them a face mask. "You'll need it," he tells them.

The Brimfield July show closed a couple of weeks ago, and Roberts has assembled his crew to begin cleaning out the house just off Philadelphia's Main Line. The men are looking at him a little dubiously, wondering if these precautions are really necessary. The house does not look threatening. It is a modest Cape, about sixty years old, with a small front porch, an enclosed side porch, and a single-car attached garage. The exterior is shabby, the grass is yellow and unmowed. It sits on a quiet lane near the end of a cul-de-sac, with tall, slender graceful trees. The only hint of prosperity is the houses nearby, new mansion-size estates that crowd their small lots and scream new money. Roberts tells the men that there is so much in this house, both furnishings and dirt, that it may take a week to clean it out.

When they enter, what first strikes them is the smell, an indescribably rank, foul odor. Eddie, or Eriberto L. Roman, begins to gag under his face mask. "Oh my God, what is this," he says to himself. "What am I getting myself into?" As he looks around the living room it soon becomes obvious. Dust and dirt must be a quarter-inch thick and seem to be plastered on, almost like a crust. It is not just dirt but also strands of hair. He wonders where it came from, until Roberts points out the picture of the Saint Bernard. And what are those green spots on the rug, dog piss? Having trouble breathing, he retreats outside.

Michael Bernstein can tolerate the stench but only because Roberts has assured him the house has no black mold. Bernstein does not trust black mold and he is ready but wary. The men have another reason to feel uneasy about the house. It not only is filthy but it also has a reputation. The seller inherited the house from his father. The story that Roberts has heard is that the father went down to the basement one night, arranged the band saw in a particular way, and tried to cut his head off. He made a mess, and he did kill himself, the Realtor selling the house tells Roberts.

Roberts is not bothered by that story, and he barely senses the heat, the dirt, and the stink through his excitement. Long after this day he will admit that the house, with all its history, its squalor, is so foul that perhaps he should never have ventured in. "But I was so excited after being up in that attic, and beginning to find things," he said. "The lust for the hunt and the greed will send you in all kinds of directions."

It sends Roberts to houses, into the inner sanctums of strangers. He is asked to pack, remove, sell, and dispose of all vestiges of one life so that a house can make way for a new occupant with fresh possessions and memories. His is a prurient task; what he is asked to do can be so personal and revealing. He is invited to open drawers and remove the rolled and darned socks knitted lovingly by a grandmother, toss out a child's faded and crackling valentine saved since 1957, and dump the jars of preserves that have turned curious colors. Those whose pasts are being dismantled rarely feel the assault. By the time Roberts arrives they are dead, in a nursing home, or living thousands of miles distant. For Roberts, it can be a sad task but also an exciting one. Mixed in with a lifetime's personal mementos he may find the valuable, the unusual, and the unexpected.

We all have a streak of voyeurism, of wanting to know how others live. It surfaces when we want to know more about the rich and famous, when their personal effects become objects we can hold or possess. When portions of the estates of Garbo, Dietrich, and Monroe were auctioned, the results were fierce bidding wars and high prices. Fans want to own a piece of what their idols once possessed. In 1998, forty-four thousand items from the estate of the Duke and Duchess of Windsor sold for $23.4 million, more than three times what people expected. Someone paid $29,900 for a frozen piece of wedding cake. But that bidding was still less than the bidding when Sotheby's auctioned off pieces of Camelot in 1994. The Jacqueline Kennedy Onassis estate came up for auction two years after her death. By then all the documents or records of historical significance had already been donated to the John F. Kennedy Library Foundation. The rest was picked over by her two children. That left twelve hundred lots of personal possessions, from her engagement ring from Aristotle Onassis to the late President's golf clubs to her monogrammed tape measure. Buyers bid ten, twenty, or thirty times more than the pre-auction estimates. The tape measure went for $42,000, the golf clubs for $700,000, the engagement ring for $2.35 million. Ultimately auction-goers spent $34.5 million on what has been called "the sale of the century."

Roberts finds value among the possessions of the less famous. He is willing to make a deal. He can inventory and appraise the contents of the house. He will pack and move them, sell them through an auction, estate sale, or consignment, buy them all outright for a set price, give everything to a charity or other organization. He will even dispose of the trash. He'll take a commission, a fee, or the contents. It's up to the owner. No matter the decision, Roberts enjoys finding and cataloging the rare, the unusual, and sometimes the bizarre.

This is not the career Roberts planned in college when he was studying entomology or later when he was a landscape designer. Entomology was never going to work; he hated bugs. He also tired of plants. Somewhere along the line Roberts developed an interest in European porcelain. He fell in love with ornate hand-painted Victorian porcelain. "I just loved it for the artwork, for the fact that it was not factory-produced but handmade and painted by women at a time when they were prohibited from doing hardly anything else," he says.

That was more than twenty years ago. The hobby became a collection and eventually an occupation. Dealing in porcelain proved too specialized, too confining. He branched into European and American furnishings, and he started cleaning out houses and selling what he found at antiques shows throughout the eastern half of the country.

He learned early on that you never know what you are going to find when you step over the threshold into a stranger's house. Roberts was still in the plant business and only beginning to dabble in the antiques trade when an acquaintance called. He wanted Roberts to look at several antiques at his father's place. If the price was right, he would sell them to Roberts. He asked Roberts to come over immediately. An odd request, but Roberts was young and eager.

Roberts's acquaintance, a stocky young man, answered the door. He explained that his father had died and he wanted to begin cleaning some things out. Most of the furniture, he explained, was in an upstairs bedroom.

When they entered the bedroom, Roberts learned how recently the man's father had died. The body was still in the bed. The father had died the night before, the death certificate had been completed by the doctor, the funeral director had been called, but no one from the funeral home had arrived yet.

Before Roberts could recover from his shock, the man explained that he wanted to sell the bed, now.

"No, I don't think this is a good idea," said Roberts.

"It will be OK," responded the man.

They debated what to do. Somehow the man convinced Roberts to help move the body off the bed so that they could examine it.

"He's dead already, he won't mind," explained the son. "Don't worry about it."

They had to clear some furniture to make room for the body. Roberts took the legs, the man took the shoulders. Afterward, Roberts began to inspect the bed, which as an antique, he was beginning to realize, had only a modest value.

That's when the funeral-home workers arrived. They had a gurney to move the body, but they could not get it into the room now that the body was on the floor and the furniture was blocking the door. With help, the body was moved back onto the bed, eventually onto the gurney, and away.

Roberts bought only a couple of small pieces of furniture.

For this latest job with the Main Line house, a Realtor had called Roberts. Roberts had met the owner a few weeks before when he first inspected the house. The man was middle-aged and had a good office job with a prestigious company in Philadelphia. Roberts assumed, in walking through the house the first time, that it had been vacant for years. However, the seller and his Saint Bernard had just moved out. At first, Roberts was not sure whether the possessions had much value. The furniture was promising; it looked Victorian and original. On the second floor, Linda Roberts opened a blanket chest and found silver wrapped in a blanket. It was a service for twelve, Baltimore Rose. Then Howard Roberts was taken aback when he reached the attic. He found barrels, the tall type that coopers still made at the turn of the last century, that were commonly used for shipping. These days you never see that kind of barrel. He opened one barrel and found fine silver, including the 1806 tea set. In another was china. In the third he found the leopard fur. Why were such fine objects hidden in the attic, he wondered, looking around. And what else was buried here in the dust?

On this first day everyone begins to realize that cleaning this house is no simple task. Every single item has to be carried out into the front yard and carefully cleaned with lemon oil and other cleansers. The smaller pieces each take at least five or ten minutes. The larger pieces of furniture can take twenty minutes or longer. Michael Bernstein and Eddie Roman take turns working outside. Bernstein wants to stay outside because he still worries that the house might have black mold. Two years ago Bernstein got sick. He and Roberts were cleaning out a house; it was not anything like this house, but there was a huge mound of old laundry that had been dumped down in the basement. The owner told them that beneath the moldy clothes there were some toys. That's all Bernstein wanted to hear, since he collects toys. It took him, off and on, four days to sift through the old clothing looking for the toys. Often he was on his hands and knees working. While they both saw the mold on the edge of the wall, they didn't think anything of it. After the job was over, Bernstein got sick. A slight man, he does not have the strongest constitution to begin with. He just seemed to get sicker. By the time he got to the hospital, he was beginning to swell and had difficulty breathing. Finally, he went into a coma. He fought off the infection, he still does not know how. He knows better now than to go near anything that looks like mold.

The Realtor comes by later in the day, and everyone notices that she refuses to come inside the house. She wants nothing to do with being inside. That night, when Roman gets home, he quickly removes his sweatshirt and pants, which are coated with sweat and the stench of the house. He can't ask his wife to clean them and he does not want his children near them. He throws them in the trash outside.

There are cleaner ways to acquire antiques and valuables, but they are not always easier. Roberts used to go to estate sales in the greater Philadelphia area in what could become fierce competitive battles with other dealers and collectors. He would search the classified ads, check carefully for items of interest, and then set a strategy. If the sale began at 9 A.M. and he wanted to be one of the first in, he knew he would have to get there by 5. If he wanted to be first, he would probably have to sleep in his car overnight. That was the reality of the competition, if he wanted to get the best stuff. Those running the sales are particular; they allow only a few in the house at any one time.

If he was the first to arrive at a house, he would also have to pass out the numbers. Big house sales that attract professional antiques dealers usually have a numbering system. Sometimes it is a voluntary system set up by the buyers. The first person to show up at the house gives himself number one and then distributes the remaining numbers to those showing up afterward. Buyers enter the house, when it opens, by number, the lower the sooner. Sometimes whoever is arranging the estate sale, a real estate agency or a liquidation company, will have its own numbering system. A company official will pass out the numbers, based on his best judgment of who was first in line. This can be a challenge, because often the agent for the sale is not the first at the house.

Sometimes the first buyer arrives and starts his own numbering system, not knowing that the company running the sale has plans to distribute its own numbers. Sometimes the company will honor the voluntary system, and sometimes not. This is especially a problem for someone who has picked up a number early, and then gone off for coffee, missing out when the company begins distributing the real numbers. To make sure this does not happen, some managers of estate sales also require buyers to stay in line, even after they get their number. Once Roberts misunderstood that rule, left to go to the bathroom, and lost his place, even though he could show his number.

The honor system does not work very well when professionals are competing to get into a good house sale. Sometimes those competitive pressures really cause havoc. It happened recently in New York, according to several antiques dealers. It began when the volunteer numbering system was used to play favorites. A buyer first to arrive decided to distribute low numbers to others whom he liked, and high numbers to those he did not like. After a while, those getting stuck with the high numbers began their own rival numbering system. The upshot was that when the individual or company running the sale arrived, there were two individuals for each number. Antiques dealers were soon calling the two rival gangs "the tag-sale mafia." Arguments have led to fights that resulted in calling the police.

"There is not a whole lot the cops can do, as long as no one punches anyone," says Brandon Levine, a Long Island antiques and art dealer who sometimes runs the sales. "The number systems are not illegal."

The situation is spiraling out of control, forcing everyone to consider abandoning the volunteer number systems. But if volunteers will not implement a fair system for getting into a house, and honor it, the only other option is to have those running the sale distribute the numbers. Says Levine: "You need to spend all day setting up and pricing things, then you have to get up at six or earlier on the day of the sale to hand out tickets. It just extends the day that much longer. But on the other hand, the system we have now is not working either."

Roberts has not seen that kind of dual numbers rivalry in Philadelphia, but he has experienced other problems. Sometimes he notices that items advertised at sales are not in the house, no matter what time he has arrived. Usually the people running the estate sale explain that the item he was interested in has been pulled.

One day a friend, who also collects porcelain, invited Roberts to go to an estate sale. The invitation was unusual in that it was scheduled for the day before the sale was to begin. "We went over there, and my friends were greeted like long-lost companions," recalls Roberts. "Then we were invited to pick through the house. We did very well that day. So did everyone else. Dealers were coming and going, I saw lots of furniture leaving, all going out the back door. All the favored dealers had been called so that they could pick the house clean before the sale."

Another gimmick is to run false advertisements, promising items that are not there. Those running the sales might also add their own goods in an attempt to get rid of them. Dealers and collectors know that anything is possible at an estate sale, although their levels of acceptance vary. All the games and tricks wore on Roberts, who finally decided the only solution was to find his own houses, even if they were filthy. "I became frustrated going to those sales," says Roberts. "You never knew what you were going to find. You were lucky to be able to do two of these in a day. It just was not worth the hassle."

By the third day of cleaning the Main Line house, Roberts and his crew are getting to know the family that has owned this house. They are finding some items of value, although not as many as Roberts had hoped. It appears that some of the most valuable was in those barrels and in a nearby steamer trunk. There is the furniture, including a four-poster bed. There is Dresden and Wedgwood china, and the Limoges porcelain. There are leather goods and clothing, men's and women's, dating back to the 1940s. A diamond wedding ring had been left in a dresser, and the owner has already told them to sell the ring. No one asks if it was his mother's.

There are also a number of strange items. Someone had a fascination with World War II and the Nazis. There are art books on the Nazis featuring grotesque drawings from a 1967 exhibit, a catalog of German propaganda posters, and an illustrated history of Germany from Bismarck to Hitler. There are the piles of yellowed newspapers from the 1940s, the cabinet full of papers from the war, the books from the Army signal corps and detailing Morse code. The men also find an antique railroad lantern, a duck decoy, and two handguns, wrapped in a chest. One is a .32 caliber police revolver. It is fully loaded, although when Roberts pulls out the clip he notices that the bullets have turned green with age. The other is a World War I side-arm pistol. This one, he is relieved to see, is not loaded. The chest also has two toy grenades. Roberts has seen grenades like this before in an Army-Navy store. They look identical to the real thing, even down to the pin. He notices that the pin in one of them is crooked. He pulls it out, surprised that it comes out so easily. He quickly pushes it back in, so that is now much straighter. With that adjustment, it really looks like a grenade.

Roberts is down in the basement. He never has felt entirely at ease down here in this house; there is something
creepy about the room besides the filth. The room is partially occupied by a large table that has a toy train set and
tracks set up. It's hard to see the little village amid the debris. Roberts sees what he thinks is loose change, until he realizes they are red and black plastic medallions of some
kind. He picks one up and tries to rub the dirt off it. An insignia appears on the face. He supposes these must be toy
checkers. He rubs a little bit more and now he can make out
the insignia. It is a swastika. He rubs another one and another. All the red and black checkers bear swastikas.

Entering someone else's abode can uncover all kinds of
secrets. Sometimes Roberts is hired only to pack. He never
advertises that he will pack antiques for a price, but somehow people keep finding him and paying him amounts that
make it difficult to refuse. One of the families that hired him
to pack had a lineage dating back to William Penn and antiques with as burnished a legacy. The parents had died, and
the five children were closing up the old family home. Most
of the antiques were going to the oldest brother, who lived
in New England and who had successfully convinced his
siblings that it would be a shame to break up the sets of furniture. It was a big job that was going to take Roberts several
days. He brought crates, boxes, and rolls of bubble wrap.

Surrounded by fine antiques one day during a lunch
break, Roberts found an appraisal that had been completed
by a local auction company. Roberts was puzzled as he read
the statement. The Chippendale chairs were listed as being
worth $100 apiece and a highboy cabinet was appraised at
$500. Roberts had been hired by one of the brothers who

lived in Philadelphia, not the one in New England who was going to get most of this furniture. Roberts had been retained only to pack, but the figures seemed so unfair to the brother who had hired him that he could not resist calling a colleague, an expert in eighteenth-century Chippendales and other American furniture. Roberts wanted to know if these figures could be correct.

When the dealer arrived, Roberts asked him for an estimate on the chairs and the highboy. The appraiser warned Roberts that some of the chairs were Boston Chippendales and others were a Philadelphia-style Chippendale. There were only six of the Boston style and twelve of the Philadelphia vintage. The Philadelphia chairs were more valuable, the dealer explained, probably worth 50 percent more.

Roberts asked for a figure.

The Bostons were $8,000. The Philadelphia chairs were $12,000, his friend said.

Apiece, he added.

That was what Roberts had suspected. He asked about the highboy.

$50,000.

Roberts called the brother who had hired him. "I think we have a problem here," he told him.

The packing stopped until the siblings could have a conference. Later, Roberts was told that the auction company had been trying to do a favor for the family by estimating low on the values to cut estate taxes. If family members were upset, Roberts never heard about it. The siblings worked out a new arrangement to distribute the antiques, and Roberts went back to carefully packing the furnishings. When he was done, the brother from New England, a highly paid corporate lawyer, arrived at the estate in a rented U-Haul truck. Roberts helped him carefully pack the vehicle with the reduced number of pieces he was taking. When they were done, the lawyer climbed onto the seat of the truck, waved to Roberts, and drove off.

It can be that no one in the family realizes the value of their parents' belongings. Roberts has seen that happen often. One day he was working in the kitchen of a house when the elderly woman who was selling it brought him an old paper bag. The bag was knotted at the top, dusty and wrinkled from age. "I found this old lamp down below the cellar stairs," she explained. "I'm not sure you can use it, but I thought you should know about it."

Roberts looked inside the bag. Cautiously, he pulled out the lamp. It was a Tiffany, worth tens of thousands of dollars.

Sometimes it is even difficult for a professional like him to recognize value in certain possessions. On one job, he was cleaning out a palatial house that had been owned by a judge. Roberts and his crew had been there for what seemed like weeks finding and packing antiques and furniture when the widow came by one day.

"Have you done anything about the wine cellar yet?" she asked.

What wine cellar?

"Go down to the base of the stairs in the cellar and you'll find a hole," she replied. "Stick your finger through it."

Roberts did as he was instructed and an entire wall moved, revealing racks of wine along the walls. There was so much wine that Roberts had difficulty getting rid of all of it. The judge's wife had no interest in it, she just wanted it gone. At first, Roberts tried to give it away. He gave it to friends, to the movers, to anyone who liked wine. He reserved a case of Bordeaux for himself, and he knew enough to set aside the Dom Pérignon and a few bottles for family members. The rest, bottle after bottle, was thrown into a dumpster.

Months later, he had only one of the twelve bottles left from the case of Bordeaux. He and his wife were going out to dinner with friends and Roberts said he would supply the wine.

The friend looked at the bottle and then looked at Roberts.

"That's a very good bottle of wine," he said.

"Yeah, I know, I've drunk nearly an entire case."

His friend looked at him a little strangely. "Are you sure you want to drink it?"

"Yeah sure, come on, it didn't cost me anything. Relax and enjoy it."

They did.

The bottles and their labels were so nice that Roberts wondered if he could sell them. He brought one to Brimfield and one day a man caught sight of the bottle.

"Do you have any more?" he asked.

"Not on me," replied Roberts.

"Too bad, it's a good wine."

"Yeah, I know. I drank it."

The questioner gave him a quizzical glance. He explained that he was a distributor for the wine, and that the Bordeaux label was exceptional. Roberts by this time was intrigued and pestered the distributor to tell him how much a bottle was worth.

"You don't know?" the dealer asked in surprise.

Roberts shook his head.

"Unopened?" The dealer asked.

Roberts nodded this time.

"Honestly?"

"Yes, tell me."

"A thousand dollars a bottle."

Friends sometimes ask Roberts if he regrets drinking the wine instead of selling it.

"It was really good wine," he replies.

It is noon on the fifth day of cleaning the Main Line house before the men finally haul out the last items of value. All that is left now is dirt and trash. Roberts estimates it will take an additional three days to thoroughly clean the house, and he has purposely stretched that estimate because he really does not want to do it. The Realtor, who has yet to go inside, says the new owner plans to have a contractor gut the inside. That means the men don't need to spend three days cleaning it. Everyone is pleased. The temperature today is in the nineties again and it feels like a sauna.

Because nothing could be stored in the house after all the goods were brought out on the front yard, it has all been moved to a warehouse. Roberts plans to sell some of the furniture at his shop, auction off some pieces, and take some of the offbeat stuff like the Nazi books, the Morse code manuals, the duck decoy, the antique railroad lantern, and the swastika checkers to Brimfield. He knows a dealer who will take the guns. He's not sure what to do with the toy grenades.

He makes one last round through the house, and when he gets to the steps to the attic he trips slightly on a raised board. He looks at it closely, and then lifts it up. It is a hidden compartment. Inside is a box of sterling sliver.

Late that afternoon he drops off several boxes at his antiques shop in Malvern. He hopes to find Linda, but she is not there. Just then, he spots a police car parked down the street from the shop. He can see a Pennsylvania state trooper inside. The toy grenades have been rolling around in the truck. He wonders if the cop might know where he can get rid of them. Perhaps he might even want to buy one.

Roberts walks up to the cruiser. The trooper inside is busy writing. It is his first day on the job since being sworn in. Roberts knocks on the car door. The window is down and Roberts holds up the toy as the trooper looks up.

"Would you like to buy a grenade?"

It is meant as a joke, sort of.

The cop is looking at him funny, so Roberts decides he should explain.

"It's a toy," he says, pointing at the grenade.

The trooper slowly asks Roberts to hand him the grenade, and Roberts complies. A moment later the trooper asks Roberts to get inside the car. Puzzled, Roberts obeys. At the trooper's urging, Roberts explains how he found the grenades, how he cleaned out the house, and how the toys are kind of a nuisance because they keep rolling around the cab of his truck.

When Roberts is finished with his explanation, the trooper tells him that he is going to have to take the grenades from him. Roberts asks why. The trooper tells him that he is all but certain this one is not a toy.

He's right. The grenades are real.

September

The idea of taking up art as a calling, a trade, a profession, is a mirage. Art enriches life. It makes life worth living. But to make a living at it—that idea is incompatible with making art.

JOHN SLOAN, *GIST OF ART*

I never strike bargains in the night.

SUSANNAH CENTLIVRE,
THE PERJURED HUSBAND

CHAPTER 13

eBay

WHEN RACHEL RETURNED to Pennsylvania in 1997 her career seemed to be at a standstill. She had gone about as far as she wanted working for auctioneers, and after she left McClintock's she could not find a job in another art gallery near home. Other dealers did not want to hire a former employee of a competitor and friend.

"I had no idea what I was going to do," she says. "I was terrified."

She asked her dad for advice. He was dealing antiques but did not have enough work for the two of them. He suggested she approach his old friend, dealer Jim Meyer. Dealers were beginning to talk about the Internet and whether they could use it to buy and sell antiques and collectibles. Meyer was always finding things at yard sales and auctions, and he needed a sales outlet. He was interested in trying out the Internet, although he really did not like to get involved with very many people or computers. The age difference between Meyer and Rachel made this a mutually profitable relationship. Rachel grew up in the dawn of the computer age. Meyer is fifteen years older, less comfortable with computers, retailing, and the nuisances of shipping. They came to an understanding. He would supply the goods and she would post them on the Internet and ship what sold. They would split the profits evenly. Arrangements to sell on eBay were fairly easy. Items did sell, although profits were not always great. Sometimes her share could be as low as two dollars. That first year she worried whether she would make enough money. "It's scary, totally scary, to work on your own and not have any kind of a weekly income that you can count on," she said. At the same time, her expenses were very low and she was sharing housing and other expenses with a boyfriend. By the end of the year she was pleased to discover that she had made $7,000. It was enough money to get her started.

"That was a big breakthrough for me," she says. "I realized I could make a living, working independently at very little cost, and that I would not have to work for someone else."

Like Gordon Reid Sr., Pierre Omidyar had no idea what he was creating on Labor Day weekend of 1995 when he launched what became eBay in the spare bedroom of his home. Based in San Jose, California, and originally called AuctionWeb, eBay's AuctionWeb, and finally eBay, it evolved and grew from hobby to business to what Omidyar saw as a philosophical statement. As he later described it, he envisioned the Internet, and more specifically his site, as a perfect marketplace. Buyers and sellers, with no restraints or middle merchants, could meet electronically and strike a deal. It would be a democratic marketplace, a community where members could freely communicate by e-mail to learn more. In many ways it was identical to the historical marketplace, the bazaar, the souk that Brimfield and the antiques flea markets are modeled on. The difference was that it did not have a physical location but a digital setting with a global reach.

At first eBay struggled to attract attention. One of the early stories about eBay's origin has to do with PEZ dispensers. Omidyar's fiancée, Pam Wesley, who later became his wife, collected and traded PEZ dispensers. According to various accounts, Wesley mentioned to an eBay official responsible for corporate communications that she had been frustrated in trying to find other collectors since moving to the West Coast. Meanwhile, a public relations campaign launched to promote the company was faltering. Reporters were not very interested in Omidyar's far-reaching visions of a new marketplace. To get better press, the eBay official, with Omidyar's approval, cooked up the story that the founder had created the site to help his girlfriend collect PEZ dispensers. Reporters and others have liked the tale so much that it continues to circulate, despite attempts by eBay officials to downplay it.

In the early years of its development, collectibles and some antiques dominated the sales on AuctionWeb and then eBay. A big breakthrough for eBay's development occurred in late 1996 when parents struggled to find the hottest Christmas toy—Beanie Babies. The one place they could find them was AuctionWeb. Collectors helped get the word out to the antiques and collectibles field. One member of a collector group would find eBay and quickly tell other members.

Joel Schiff remembers the site growing in popularity. He's not quite sure when he looked at it the first time, but he remembers searching for cast-iron cookware and coming up with only thirty-two listings. "It was absurdly low," he remembers. Still, even in the first days, some unusual items could surface, such as an interesting Griswold waffle iron. "Who knew anything like that even existed?" asks Schiff.

When Schiff looked again a few months later, he found there were a thousand listings. As time went on, the number just kept rising to the point where he was finding five thousand new listings for cast-iron cookware. Schiff began to spend more of his time on the computer and less of it going to shows.

As eBay became more popular, prices for antiques and collectibles rose at first. Schiff noticed that Griswold items in particular were drawing strong bids. A Griswold skillet that should cost only nine dollars would go for double that, and sometimes even higher. Intense bidding would sometimes erupt for rarer items, and it was not unusual on eBay to see prices of $300 for an item that previously would have sold for only a fraction of that.

Dealers saw what was happening to prices and were soon posting entire inventories, at inflated reserve levels, and often getting more than what they asked. They quickly learned the importance of marketing on this new technology. One seller sold his ex-wife's wedding dress by modeling it and posting the picture, along with a humorous account of what happened. Another auctioned off odd things and found enough funny stories from the experience to write a book. An online community began to develop. Some buyers and sellers became fiercely loyal. When eBay began hosting annual conferences of loyal users in California, hundreds would come from as far away as Alaska and Australia. Many would line up for an opportunity for an autograph and if possible the briefest of chats with Meg Whitman, Omidyar's successor as eBay's chief executive officer.

Rachel soon was selling not only on eBay but also on her own website. A friend who had space on his server convinced her she needed a website. She did the design work on her website herself and sold only art, while also directing traffic to her eBay auctions. She called it Griffin's Hoard. The griffin is a mythical character with a lion's body and an eagle's head, claws, and wings. She added "hoard" because griffins were said to protect their cache of valuables. Friends teased her about the name. They said it sounded like Griffin's Whore. "So after a couple of months I changed it to Griffin's Gallery," she explains.

One of Rachel's most important e-mail contacts occurred when she received an inquiry about a lithograph she was selling online. It was by Zella deMilhau and Rachel was asking $225. She had bought it at Brimfield for $125. She did not have any biographical information on the artist, but she liked the image, which showed a cluster of Southwestern Indians near their adobe houses. She exchanged e-mails with the buyer, who decided against purchasing it, but he did offer a detailed biography of the artist. More than a year later he e-mailed Rachel again, this time about some California paintings by Everett Bryant, the husband of Maude Drein Bryant of the Philadelphia Ten. "We arranged to meet at a New Jersey auction," recalls Rachel. "It turned out he was a handsome gentleman a few years older than I who was quite passionate about art. His name, of course, was Joe Laskowski."

Collectors and dealers first began to become uneasy about eBay when prices began to swing. While prices rose early in the company's history, many took a nose-dive after a short time. A survey in 2001 by *AuctionBytes,* an online newsletter that monitors eBay, showed that prices for a range of collectibles fell 25 percent in one year. Two years later prices were down 35 percent. Even worse, fewer items were selling on eBay. In 2000, 72 percent of the items placed up for auction had sold, compared to only 45 percent by 2003.

It was obvious to most what had happened. eBay had transformed what had been primarily a set of regional markets that were based on a limited supply of items into a national and at times international market that had been overwhelmed with supply. "For better or worse," says David Steiner, who produces *AuctionBytes*, "eBay has redefined the value of collectibles. Many dealers feel they can essentially throw away the price guides. What people want to know is, how much will it bring on eBay?"

Adds Gary Sohmers, the Brimfield dealer who specializes in pop culture: "The market place changed as vendors realized they had a larger audience. All of a sudden we began to learn what was rare and what was not."

Joel Schiff watched cast-iron prices plunge. "You just knew that those [high] prices were not going to last," he says. "The Net completely destroyed the feeding chain that had been set up where things moved from someone's attic to a shop or a flea market. And it also destroyed the regional markets." Schiff found that while low-priced items and high-priced items were not affected, the middle range of cast-iron cookware fell significantly.

Over time Rachel has built up her Internet business. She calculates that she sells about 75 percent of her paintings online. The rest are sold through personal contacts at shows such as Brimfield, at auctions, or through connections made through the Internet. Joe has been nearly as active. They both like eBay's ability to reach individual buyers across the country. Much of Rachel's Philadelphia Ten business has been generated by her website, which advertises her interest in the women artists, lists them by name, and provides biographies. "I tend to be shy at times, so the Internet can be great," says Rachel. "You don't have to deal with people immediately; you can be on your own clock. If someone contacts you by e-mail, you don't have to respond immediately if you don't want to. The time pressure is off."

To a certain extent Joe and Rachel have been insulated from the falling prices, because original artwork, by definition, is unique. But regular eBay users have also found so much art out there that they have begun to refine or limit the meaning of "unique." If Joe and Rachel put up for sale an Impressionist painting of a country road, it is now competing with as many as fifty other images of country roads also on eBay. Comparing the compositions and the prices of the paintings is now just a click away.

Moreover, Joe and Rachel have noticed that fewer of their paintings are actually bought. And the seasonality of eBay can drive them absolutely crazy. In the summer it is much tougher to sell on eBay. People do not want to be inside, looking at a computer, on a pleasant summer day. As September approaches, Joe and Rachel find it is far easier to sell at the shows.

Rachel sometimes has difficulty understanding why some things sell on eBay. One day she checked on her latest sales. She noticed that an Edward Quincy watercolor had drawn strong interest from two buyers. She was surprised. She had had the watercolor up on the Griffin's Gallery website for years, trying unsuccessfully to sell it for $350. She had tried twice before to sell it on eBay and had not gotten any takers. Now, the final bids were in and it had gone for $450. How could you figure that?

Sohmers says the easy answer is that eBay has become simply too big a market to sell specialized items efficiently. He tells about how a dealer put three vintage concert posters up for sale on eBay on consignment for the owner. The beginning reserve price was $9.99. Neither the owner nor dealer realized they had rare collectors' items, and soon dealers were offering $40,000 and $50,000 to take the posters off eBay and buy them outright. Sohmers says he and a partner offered a guarantee of $70,000 and suggested they could sell them for as much as $125,000 on a commission basis. The owner said, "No, let's let it ride on eBay." The final auction sale on eBay was around $50,000. "People get greedy," says Sohmers. "They don't understand how eBay operates these days."

While eBay has liberated Rachel, allowing her to find a way to make money dealing art, she is still leery of the medium. Although she sells on eBay, she is reluctant to buy. There are just too many risks. It is important to understand the dealers and to understand the works of art. When she goes to auctions, she has a sense of the auction houses and how they handle suspicious paintings. She knows exactly which dealers might add a signature to an unsigned work, and which will not. She usually can't tell that on eBay. Her concerns have prompted her to offer a guarantee for the work she sells on eBay. She offers a full refund within a week after receipt for any reason and up to three weeks if the buyer argues convincingly that she has somehow misidentified the painting.

Joe is less afraid to buy on eBay, although he knows the

risks. One of the first purchases he made on eBay was a painting that was advertised as an oil, which he bought for $500. He knew it had to be worth at least $20,000—until it arrived in the mail and he realized he had bought a very large, framed print of the original. He was lucky. He put it back on eBay and sold it for only $20 less than what he had paid. It taught him to be careful.

The reaction to the Internet at Brimfield and elsewhere in the early years was a mixture of curiosity and fear. Phillip Davies recalls setting up a booth at the Central Park field at Brimfield, offering dealers and collectors a drink and an opportunity to find out more about the Internet. Davies had just quit his job as a newspaper photographer for *Newsday* on Long Island to start an Internet site, TIAS.com (The Internet Antique Store). TIAS.com offered dealers an alternative to eBay, where sellers did not auction off items but set fixed prices in what amounted to an electronic consignment shop. These kinds of outlets have never taken off the way eBay and online auctions did, although Rachel says they can still be handy. For the first couple of years dealers flocked to the site. "I don't know if we converted people," recalls Davies. "They wanted to know what people were doing. There were stories about what was going online, what was selling, what was not selling. But it did get us in the door."

Actually, Davies had been lucky to get that far. Other field promoters at Brimfield, and other markets too, literally chased him off their fields. "They did not like the whole idea," he recalls. "They saw us as competition. They were just very negative about the whole thing. The Internet was a threat, therefore you did not deal with it."

eBay has been a little more successful in getting onto

Brimfield, but it had an unusual advantage. Eric Moriarty got a great location for the tent he set up for eBay at Heart-O-The-Mart. His dad, Don Moriarty, runs the field and made sure of that. Eric had grown up on the fields, making money each summer that he put toward college. After he graduated, he came to his father with a dilemma. He had two job offers, one from a prominent national accounting firm and the other from a tiny upstart computer company called eBay. He told his dad he preferred the computer company, but it somehow seemed traitorous to work for a company that some had already begun to suggest would destroy Brimfield and all the other great antiques markets. Don Moriarty told his son to go where his heart was, and Eric chose eBay over Arthur Anderson, the accounting firm that a few years later was so tied to corporate scandals that it folded.

Don Moriarty has long argued that Brimfield should not fear eBay, that the online company is too remote, too sterile, and ultimately too clumsy ever to win over everyone in the antiques and collectibles field. Over time, as eBay began to stumble and antagonize some antiques and collectibles dealers and collectors, other field promoters began to agree with him.

"eBay has had a huge impact at places such as Brimfield," says Steiner of *AuctionBytes*. "I believe that most of the antiques dealers at Brimfield have a love-hate relationship with eBay and the online world. On the one hand, they know they can't live without it and eBay can be very convenient. But on the other hand, eBay has made life more difficult for them. Now everyone knows prices far better than in the past, prices in many areas have fallen, and there are real fraud issues when you are dealing with eBay and the Internet."

Gary Sohmers says: "eBay began as an opportunity in our business for both buyers and sellers. It has become a big, giant flea market. I like to call it flea bay. It's like walking through Wal-Mart and you are looking for something you really need and you can't find it."

Steiner argues that eBay does not understand or really care to deal with the sort of people who come to places such as Brimfield. eBay staffers, he notes, "are a bunch of Stanford grads. They would rather sell a piece for ten thousand dollars as opposed to a piece that sells for two dollars. It's the same amount of bandwidth, the same amount of service space, and I don't think they have ever been able to deal with the multiple set of personalities that come along with these antiques dealers. These dealers are a very feisty group of people."

eBay has long maintained that fraud on its site is a minor issue, representing less than one percent of all sales. Still, that number could be significant, given that annually there are more than a billion auctions. Steiner says that fraud remains eBay's major impediment to future growth. "It has been the Achilles heel for the entire industry," agrees Davies of TIAS.com. Sohmers believes the real extent of the problem is still unclear: "People are so stupid, they may not yet have discovered that they have been duped. In some cases, it may be years before they discover it."

The Federal Trade Commission reports a steady increase in the number of complaints it has received about fraud over the Internet, primarily concerning Internet auctions. Internet scams reported to the FTC in 2004 totaled 205,568 incidents, costing consumers $265 million. Problems involving Internet auctions have ranged from sellers never sending the merchandise, to shill bidding where sellers artificially drive up prices, to delivering goods that are fake.

eBay and its top sellers have long been irritated by such stories, maintaining that they do not fairly represent what is going on. "Their biggest concern is that eBay is getting a black eye," observes Steiner. "Every time they see a headline in a newspaper about fraud, they take it personally, they feel that the market is being attacked. They want people to come to eBay and eBay has not been able to stem that tide of fraud. It is so easy to get anonymous e-mail accounts. The fact that they tout over one hundred and thirty-five million registered users is a huge joke. I have a dozen eBay accounts myself. There are very practical reasons for having them. If you are a dealer and you are looking for a bargain, you do not want people tracking your movement on eBay."

eBay has launched a buyer protection plan to provide refunds of up to $500 to buyers who, in some cases, do not receive the goods they purchased or who receive goods substantially different than those represented by the seller. The company also claims that it has increased the number of fraud investigators to one thousand. It does not provide a breakdown of these investigators' responsibilities or of how much of their time is devoted to fraud as opposed to other duties.

Buyers such as Schiff, who has seen his share of fraud, are unconvinced that eBay has done enough to police its marketplace. Ultimately, eBay maintains that it cannot be a cop and cannot be liable for what happens. eBay claims that it is "only a venue."

Adds Steiner: "I think fraud is a huge problem that no-body has figured out yet how to stop. And it is going to take more than eBay. It is going to take regulation, it's going to take cooperation from Web-based companies, it's going to take eBay and payment companies, and they are not even close to having that kind of cooperation."

One day Joe was scanning eBay when he discovered a woman in the Boston area who had sold two paintings, one of which was a John Singer Sargent for $5,000. She indicated in her advertisement that she had full provenance of other works, which had been owned by her parents, and that she would soon be putting more works up for sale.

Joe e-mailed her and learned that she had another Sar-gent. The photo she sent him was of a painting of a beauti-ful woman standing by some rocks on a New England coastline. It looked like a work that should be in a museum, and when she wanted only $3,000, Joe wired her the money. The moment he unwrapped the painting he felt a little sick. It looked nothing like the photo the owner had sent. Instead, it was hardly more than a stick drawing by a child, it was so poorly executed.

In the beginning Joe tried to reason with the seller. In the first phone calls, he stuck to asking fairly innocent ques-tions about the missing provenance papers. The woman promised to send them. They never came. After weeks of delay, when he finally demanded his money back, the con-versations took a turn for the bizarre. Sometimes he would call and be informed that he had the wrong number, or the person on the other end had never heard of him, or he would be told he was calling a doctor's cancer line. Later, when he was convinced he had the correct woman and she acknowledged who he was, she would tell him that she had been a victim of identity theft. Someone else using her name had sold him the painting. She had no idea how she could help.

Joe considered going to Boston and knocking on the door of her house. He was afraid he would lose his temper and wind up in jail. He had tracked down a lawyer in Chicago who had also bought from the woman. The lawyer reported that he was out $20,000. Joe could not file a complaint with eBay, because the woman had sold the painting privately, and, further, she was no longer listed on eBay. He could either try to get law enforcement authorities interested or he could write off the buy as a deal that had gone bad—$3,000 bad. He called the FBI, but they did not seem interested. In some ways, he felt the mistake had been his. He had not done his homework. He had not researched the seller or the painting thoroughly enough. Had he done so, he would have discovered that the painting was indeed of museum quality; in fact, that's where the original now hung.

"I just have to be more diligent and less greedy," he told Rachel.

The experience did not stop him from buying on eBay, but it did teach him that he had to be more careful. But not too careful, for the gamble, the thrill of the risk, is partially what makes the game so much fun for Joe.

CHAPTER 14

The Toothache

RACHEL HAS A toothache. It's in the lower left molar. The dentist told her that she needs a root canal. That costs $2,000 and she does not have it. She barely has medical insurance, let alone dental coverage. She pays Mennonite Mutual Aid $2,400, which covers only medical problems. Even then she has to pay the first $500 and half of the next $2,000 in bills. Before she leaves the dentist, she asks if she has any other options. He says an extraction would cost $200.

"Poverty sucks," she tells herself.

It is a warm summer day in late August. Joe is out at an auction and she has only Ryzo, her rottweiler, to keep her company. The Perkiomen Creek is low this time of year; she can see its languid and lazy flow from her porch. She thinks about returning to stripping the woodwork in what will eventually be the guest room. And, maybe, just maybe, if things work out with Joe, someday the nursery. But her tooth hurts too much and besides, she is upset. She's been in a funk for what feels like weeks.

This year's final Brimfield show is in two weeks. She does

not know what to expect from Brimfield. Certainly this summer has not met her expectations. She likes the house, and her relationship is fine with Joe, except for a few bumps as they have settled in. But the mortgage has become a real concern, especially since they have sold far less art on eBay than she had hoped. She knows that situation will change after Labor Day, but even then the checks won't arrive for weeks. They have made some sales. She has sold three of the fourteen Charles Wachter paintings that she picked up at the May Brimfield show and netted $1,400 from the sales. That's what she paid for all fourteen. So far she has only broken even, and several of the paintings have to be cleaned before they can bring good money. Joe has also sold a few paintings, including one by a Connecticut Impressionist, Oscar Anderson, which they bought at the July show. It cost only $150 and he's going to get $600 for it. The problem with this deal is that they will not get their money until they deliver the painting on their way up to Brimfield in two weeks. Knowing Joe, he will probably use the money to buy more art. They also sold a couple of paintings to dealers who have galleries. But it hurt a little to get $400 for a painting and see it marked up to $1,200.

Rachel always worries about finances. It is something she got from her mother. It just feels more acute this time, something like the toothache. Even though she never has had very much money since she left college and went out on her own, her financial record is spotless. She has never been late with a bill, not even a credit card bill. She has bought and sold two houses before acquiring this latest one, quite an accomplishment considering that she has primarily worked for herself. She knows how to be creative. When she applied for the mortgage for this house, she put down, accurately, that her income last year was $60,000. What she did not mention was that her expenses were $45,000. The bottom line was, she got the mortgage. The problem is that now she and Joe always seem to be short of cash. They have to extend themselves partly by using credit cards. It is a juggling act that she does not like. It is really bothering her. How much longer will she and Joe have to squeeze every penny? When can they live like most couples?

In contrast, Joe never seems worried about their finances. He always has faith that he will find the art that will pay the bills. So far their finances are separate, which is both good and bad. It helps that Rachel does not have to worry about what Joe is spending, but she does anyway. She especially worries that he will not be able to pay his share of the mortgage. She has noticed that Joe has become more cautious lately. It is Joe who pointed out that perhaps they should not bring any paintings to Brimfield. What is the point? They are having so much trouble selling online, he wonders if they can find buyers at the flea market. Joe is still feeling out the Brimfield market. To him it is more a place to buy than to sell.

As much as money has raised her anxieties, it has also triggered other questions in the last few weeks. Her college, Antioch, has a motto from its first president, the nineteenth-century educator Horace Mann: "Be ashamed to die until you have won some victory for humanity." Rachel has been thinking of that challenge and wondering what she, as an art dealer, is doing. She works with other dealers to promote art and to find a market for it. She knows this is an important role, especially in a capitalistic system. What art and culture would survive without dealers? It certainly would be different.

Humanity needs culture, but art is generally the province of the privileged. A friend recently talked to Rachel about the idea of promoting art among prisoners. It began innocently with the friend asking if Rachel could help research whether there is a market for art produced behind bars. But it got Rachel thinking. Perhaps there is a way she can work with art to help the people who need the most assistance. For that matter, maybe she can focus not just on people in prisons but in ghettos and barrios too, the poor, the mentally ill, the unfortunate, wherever they are. It must be her Quaker heritage, not the money problems, that prompts these questions.

Perhaps that is what is also awakening another nagging concern—the matter of the ethics of her profession. When she gets into these moods she seems to confront a range of qualms. It sounds strange to raise a moral compass on something as basic as buying and selling art. But for an art dealer to succeed, she has to play particular roles both in acquiring and selling. When she buys art, she has to hide her knowledge of what she is buying in order to acquire it at the lowest possible price. Once she owns it, she needs to use that knowledge to promote the piece and sell it at the highest price. Someone is going to get hurt in this process, and it is not going to be the art dealer if she wants to remain in business. In most cases the initial seller is going to lose, but Rachel knows that if the dealer tells the truth upfront, the outcome will be far different. Few care if the profit is only a few hundred dollars. But what if the difference is between a buying price of four dollars and a selling price of two million or more?

It always seems to come back to money. Rachel isn't really poor. Both she and Joe are sitting on a huge pile of money. But like the hungry child staring up at the cookie jar on the top shelf, it is so close yet so far away. She isn't thinking of the house or property; they are heavily mortgaged. The money is all in the paintings. In every room paintings are propped along the walls, ready to be hung. She has been dealing—or is it collecting?—art for years. She has maybe a couple of hundred paintings. They are worth well more than $150,000, maybe $200,000, perhaps even $250,000. What if she sold all her paintings? That might be enough to retire the mortgage. She loves the paintings, but she is tempted to be free from these financial worries.

"They're just pieces of canvas and oil with pigment," she tells herself. "That's all they are."

She remembers a dealer who specialized in Pennsylvania art, to whom she had sold one of her Philadelphia Ten paintings, a landscape by Fern Coppedge. That dealer has seen what she owns; perhaps he would be interested. Maybe others would be too. She begins working on a detailed inventory.

There are different definitions of what constitutes success within the art and antiques industry. One yardstick is knowledge and respect in a field where information is paramount. Most hide their knowledge, but some, such as Harry Rinker and Ralph and Terry Kovel, tout it. Rinker, based in Pennsylvania, publishes his own price guide on antiques and collectibles, appears at workshops, and has hosted several radio and television programs, including one called *Whatcha Got.* The Kovels have published more than seventy-five books, including a "complete price guide" on antiques and collectibles that has gone through thirty-five editions and sold 2.7 million copies. They have written a syndicated newspaper column, produced a newsletter with 150,000 subscribers, and been on television hosting *Flea Market Finds.*

When the Kovels and Rinker show up at Brimfield, people recognize them from television.

The same thing happens to Gary Sohmers. One day a middle-aged woman was browsing the booth and caught sight of Sohmers with his long gray pony tail and his trademark Hawaiian shirt.

"Don't I know you?" she asked.

Her partner knew immediately that Sohmers is a regular appraiser on the PBS program *Antiques Roadshow*. She nudged her friend and said, with a note of pleasure in her voice, "You know who he is."

"Oh, yes!" exclaimed the first woman in an excited voice as the recognition hit. "Yes, yes!" she said even more excitedly.

Sohmers gave them each an oversized postcard of his smiling face and signed his name on the front.

Sohmers says this happens all the time, because of the magic of television. Actually, Sohmers brags that he has been in the business since he was eight, when he tried to sell some of his toys at a yard sale. Except for stints in a rock-and-roll band, he has been a dealer, based in Hudson, Massachusetts, of everything pop culture, from toys to campaign buttons and from old record albums to the Hawaiian shirts he wears on television. He quickly recognized the value of *Antiques Roadshow*, although he failed to get on the show in its first season. He says it was only after the producers went out on the road that first year and saw the volume of pop culture collectibles that they realized they needed someone with Sohmers's background.

Antiques Roadshow is the most popular program on PBS, and its appeal is very similar to the lure of Brimfield: the search for lost treasures. In the show, which is based on a similar British program, a group of antiques experts appraise objects owned by residents in a featured community, which changes with each episode. A couple of dozen pieces are so unusual or valuable that they are aired. The news that an heirloom or object bought for 50¢ is now worth $5,000, $50,000, or $500,000 brings tears of joy to the owners.

The biggest stars of the show have been two men whose roots run deep at Brimfield. Leigh and Leslie Keno, known as "the twins," still return occasionally to Brimfield with their dad, Ron Keno, and reminisce about the antiques market. Ron Keno is an antiques dealer from near Mohawk, New York, who for years brought his two precocious sons, who are identical twins, to Brimfield. The twins were always seeking antiques. Ron Keno recalls one time when the boys had been up at six-thirty in the morning, out scouting a field, when they returned, excited, insisting he get out of bed and see what they had discovered. The elder Keno got into his pants and followed the two energized boys back to a dealer. They had placed a ten-minute hold on the objects: two busts of animal heads, a giraffe and a rhinoceros, covered entirely in bottle caps.

"Boys, this is great, you have found two genuine examples of folk art," Ron Keno remembers telling his sons. He paid the dealer $800 and sold them to another dealer, who eventually donated them to the Smithsonian.

The boys remember another time when they hopped the fence at J&J's, beating the 6 A.M. rush, and found a stoneware mug. They paid $200 for it and sold it for $800. As teenagers, they became serious collectors of eighteenth-century stoneware, selling much of it to help pay their way through college.

The other story they like to tell about their Brimfield education is the time, when they were about thirteen, that they found a wooden burl bowl on a dealer's table. It looked authentic, so they bought it. A few minutes later they came across a dealer who had a table covered with identical bowls, for a fraction of the price. They had been had—the bowls were reproductions.

The twins today are recognized experts on American furniture and decorative arts, although they have gone distinctively separate paths. Leslie Keno is a senior vice president with Sotheby's, while Leigh Keno has his own New York gallery.

Having your own gallery is a measure of success for Joe and most other dealers. It has been a dream for years, albeit a distant dream. Joe loves the wheeling and dealing of being a picker, of having the freedom to go wherever he wants, of not being tied down to a building. But he seems to always be talking to people about their businesses. More than once he has been tempted to buy a business, and his interests have run from used-book stores to far more exotic ventures. Once he was with Rachel and some friends at a large antiques store in New Jersey that was liquidating its entire inventory. He fell into an increasingly complex conversation with a saleswoman about buying an antique popcorn wagon. It was from the turn of the century, had been fully restored to its bright red-and-gold-lacquered surface, and needed only the horses to pull it. Joe talked about buying the wagon, which at that moment cost $25,000 less the 15 percent liquidation discount (scheduled to fall farther in subsequent months), and taking it to Phillies and Eagles games. Joe has a tendency to tease, but this time he appeared serious. He has a strong entrepreneurial streak. Rachel has been content to be a picker, but she is beginning to warm to Joe's dream.

Most dealers Joe and Rachel know do have their own galleries. Even Fran Smith, who does not have one, can park his inventory at his daughter's shop.

Mike McClintock says he loves being on the road. A wistful look comes into his eyes, even as he thinks about the four or five years that he traveled from show to show. "It was a good time," he said. "The routine was never the same; you never knew what was going to happen in a day." Despite that, he left the circuit of shows and opened his gallery to establish more legitimacy. "Opening a shop gives you more believability. It takes you to the next level."

The economic differences between selling retail and wholesale are vast. But along with them come some trickier questions. Rachel knows that a storefront will draw annoying people who will want free appraisals of their artwork. Rachel used to have more patience to deal with such requests, and sometimes she still does. But whether they know it or not, these people are raising ethical issues every dealer has to face. What should Joe and Rachel pay if someone brings in something of value?

"I feel the most ethical way of dealing with this is to offer to take it on consignment or offer them a price where we feel we could make money, but not so low as to rip them off," she says. "The problem with this is if you offer two thousand dollars on a painting that has an auction value of four thousand after it is repaired and cleaned and reframed, that may seem like a lot to them and they then think, 'Wow, I didn't know it would be worth that much. I better check into this further.' So sometimes you are better off offering them a hundred dollars."

But is that ethical? In one sense, the obvious answer is no, because the piece is worth $4,000. At the same time, dealers such as she and Joe need to be able to make money. "We have spent years reading, researching, educating, and investing in our profession," she said. "How are we supposed to get paid for our knowledge? You do not say to a doctor, 'Well, you should just tell me what is wrong with me because it is the ethical thing to do.' You pay that doctor because the person spent time in learning, reading, researching, and has experience in the field. Doctors also invest in machines to help diagnose problems. Antiques dealers are spending money investing directly in merchandise."

Antiques and art dealers also offer other services. In a way, antiques dealers are market makers in their fields of expertise. Just as different brokerage houses buy and hold specific stocks they favor, so do antiques dealers. This gives stability to the market. What would antiques be worth, wonders Rachel, if there were no antiques dealers to know what the items are, know something about their history, know how to restore them, and be willing to buy them at a price?

It is dealers who are often creating new markets for antiques and collectibles. Rachel knows someone who is collecting earring holders. The holders were probably made sometime between the 1950s and the 1970s. They are usually about six inches high and are created in some sort of figure—banana, bunny rabbit, heart—and made of metal or plastic. There is a market for these, but not much of one. One day there will be. Someone will publish a book, and then the prices will escalate. When you have a yard sale and sell "that old thing you bought when...," you put a very low price on it to get rid of it, and maybe one of your neighbors will want it, but instead of getting a dollar you get fifty cents. Or if an antiques dealer comes by, he or she will give you that dollar and then might hold onto the item for years, perhaps collecting more, perhaps writing the book. Then in twenty years that thing will be worth $50, but only because of the dealer/collector.

Dealers often hold the upper hand. Rachel knows of a dealer/restorer who cleaned a group of paintings for a customer. Instead of charging the woman a few thousand dollars, he made an agreement to trade one of the paintings for the cost of the restoration. She may have been a wealthy woman who did not need the $30,000 to $50,000 that the painting was worth. At least that is what Rachel likes to think, since many in the field would say that the deal was ethical: the woman had agreed to the arrangement. Still, it bothers Rachel because the dealer used his superior knowledge to take advantage of someone outside the profession. In contrast, it does not bother her when she or Joe, or any dealer for that matter, acquires a painting from someone inside the profession. The rules, Rachel believes, are different and other dealers are fair game.

Still, the rules for selling retail to nonprofessionals are far from simple, and Rachel is still struggling with what she believes is acceptable and what is not. "When retail people put a price on things, and we make money, I have no ethical quandaries," she says. Once, Joe and Rachel bought a watercolor for $100 directly from someone. The artist who had signed the piece had no record of recent auction sales. The seller wanted $300 but took their $100 offer. They tried but failed to sell the painting to other dealers, even when they dropped the price all the way to $100. Then they put it on eBay and got $2,000 for it. Rachel had added a summary of the painter's biography, culled from one of Joe's art books, to the listing. It attracted the attention of buyers in the area where the artist had lived, and suddenly there was strong interest in the piece. Rachel sees no problem with this. "We were doing our job of properly researching and writing the description to the best of our ability," she explains.

"When we have to make offers, honestly, it is up to the seller to say yes or no, so the ball is in their court. But when I hear of other dealers doing this and making money off of someone, it makes me think less of them. Why? Maybe because society doesn't appreciate antiques dealers the way they do doctors or teachers. People should appreciate that we do fix and restore old things and we do educate and preserve history. And like the stock market's market makers, we do provide a baseline that makes their old things valuable."

Perhaps she would not question the ethics of the antiques business as much if there weren't so many rumored and documented problems. Rachel knows that the vast majority of people she deals with, especially the professionals, are honest and ethical. She is able to handle those she doubts. Every profession has people willing to cheat the system. In the world of antiques it has happened at the very top.

It isn't just Brimfield where caveat emptor prevails. For years dealers have told stories about some of the auction houses that bend the rules when it suits them. Howard Roberts's experience with the Chippendale chairs appraised at a fraction of their real value by a reputable firm typifies such stories. The behavior persists despite formal organizations that encourage education in appraising and ethics and that have established ethical codes.

A criminal investigation of price fixing and collusion implicated the world's two most prestigious auction houses, Christie's and Sotheby's. Sotheby's board chairman, A. Alfred Taubman, tried to fight the charges, but a New York jury convicted him of plotting with Christie's to fix commissions. He was sent to jail for a year and fined $7.5 million. His counterpart at Christie's, Anthony Tennant, who lived in England, was also implicated, but the United States was unable to extradite him to stand trial. The two firms, as part of a court settlement, paid out $512 million in settlements to 130,000 customers in the United States alone who had lost money as a result of the scandal.

Rachel is comfortable with some of the informal codes that have been passed down by her father and other mentors. They are designed so that dealers play fair and not hurt each other. From what Rachel can tell, they seem to have developed through gossip and social pressure.

One of the most basic tenets is that dealers should not brag when they make a score. Dealers interpret this in different ways. Some never talk about their scores, feeling the less said, the better. Others believe they can discuss a triumph, especially in answer to a question. Sometimes it is impossible to hide the results if a sale is made at public auction or makes the trade press. But a dealer should never be smug or cocky to the person who sold the object.

At the same time, the dealer who makes the score is not required to share the wealth with the party who sold the object. However, the code does obligate the dealer with the windfall to take some business back to the seller. Often the buyer never tells the seller why he is back, or why he is buying from him. But sellers can sometimes guess. It's all part of the code.

Dealers who lose big on a score have no recourse, and anyone who makes a deal needs to stand up and accept it, rather than having second thoughts after the terms are settled.

After Bidge McKay and Jim Meyer sold the Martin Johnson Heade, they decided not to tell anyone about the score and certainly not to brag about it. But the Christie's auction was so well publicized that eventually the dealer who sold them the Heade heard about it. Bidge McKay will only identify that dealer by his first name, Joe.

"Gee, you made all of that money off that painting," the dealer named Joe told McKay when he next saw him.

"Look, Joe. You approved the sale and we paid you what you asked for it," pointed out McKay. By then McKay had learned that Joe had paid only $50 for the Heade, so he knew that Joe had tripled his money. Still, McKay must have been thinking about the code, because he offered to do the dealer a favor. He knew the dealer had an old clock that needed work, so he agreed to refinish it for him. When he delivered it, he told the dealer, "You know, if I knew somebody who had made a lot of money off of me, I would see how much of it I could get back from him."

"What do you mean?" asked the dealer.

McKay said he knew that the dealer acquired quality antiques. He suggested that the dealer call him when he found a good piece. He also told the dealer to write down on a piece of paper the sum for which he would sell the piece and put it in an envelope. McKay would look at the antique and, if he liked it, he would write down a sum and insert it in a separate envelope. Then they would open the envelopes, and the dealer would be obligated to sell to McKay, without any more haggling, at the higher price. "You mean if I put down a thousand dollars and you put down two thousand, then I get the two thousand?"

"That's right," responded McKay.

They made several sales like that. The one McKay remembers best is the 1740 Philadelphia bent-back ladder-back armchair. The dealer wrote down $1,800 and McKay wrote $2,800. Later McKay sold it for $5,000. A little bit later he traded a painting to get it back. He had learned more about the history of the chair, and he was able to sell it the second time to another buyer for $11,500. It was later exhibited at the Philadelphia Museum of Art.

Rachel has heard the story several times and believes the code works well for everyone in this situation. She adds one postscript. The painting that her father traded was by George Sotter, a Bucks County artist whose work has risen significantly in value and even then was worth somewhere between $5,000 and $10,000. Today, the Sotter is potentially worth far more than the 1740 Philadelphia chair.

Rachel is still wrestling with the ethics, but as she remembers the code she feels a bit better. She will have to think it through some more. While she gets discouraged and often has doubts, they rarely reach the point where she would consider getting out of the profession. Still, she might like to sell her inventory.

It takes Rachel several days to see whether there is indeed a market for her painting collection. A dealer in his fifties from Florida often calls Rachel to see what she has found and to brag for an hour about what a great buyer he is. He has never bought anything from Rachel and his calls have gotten annoying over the years. Still, she wonders if it could have been that the merchandise she offered was not good enough. She sends him a sheet of her best paintings. He e-mails back that he is interested. She also sends the list to that local dealer who bought the Fern Coppedge.

The Florida dealer offers her $50,000 for everything. The Pennsylvania dealer is not certain that he even wants to buy her stock, or that he has the money for it. If he can come up with the cash, the best he can do is $100,000.

Rachel is disappointed. No, she's upset. It would be a huge loss to sell the works for either of those prices. They have to be worth more than $150,000, and even that is on the low side. It definitely is not enough. Maybe it's just as well the prices came in so low, for she really does not want to sell her paintings. Over the last few days that has become increasingly clear. But what is she going to do about paying the mortgage? Brimfield is now only a week away, and both she and Joe seem so unprepared for it.

Rachel solves one problem. The dentist pulls her tooth. She is no longer in pain. She's just upset. And she's worried. It's not just the money. Others have made their mark—will she?

CHAPTER 15

Discovering Maxfield Parrish

THERE IS NO sign of Joe and Rachel. The September show is underway, and they have missed the Monday night flashlight walk when dealers surreptitiously sell before the market officially opens, the dawn rush at Sheltons, and all the other early Tuesday field openings. They arrive on the fields at midmorning on Tuesday and look exhausted.

The couple left Collegeville late on Monday. They had an argument but that was all right; Joe remembers that they had others in May and July just before leaving for Brimfield; usually everything works out fine. The Labor Day traffic around New York was awful.

They had to make a stop in Connecticut to drop off that painting by Oscar Anderson, the Connecticut Impressionist. The buyer is a dealer who specializes in furniture. He has a shop near his house and a few paintings, including an interesting, large French one. Even though they came to sell, Joe and Rachel could not resist seeing what they might buy. When they got to the shop, they decided they could not buy the painting, which was a war scene. It was well done but it had too many dead people. It is hard to sell paintings depicting the dead and wounded. Joe saw an illustration, up on a back wall. He asked the dealer to bring it down. The black-and-white illustration showed a young man sitting in a chair eating a sandwich. The dealer said it was a lithograph by Maxfield Parrish.

The name Maxfield Parrish still rings a bell with many Americans, but his familiarity is fading. Born in 1870, Parrish flourished as an American illustrator from the dawn of the twentieth century through World War II, an era that has been called the golden age of American illustration. Parrish was prolific, producing idealized and romantic images in vibrant, luminescent colors. It is said that Parrish so dominated the images Americans loved in the 1920s that a poll taken at that time named him along with van Gogh and Cézanne as the three greatest artists of all time. One out of four American homes in that period displayed a framed Parrish, and more of his images were sold than of any other artist of his era. Parrish followed a rich heritage of illustrators led by Frederic Remington and Charles Dana Gibson. Over time his reputation and his art fell out of favor, critical opinion holding that he was too commercial and his subjects hopelessly naïve and outdated. But in the art world, good reputations are often revived, and in recent years the values of original works of many illustrators, including Parrish, have soared.

Joe and Rachel both studied the composition. The dealer wanted $295 for it. Joe looked at Rachel: "What do you think?"

Rachel, who is always the pessimist when asked that question, replied, "I like it."

So did Joe, although he worked to maintain his neutral look.

Rachel could see the sheen of thick ink, a characteristic foreign to lithographs. Lithographs also have tiny dots. This one had them, but they did not appear to have come from the printing process but rather from pen and ink drawn by the artist. She noticed that a white space on the drawing contained white pigment, which never would have occurred in a print. She thought it could be an original, and at that price they could hardly lose money. Prints sell for anywhere from $100 to $500 and she had not seen this one on the market. It also had a nice oak frame worth at least $50.

Joe was thinking the same thing. It was almost too good to be true, he thought. Maybe it was. Maybe it was another Alechinsky. Joe had not yet done any work toward learning whether the painting he had bought in May was authentic, but he intended to do it someday.

They bought the Parrish for $275.

At Brimfield the weather today is foul, as dark as Rachel's mood has been for weeks. It rains hard most of the day, a thick downpour that will recur throughout the week. Brimfield shoppers expect the worst; there are stories that the harder it rains, the more determined they become. If it seems perverse to set items of value in a field that easily floods, then that is the contrariness of Brimfield. The weather is always a factor, be it the threat of frost or even snow in early May, the very real likelihood of suffocating heat and humidity in July, or the prospect of a hurricane in September. A brilliant sunny day can draw huge crowds and boost sales. But no one is surprised when it rains.

It is still raining Wednesday morning and at five-thirty Howard Roberts is hurrying to get to his tent to set up before the rush. He wonders what he will find there, because the rain came down hard during the night. He has one of the lowest, wettest places on the field. The tarps he put down as a floor tend to act like a bathtub. He peeks through the canvas tent flaps and sees about an inch of water in the bottom. He's relieved. He can sweep it out quickly and take down the furniture he stacked before leaving last night. It could be worse, a lot worse. He remembers another stormy Brimfield show. He had been heading to his tent when two other dealers told him they had already gone inside and moved a few things off the floor to get them away from the water. But it must have rained some more after they left, because when he opened the tent flap, water began pouring out. It made a rushing sound as it exited. There must have been seven inches standing inside. Items had been stacked on top of a large dining room table and they nearly touched the top of the tent. Several blue plastic storage tubs were floating in the water. It was late in the show. He simply began packing to leave early. He was lucky; he hardly lost anything.

The water is bad enough, but the mud is the real challenge. The thick, gooey muck is so powerful it can suck shoes off feet and yet is loose enough to fall off shoes that come in contact with a clean surface. Thick alluvial deposits of rich, dark loam have been deposited for ages from the modest Mill Brook and its smaller, unnamed tributaries in this low river valley. The result is a high water table that will flood even at the mention of rain. It causes tent stakes to melt in the slime and automobile tires to sink deep into the muck. Some field owners have installed underground pipes and gravel to drain the water. On other fields the mud can capture anything with wheels, and the only means of rescue is to hoist whatever gets stuck with heavy-duty winches and cranes. It is not a pretty sight. There have been Brimfields at which Rachel has been unable to find any paintings because dealers do not want to take them out for fear of the rain and mud.

July is usually the hot show. Dealers have few options for coping with the heat. They can stay away, which about half of them do. Or they can complain. Rich Conley, the dealer who calls himself Santa Claus, counters on such days by setting up a bobsled and skis before a huge mural that depicts a scene of the Canadian Rockies. Then he takes pictures of visitors as they pose in front of his mural. Or he serves snow cones. "It always makes people feel cooler," says Conley. To Conley an antiques show in a field is really no different from a rock show in the open air. "Brimfield is as close as it gets to the original Woodstock."

Of all the elements of weather, wind is the one most feared. Even a mild breeze can cause glass and pottery to topple. Higher winds can be potentially deadly. Tents need to be secured. One time a high wind pulled a tent with its stakes out of the earth. As the tent rose in the strong gust, it hurtled toward the road, its metal stakes suddenly dangerous projectiles. It flew directly into a school bus, with several stakes smashing windows but leaving ducking passengers uninjured. Observers noticed that some of the ropes and stakes just narrowly missed wrapping around high-tension electrical lines that bordered Main Street. Photographs inside one of the permanent buildings at Heart-O-The-Mart show tents wrapped around buildings and utility wires during a 1989 storm.

In 1999 when Hurricane Floyd roared toward New England and Brimfield, the Massachusetts State Police and Brimfield selectmen officially closed the show. Yet some dealers and buyers were reluctant to leave. "I had a terrible time getting people off the field," says Marie Duldorian, who runs the New England Motel field. "The state police wanted them off right away, but it wasn't easy." Rachel remembers going to that show and being surprised there were so few dealers. "I did not know it was officially closed," she says. By the time Floyd arrived on Thursday it had been downgraded to a tropical storm, but it was powerful enough to drop five inches of rain and knock over trees and tents. By Friday, the fields were officially re-opened but much of the business was gone. "I went to J&J on Friday and there were about six people set up," recalls Rachel.

For this show, Robert Cheney is trying to stay away from the fields. The board of selectmen in late July hired a new police chief, Charles T. Kuss, who has assured Cheney that he has a plan for this September show. He has not shared it with Cheney, and the board chairman has not asked for any details. It apparently does not include hiring any new police officers. Kuss is the only permanent law enforcement employee the town has placed on the payroll. While no picket lines have been set up, other police departments are taking the same position they took in July. They will stay away from Brimfield this week. Cheney does not mind; he thinks the July show went well. "There were no sirens, no screaming policemen, and no speeding police cars during the week," he says. "It was pretty quiet, which is the way it should be."

Cheney and the town are also still not taking any responsibility for the silver heist at Mark and Lee Gillespie's booth. The Gillespies, after thinking about skipping the show, are back in the same location. Now they have bars and grills on all their cases, and they spend an hour each evening packing up the cases and bringing them back to their motel. Each morning they spend another hour unpacking and setting up. "They are secure, but if someone wants to get in they still will," says Mark Gillespie. Police have not said anything about the case. The Gillespies are convinced that the thief was a professional who had scouted out the booth and knew exactly what he was doing. They never expect to see the objects again. The other silver dealer whose booth was burglarized back in May is not at the show, but Robert Lloyd always skips the September Brimfield for a big show in Baltimore. Some dealers wonder if Lloyd will return next year.

Later on Wednesday Joel Schiff and a friend are carrying a very heavy cast-iron pressure cooker. They move slowly up the muddy aisle, passing the booth with the hammerhead shark atop it, until they reach Howard Roberts's booth. Schiff asks if he can store the pressure cooker here, since it is along the side of the road. Roberts agrees. Schiff shows Roberts how the pressure cooker works. He estimates that it is at least two hundred years old. After he leaves, a man comes in and spots the checkers with the swastikas removed from the dirty house back in Pennsylvania. Roberts is surprised that the buyer has found them. He has not hidden them, but neither has he displayed them. The buyer asks how much Roberts wants for them.

Roberts shrugs. Twenty-five dollars, he says.

The man is about to agree when he counts the checkers. "This set is incomplete," he says.

"What do you want for twenty-five dollars?" asks Roberts.

The buyer apparently agrees, because he closes the deal without haggling over price. Roberts is relieved; he did not like those checkers.

The rain begins again as May's opens on Thursday. Some dealers are grumbling louder. But the scores of shoppers are still out there. Mike McClintock finds a William Trost Richards watercolor for $2,000. Richards was a Philadelphia-based painter who flourished in the late nineteenth century, specializing in watercolors and landscapes along the East Coast, especially the Jersey shore. The piece McClintock buys is from Richards's later days, when he was less popular. He knows he can sell it for $8,000.

McClintock has always been a gambler, one who trusts his own judgment. The Richards painting reminds him of another time he wagered on a nineteenth-century American painter. Years ago, when he was still on the road, he went to an auction with a little more than $2,500 in his pocket. While he was reviewing the paintings, he came across a pair by the same artist. He studied them for a long time and then turned to his partner and said, "You need to trust me on this. I want to spend every penny we have, if necessary, to buy those paintings. We may not be able to eat tonight, but we need those paintings."

It came down to him and one other bidder. The bids went back and forth, climbing by $100 each time. When they passed $2,000, McClintock never paused. He bid $2,100.

The other bidder responded at $2,200.

The auctioneer's singsong chant invited McClintock to respond at $2,300. He did.

"We have twenty-three hundred, twenty-three hundred, twenty-three hundred. Do we have twenty-four hundred?"

For once the other bidder was quiet.

"Do we have twenty-four hundred?"

The bidder shook his head.

McClintock bought the pair of paintings by Robert Loftin Newman, a nineteenth-century painter noted for his dark landscapes, and still had enough money for dinner. McClintock sold the paintings for $5,000. While he was pleased with the profit, what he had really proved was that art dealers sometimes have to gamble everything in their pockets if they believe in their judgments.

Santa Claus may have a big hit at the show. Actually, Rich Conley has not discovered the piece, but he is perhaps even more excited than the man who has. Conley is walking down Route 20 on Wednesday afternoon when he sees a crowd around a booth at Collins Apple Barn. Dealers are examining a wooden cradle. It is oak, looks old, and has an inscription on the side, "Suffer Little Children To Come Unto Me, Forbid Them Not For Such Is Ye Kingdom of God 1675." Several are asking the dealer, everyone calls him Larry, what he wants for it. Larry is getting nervous; he is not sure what he has, and finally he tells the dealers that it is not for sale. He carefully places the cradle inside his truck. The crowd begins to disperse, except for Conley, who wonders how Larry found it.

Larry, whose actual name is Gary Zaczyk, tells him. Earlier in the day Zaczyk bought a schoolmaster's desk with a lift-top lid from a dealer during the rush at Heart-O-The-Mart. He paid for the desk and returned in the early afternoon to pick it up. He noticed something wooden beneath a beanbag chair toward the back of the tent. The dealer explained that it was a cradle from the 1800s. Zaczyk examined it closely and noticed the numbers at the end of the inscription—1675. The cradle looked older than nineteenth century, and those numbers appeared to be a date. He saw that it was in good condition, although a bottom board had been replaced some time earlier. The dealer said he wanted $850 for the cradle. He explained that he had bought it from an estate near New York City, where it had been stored in the attic. The previous owners said that the cradle at one time might have been owned by either a parent or grandparent of someone who had signed the Declaration of Independence. That person's name had begun with a *W*.

Zaczyk looked around the tent. He was surprised that he had missed it, that everyone had missed it during the rush, but it was in a back corner covered by other things. The dealer's tent mostly contained jewelry and sterling and few pieces of furniture. Not only had the dealer been off as much as two hundred years on the vintage, but the price was ridiculously low. Zaczyk has been in the antiques business nearly forty years, more than half of them with a shop in Albion, in the farmlands of western Pennsylvania. He has a sense of what is authentic and good. This piece fit. He bought it for $750. The crowd of dealers had gathered the moment he had gotten back to his booth. Dealers seemed to agree with Zaczyk's judgment.

Zaczyk and Conley begin speculating about the piece. Conley thinks it might be related or from the same era as a Hadley chest. Named for a nearby town in central Massachusetts, the chests were made by a small number of woodworkers between 1680 and 1740 in a five-mile stretch of the Connecticut River Valley. They featured carved inset panels and low, heavy-framed shapes modeled after medieval construction styles. Built as showpieces, they fell out of favor even before the American Revolution and were rediscovered by scholars and antiques buffs in the late nineteenth century. Hadley chests sell at auction for up to hundreds of thousands of dollars. Conley is still excited by the discovery. Za-czyk, who has known "Santa" for years, tells Conley that if he helps him authenticate the piece and find a buyer, he will cut him in on the deal. Conley is excited. He's going to spend the winter finding curators and auction houses that might be interested. He is convinced that the cradle is original and that it is museum quality. "It could be the biggest score ever made at Brimfield," he tells friends, including Rachel.

News of more scores only makes Rachel feel worse. It has been a terrible show. She and Joe brought hardly any paint-ings to sell and they really are not buying much of anything. Sure, Joe is still finding a few bargains and then flipping them. They brought their bikes instead of additional paint-ings to sell, and when it is not raining too hard, Rachel spends much of the week riding, visiting with friends.

On Thursday afternoon Don Vandeemark, a New York dealer who has set up next to Joe and Rachel at Heart-O-The-Mart, tells them he is moving to J&J that night. He won-ders if they will help him set up. He will give them dealer passes in return, so they can scout J&J before it opens in the morning. Joe immediately agrees. Rachel is surprised. It sounds like a lot of work for only an hour or so of opportu-nity before the gates open. She also suspects that they will be lucky to get back to the motel by ten. The trucks and vans line up outside J&J through the late afternoon on Thursday, but it takes hours to check in and get to an assigned space. Then it takes hours to set up. Many dealers complain that it is just too much, especially as they get older, because Friday is such a long day. Joe wishes he had known how long it would take; he probably would have begged off. It is mid-night before they get back to the motel.

They get a few hours sleep and are back at J&J by four-thirty Friday morning. Vandeemark asks them to take a few things out and then suggests that they get on the fields to look for bargains. He can finish. Joe and Rachel split up. It is hard to see in the darkness and J&J has never been a good field for Rachel. Still, she is here; she worked hard for this opportunity; she should make the most of it. She feels as though she has gone up and down every path at least twice and now it is almost 6 A.M. In just a few minutes the crowd will surge in. Bargains will begin to disappear.

That's when she sees the painting. It is a landscape, a farm scene of waving, amber hay and lush, green fields in the distance. The painting is not large, perhaps twelve inches by twenty, for sale by an older woman with plenty of pottery, glassware, and other antiques but few paintings. Rachel takes a closer look and her heart leaps.

The signature says Ranulph Bye.

She wonders if the dealer knows who Bye is. She asks the price. The woman says she can have it for $585.

Obviously the dealer does not know Bye. Either that, or the dealer must think it is a print. Rachel examines it more carefully—it is an original. The dealer explains that she found the painting while cleaning out an old house in up-state New York. Rachel tries to stay calm, but she can feel her excitement building. She fights it off and again studies the painting, this time even more closely. She can see the artist's brush marks.

The time is just six o'clock. Now she can feel the crowd coming, like a marauding army, about to pillage and plunder—or at the very least to steal the opportunity for scores. But Rachel has beaten them. She lives for such moments, for the sudden recognition of a piece of art, for the ability to find it a moment before the crowd, and for the instinct to close the deal. She had forgotten just how good this feels. It is a wonderful feeling, and despite the early hour and her lack of sleep, she suddenly feels very wide awake. Actually, she feels better than she has in weeks. How could she have forgotten? This makes it all worthwhile.

"I'll take it," she tells the woman.

Just then the first buyers come by.

Ranulph Bye was a Bucks County painter, not one of its most famous, but a painter who flourished in the days of Edward Redfield and Daniel Garber. This oil is unusual because Bye was known as a watercolorist. Fifty years earlier he was called "one of the foremost watercolorists in the country," having painted more than three thousand scenes, primarily landscapes, seascapes, unusual structures, and buildings and scenes of rural America. He is eighty-seven years old and still alive. Prices for Byes, according to *Davenport*, range from a low of $1,000 up to $2,000 and sometimes $4,000. Rachel knows those figures are not accurate. Bucks County artists are rising in value. Who knows what she could get in a few years for the Bye? Assuming she can keep him. Of course, she wants to. She can see the place in the kitchen where she could hang the painting.

"I know a little about the artist," Rachel tells the dealer. She then describes how, when she was sixteen, had dropped out of high school, and was feeling a little lost, she worked for a while as a painter of houses and fences. One day she found herself painting a picket fence in Bucks County at a house that was owned by Bye's ex-wife.

It seems fitting to rediscover Bye when she is again a little lost. And it feels good to rediscover all the rewards of being an art dealer.

Joe has not found anything, but he is excited about the Bye. It has to be worth at least $5,000, he thinks. Perhaps $10,000. It is a score. Rachel doesn't tell him she is thinking of keeping it rather than selling it. That can come later. They go to the snack bar and have breakfast. It tastes better than anything Rachel has eaten in weeks. Joe is tired; he wants to get back to Vandeemark's booth and take a nap. Not Rachel. The rush is ending, but there have to be bargains out there. She's probably been missing them all week. What got into her?

The stormy weather finally breaks on Friday, and the September sun is strong but pleasant, a reminder of the summer's heat and the promise of autumn's chill. By Sunday the remaining dealers are packing. The Brimfield September show marks the end of the season. There will be other big shows this fall: Round Top, Renningers, and Atlantic City. But to an antiques dealer, Brimfield and Labor Day mean the days of dust and grit and summer heat are at an end. The end of the September show marks the time to get back to eBay, to auctions, to estate sales, to other ways of finding stuff and making a living off it. For a few this show is the end of an era.

June Secrist tells David Lamberto she will not be coming back to the Hertan field next year. She is in tears. Secrist and her husband, Bob, began coming from Ohio twenty years ago. For years they had sold antique advertising signs, until originals became so difficult to find that the market contracted significantly. That happens sometimes with antiques. Either that, or the price for certain collectibles simply falls through the floor. That was when June Secrist began experimenting with selling dolls. The first year, she was over-whelmed by the response. Women literally fought to get the homemade dolls, fashioned from vintage textiles, and Secrist sold out in ten minutes. She kept bringing more dolls and the crowds just got bigger. But she is getting older, she missed the May show because of an operation, and she and Bob have decided that this will be their last show.

Lamberto wants to boost the crowd on Sunday, so he has arranged for several bands to play at the Hertan field. He has promised Sue Adams, who runs the Quaker Acres field across the road, that this will not be like the last concert. On that occasion, a group of South American Indians wanted to sell CDs of their music, and Lamberto agreed to let them set up and play on the nearly empty field on a Sunday. He began to have misgivings when they arrived with a set of huge speakers that looked as if they might transmit music to Jupiter. The music turned out to be loud but manageable, and it was actually quite nice except for one increasingly vexing problem. The group had a very small repertoire. Soon they were playing the same songs over and over and over, and they kept on for hours and hours.

Finally Sue Adams phoned Lamberto. "Can't you stop them?" she said. "It's driving me crazy."

So he stopped them.

The band this time plays American rock music and it is fine. While the music selection is large, the crowd is small. Almost no one comes. Lamberto counts maybe a dozen people sitting on the scattered benches on the field. Maybe this is not the best way to draw people over the weekend, he thinks.

The first hint of a problem at the New England Motel field comes at midmorning on Sunday when the state police arrive at a booth run by Larry Stowell of Marco Island, Florida. The first rumors suggest that Stowell, a jewelry dealer, is the latest burglary victim. The thieves got jewelry worth only a few hundred dollars, according to the first reports. The amounts of the estimated loss build as the day goes on, eventually reaching $300,000. Stowell is too upset to talk to anybody as he packs his jewelry cases and prepares to drive home. He came back to his booth this morning and found it rifled. Someone has stolen $100,000 in jewelry, according to the report compiled by state police. No one saw anything.

Joe and Rachel usually leave on Friday and always by Saturday. Now, here it is Sunday afternoon and they are lingering in Brimfield. They have shown Fran Smith the Parrish they bought on the way up. If anyone is familiar with illustrations, it is Smith, who began his career dealing in illustrations. He once worked with another dealer, Judy Goffman, when she was getting started buying and selling original illustration art. Today Judy Goffman Cutler, as she is known, is a preeminent dealer in illustration art. She has a gallery in New York City; she and her husband run the National Museum of American Illustration in Newport, Rhode Island; and she has authored books on illustrators, including Parrish. Fran Smith may not be in the same class these days, but he knows illustrations. He takes his time, and then can't contain his excitement. It looks like an original. While Parrish is known for his color, much of his early work—beginning in 1896, when he was twenty-six, and continuing over the next decade—was in black-and-white, and this appears to be from that period. The artist produced black-and-white illustrations for books such as *Mother Goose* and *The Arabian Nights* and for mainstream magazines such as *Harper's, Collier's, Scribner's,* and *Ladies' Home Journal.* Smith asks what they will do next. Joe and Rachel suspect they will take it to a dealer who specializes in illustrations. Smith volunteers to help.

Rachel no longer wants to ride her bike. Instead, she and Joe search the fields. It should seem foolish; by now everything is gone, but Rachel can't help herself and her attitude is infectious. Yesterday on Sturtevant's field, on a day when nothing should have been left except for crumbs for amateurs, they found a painting by an obscure Boston artist, dated 1853. The dealer wants a couple of hundred dollars for it. Now, on the last day of the show, Joe and Rachel talk about whether to buy it. They do not have a lot of money left, especially after purchasing the Bye. They are hoping to spend a few days later in the month on Cape Cod, where a friend of Rachel's family has offered them a place to stay. That should not be factored into the decision, says Joe. Rachel agrees.

They buy the painting.

"You never know," Joe says. "That's what this business is all about—taking another risk."

May Again

*Buying is much more American than thinking
and I'm as American as they come.*

ANDY WARHOL

*Nowadays people know the price of everything
and the value of nothing.*

OSCAR WILDE

CHAPTER 16

A Long Wait

JOE AND RACHEL each listen twice to the phone message. Clearly it is Roger Reed from Illustration House, but his words are garbled. They immediately fear the worst. Rachel is convinced there is something wrong with the Parrish. That's the last thing they want to hear. The Parrish they bought eight months ago is scheduled to be auctioned next Saturday afternoon. They have waited so long. Joe left the illustration with Reed, who runs the New York auction company, back in November, and Rachel sent the frame to Reed last week. Perhaps there is a problem with the frame. It's now Saturday night; they won't be able to reach Reed until Monday. On Sunday Rachel spends part of the day searching for the receipt that Joe got from Illustration House. She can't find it.

They feel closer than ever to something big. Yet the reality is that, from a cash standpoint, they are broke, and Brimfield begins Tuesday. "If the Parrish goes through, we will be fine, we can pay off all our bills and have some cash," Rachel tells Joe. "But we need the Parrish to do well at this point."

They don't feel that they can afford the Ashford Motel, the worn and tired place where they stayed last September for only $42.50 a night. They'll stay in the tent. Rachel has been gathering paintings, and they will try to sell more than they buy. She has arranged to sell a painting on the way, and there may be more help even if the Parrish turns out to be a bust.

Just a few days ago Rachel stumbled onto a Cora Brooks. A woman in Georgia was selling it at an online store, Ruby Lane. Rachel found it with a Google search for Cora Brooks. This painting looked familiar: it was a still life, and Brooks was famous for her still lifes. Rachel knew a dealer friend who had recently sold a similar Brooks scene for $30,000. Rachel was certain that if she could buy this painting, she could market it and sell it for anywhere from $20,000 to $45,000.

The seller wanted $12,000.

Excited, Rachel called Georgia. The woman definitely wanted to unload the painting; she'd had hardly any inquiries and it had been posted for nearly six months. Because Rachel is a dealer, she agreed to sell the painting to Rachel for a 30 percent discount, at $8,400. Rachel found one of those checks the credit card companies send, the ones with the high interest rates, filled it out, and mailed it.

When Joe came home, she could barely contain her excitement. Joe was not as pleased. He admitted it looked like a good painting, but the timing was poor. With Brimfield coming, he thought they were going to save their money. And weren't they going to consult with each other? The couple are still trying to keep their finances separate, but it is a constant struggle because they often decide together on a purchase or sale. Deep down he worries that Rachel will want to keep the Brooks.

She has thought about it.

So much has changed since last September and yet so much has not. Joe has taken a traditional job, and Rachel is continuing to buy and sell art for both herself and Joe. They are officially engaged, and Rachel is battling Lyme disease.

Talk of marriage began last fall with Rachel dropping hints. Mostly, she just liked to discuss their relationship and began suggesting that it was time either to move to the next level or . . . She was not getting any younger; she wanted not only a partner but also children. Joe got the message. In December he saw the perfect engagement ring at S&S Auctions. It was an old-fashioned antique ring that matched Rachel's style. It would help him make a statement. He brought it home, wrapped in a little antique box, and then not too subtly suggested she open it.

Later, he does not know what to say when the issue of how much he paid comes up with friends. He likes to say the ring cost a fortune, but that does not make Rachel happy. She wants him to say he got a deal.

"Why should I say that?" he asks. They are talking about money. He knows to be careful.

"You told me you paid seven hundred dollars," Rachel tells him.

"I didn't pay seven hundred," he replies defensively.

"Well, what did you pay?"

"Around seven hundred," he says. "Less than that, but close."

The answer seems to please Rachel. They had the ring appraised for $1,400.

The wedding is scheduled for October. They'll have it at the farmhouse, pitch a big tent out in the yard by the creek, and invite all their friends.

Rachel was diagnosed with Lyme disease last fall. In retrospect, she knows she must have come down with the disease last summer. Both she and Ryzo got it about the same time, probably from playing in the yard. Lyme disease, which usually comes from a tick bite, is a serious neurological disorder that can begin with a rash, fever, and headaches and over time can lead to arthritis, memory loss, and heart problems. Rachel endured sharp shooting pains in her muscles, night sweats, and occasionally an overwhelming fatigue. Perhaps that contributed to her pessimism last summer. During the winter she would find herself at auctions or art sales unable to concentrate and too tired to care. Often she told Joe that she had to go out to the car and take a nap. She had seen a doctor, repeatedly, despite her lack of adequate medical insurance, but so far she was making only a slow improvement. The doctor told her it would take time. She had taken Ryzo to the vet, and the dog's medicine seems more effective than hers. Even now, in May, nearly a year later, she knows she has not shaken the disease.

The vet bills just seem to be getting larger all the time too, especially now that they have acquired a second rotweiller. She is called Lady, and technically she is Joe's, while Ryzo is Rachel's dog.

The other big development is Joe's job. Who would have thought when they left Brimfield last September that Joe would be pulling down a regular paycheck? He's had the job for nearly five months, but Joe has discovered once again that he really does not like working for someone else. For months now Rachel has been expecting him to come home at any time in the middle of the day and say, "That's it. I quit. I'm done."

The opportunity began last fall when Joe called Philip Rosenfeld, who owns the Pennsylvania Art Conservatory, a gallery in nearby Berwyn. Joe tried to interest Rosenthal in several paintings. In the course of the conversation the gallery owner mentioned that he was looking for a new manager. Joe was interested. Here was a way to earn some money he could set aside for the gallery he wanted to own, while also learning how to run one. That was what Rosenthal was offering. Rosenthal wanted somebody to run the gallery while he and an assistant were out buying art for the gallery. Rosenthal's operation was not only a gallery; it had a number of employees and did extensive art conservation.

"I would be very interested," Joe told Rosenthal.

Joe began at the gallery in early January. His disappointment started almost immediately. While a salary figure had been mentioned, Joe was put at a lower pay level during what was termed his probationary period. There was also the promise of health insurance, but it was unclear that it would become available. As time went on, he did not seem to get the responsibilities he had anticipated. For one thing, neither Rosenthal nor his assistant was leaving the gallery as much as Joe had expected. He was rarely in charge. In fact, mostly he was handling customer complaints. The job was like a glorified customer-relations position. Joe had become accustomed to working for himself and he liked it. He never minded work, but he liked to do it at his pace, to come and go as he wanted. Now he was expected to be at the gallery during certain hours, to be available even when nothing was happening. It was like punching a time clock, like being chained to a desk.

Joe also sensed that Rosenthal was not happy that Joe was still buying and selling art on the side. Joe had to be careful not to mix his business with the gallery's business. He worked hard to maintain a separation, to make sure he was not buying from the same people as Rosenthal. He certainly was not selling in the same forum. The customers at a posh gallery were not likely to be buying on eBay or at Brimfield. Despite the job, Joe found himself busier than ever buying and selling paintings on the side. He was using his paychecks not to pay for his future gallery but to wheel and deal art. Some of his earnings were going to inventory, but he was making money. He had recently bought an unsigned nude for $100. Joe was convinced from the look and feel that the painting was by Guy Pene DuBois, part of the Ashcan School that Joe collects. He took the painting apart and discovered a note inside that said the painting had been owned by Patrick Nartell, who had obtained it from his teacher, Guy Pene DuBois. That documentation was enough for Joe to get $1,000 for the painting, ten times his investment.

Rachel could see that Joe was unhappy in the new job; who couldn't? He did not complain, at least not much, but he had always struggled getting up in the morning and now he was madly dashing out at eight o'clock, racing to try to make it to work on time. "You can quit anytime you want," she told him. He would just shake his head.

Joe knows he is coming to Brimfield this May; he just does not know how. On the Sunday before the show he tells Rachel to go ahead and leave the next day, and he will catch up with her on Tuesday. She needs to stop on her way up to sell a painting. That's why she is at the McDonald's at Interstate 84 and Route 9, just after crossing the Hudson River. She is to meet a couple who have expressed interest online in a painting she owns. Both she and Joe are certain that it is by a Connecticut painter, Wilson Irvine, but it is not signed. It looks like an Irvine: an Impressionist painting of a stone bridge with a creek gushing beneath during a spring thaw. They have documentation that shows it was once owned by a neighbor of Jan Irvine, who was the artist's sister. The dealer they bought it from guaranteed it, and he had two other paintings he had bought from the same owner that were signed.

Rachel and Joe want $3,000 for it, and the couple have indicated they will pay that much after they inspect it. Another online buyer has also expressed interest but isn't willing to go as high. Joe and Rachel acquired the Irvine by trading another painting worth $1,000 as well as paying $1,000. The $3,000 they get from this sale is going to be the cash Joe and Rachel will use at Brimfield to get started. They are going to split the money and see what they can find.

But when she opens the trunk and shows the painting to the couple, they seem to spend an inordinately long time looking at it.

Rachel is surprised at their hesitancy. She thought they already had a deal.

Finally, the man says, "We're not interested in it now, maybe later."

Rachel is stunned. She tries to be polite, but she tells them that she is going to Brimfield. "There isn't going to be a later," she tells them. "If you don't want it, I'm selling it at Brimfield."

The couple are not moved by her comment.

Disgusted, she leaves.

She is coming to Brimfield with almost no cash and very little money in the checking accout. She can remember other years that she thought were lean, but she was still able to bring $3,000 in cash and a checkbook balance of $10,000. Later that day she finds a booth where art books are being sold cheap. She thumbs through them and finds a book on Edward Hopper and his New England art. Joe does not have this book, she realizes. She looks at the price: $8. Too much, she thinks, walking away.

Joe waits until Monday morning to tell Rosenthal he is taking the rest of the week off. The only other option would be just to outright quit, something he has considered repeatedly over the last few weeks. Instead, Joe feels that his proposition is eminently fair, as he points out to Rosenthal.

"Before you say anything, consider this," Joe tells the gallery owner. "Everything in my department is in order. I made sure everything is up to date. John is responsible and can handle everything in the department. If there are problems, you can always call me on my cell phone."

Rosenthal asks him where he is going.

Brimfield.

Rosenthal does not seem happy. Finally he tells Joe, "I have a problem with your being manager of this department and being an art dealer."

Joe repeats that line at Brimfield. "What did he expect of me, that I was just going to stop?" Joe snorts to Fran Smith, Mike Pacitti, and Mike McClintock. "That I was going to give up dealing?"

The idea is preposterous and certainly not worth it financially.

When the Heart-O-The-Mart field opens Wednesday morning, Joe and Rachel are poised to sell. Unlike last year, when they just propped up a few paintings against the car, they are far more organized. Rachel has brought a large overhead canopy to protect the art. Some works are propped against easels, others are against an antique trunk. There are far more than last year. The Irvine is prominently displayed.

A scout for a prominent New York–based dealer quickly spots it. He calls the dealer on his cell phone and he too arrives quickly. The dealer assesses the painting and says he is willing to pay $2,000 for it. Rachel tries to hold out for $3,000, but without a signature he will not take the risk. He's convinced it's an Irvine, but the painting needs that signature.

"Oh well, it's just as well," she tells a friend. The $2,000 is what she and Joe paid for it in cash and trade, and at least they have some money now.

The selling continues. For once, Joe and Rachel are selling more than they are buying. A New York designer, with four assistants to track his sales, buys two prints for $1,100. Joe and Rachel paid $300 for these two and a third print together. A large painting of an industrial scene goes for another $2,000, a profit of 100 percent. Joe, who has been out trying to buy, comes back amazed by the amount of money they have made in just a couple hours. It's nice, but in truth neither of them is concentrating on Brimfield as much as usual. They have not told anyone at Brimfield about the upcoming auction of their Parrish. While they showed the Parrish last September to Fran Smith, they have not talked to him about it since then. With the auction now only days away, it's hard to think about anything else.

After buying the Parrish last September, they waited before taking the next step to confirm that it was an original. They considered contacting Christie's or Sotheby's but finally chose Illustration House because the auction house would know more about Parrish than anyone else. Walt Reed had founded his gallery thirty years earlier in Connecticut, later moving it to New York. Reed knew many of the great illustrators, from Norman Rockwell to Tom Lovell, who was known for his Western and Civil War scenes; Jon Whitcomb, who liked to depict glamorous women; and Stevan Dohanos, whose work was often in the *Saturday Evening Post*. These days Reed's son, Roger, runs the day-to-day business.

Joe has been doing his research on the Parrish. He knows now that it was part of a book of nursery rhymes and that it is of Tommy Tucker, the poor orphan boy who must sing for his supper. What Joe had not realized was that the book where the illustration appeared, *Mother Goose in Prose*, was so popular. The Chicago publishers Way and Williams had approached Parrish about producing fourteen prints for the book, which was the first work by L. Frank Baum, who would go on to write *The Wizard of Oz*. The book was a hit from the moment it was printed in 1897, and it was quickly followed by several editions, including one three years later that was offered as a premium to users of Pettijohn's Breakfast Food. More important, as far as Joe and Rachel are concerned, the book became a collector's item. First editions are now selling for between $1,500 and $2,000.

The book sold well even though the famous Parrish colors are noticeably absent. All the illustrations, except for the cover, are in black-and-white. Parrish was twenty-seven at the time the book was published, and his illustrations already were demonstrating the fine details that would make him so popular in the twentieth century. Biographers say that the *Mother Goose* book had an unexpected benefit for Parrish, because the illustrations impressed children. Later, when those admirers grew up, they continued to seek out Parrish's work. In the copy of *Mother Goose* that Joe examined, Humpty Dumpty sits fat and egg-like on a plain ledge, while behind him fanciful turrets, gables, and towers of an elaborate castle rise to the sky. Old King Cole basks alone on a plain throne, with the most whimsical and satisfied of smiles. In contrast, the Man in the Moon appears torn between his peaceful life in the skies and the wondrous village that Parrish has created below. The figure of Tommy Tucker, who is sitting on a chair, has one important characteristic: some believe it is a self-portrait of Parrish.

Roger Reed was impressed with Parrish's Tommy Tucker and was prepared to buy it immediately. He offered Joe $13,000. Or the auction house could take it on consignment and put it up for auction.

Joe was inclined to take the money, and he was pretty sure, as cautious as Rachel could be, that she would also want the cash. Rachel wanted to know the high estimate for the work.

It was $20,000, perhaps $25,000 or at the highest, $30,000.

"Let's put it up for auction," said Rachel.

"Are you sure?" asked Joe.

"Yes," replied Rachel.

At the time Joe was surprised that Rachel wanted to gamble. They did need the money, especially in that time before Joe was working. But the longer he knows her, the more he appreciates her investment skills. Yes, she likes to hold paintings. Part of it is the love of art, but Rachel is also smart enough to know that there is a time when one has to let go. Her strategy with the Parrish is the same; she will wait to get the best price possible.

Joe was so busy at work that he did not call Illustration House on Monday. Late in the day he retrieved another call on their answering machine. All Reed said was, "Joe, call me, I need to talk to you." On Tuesday, while driving to Brimfield, he finally got Reed on his cell phone. As the call went through, Joe hoped his phone battery was recharged. It had a tendency to go dead at the worst possible moments. He was relieved the moment Reed began, because the first thing Reed said was that there was "a lot of interest in the Parrish." So much interest, said Reed, that one dealer wanted to know if he could have more than the sixty days he needed to pay.

Joe was not sure—they really needed the money. "If he is only going to pay twelve thousand or fourteen thousand for it, I'm not very interested in that," Joe told Reed.

"No, you don't understand," replied Reed. "He's authorized to bid at least to the high estimate."

Joe was feeling much better when he told Rachel. At this point he was planning to cut Brimfield short, return home on Friday, and then go to New York for the auction. Rachel had no interest in accompanying him. She might go see her mother in New Hampshire.

"It just makes me too nervous," she said.

They have been waiting a long time now. They have so much riding on this auction.

CHAPTER 17

Setting Values

EVERYWHERE MIKE McCLINTOCK goes, he takes his new walking stick. He stops at Rachel's tent to show it off. It is about four feet high and topped with a carved figure. Mc-Clintock found two clubs earlier in the day. He thinks they were made in Fiji and are authentic. He tells Rachel he paid $1,000 for the pair and immediately sold one for $1,500.

"I'm having second thoughts about selling it," he says. "I think I could have gotten more."

He shows her the one he still has.

"This is the better of the two," he says, walking away confidently.

Sometimes Rachel is mystified how McClintock can know about such obscure items. The same could be wondered about many here at Brimfield. Some say there may be more experts in more areas of antiques and collectibles for each Brimfield show than for anywhere else. Sometimes dealers bring objects they know nothing about to Brimfield. Often during the week someone will walk by, see a piece, and not only be able to identify it but often be able to provide a history lesson, too. If Rachel wants to know more about where McClintock gets his knowledge, she should ask him the story behind those fat rings he wears on his fingers.

They are impossible to miss, thick bands of gold with intricate designs of grapes, leaves, and vines. The rings are made of Black Hills gold, mined in the 1870s gold rush that swept the Dakota Territory. According to legend, they originated from a dream a young Frenchman had when he became lost searching for gold in the Black Hills. Weak with hunger, he fell asleep and dreamed of beautiful grapevines and grapes from his homeland growing near the side of a creek, and when he awoke he was inspired to craft the rings. Actually, they were designed by a jeweler in Deadwood, South Dakota, during the gold rush and sold in various places including the mining camps. Today they can be worth tens of thousands of dollars.

McClintock says that years ago he acquired them after encountering a run of bad luck. He had just spent his last thirty-two cents on a cup of coffee, although he was not worried about eating. He was traveling in a circuit of friends and acquaintances, and someone always had an extra sandwich or a cup of soup.

"A friend of mine always liked to walk with me when a show was opening, because I would help him out a little," explains McClintock. "He came over and wanted to walk, but I said, 'No, I've got to set up.' 'No, come on, let's go.' And I said, 'No, I really have to set up.' Well, he knew that if I did not want to walk, it meant that I did not have any money. So he gave me a thousand dollars and we walked a little bit, but then we had to split up. I bought a couple of little things and then I reached a dealer who was selling an

American Indian basket, it was a rattletop basket. I had to have that basket. I paid nine hundred for it. So I went back to my trailer and I was setting up and my friend came by. He said, 'OK, now let's go walk.' And I told him again that I had to set up. He said, 'You spent all of the money already?' I nodded. He asked, 'What did you buy?' So I took out the bag and showed him the basket. 'You spent all of that on that basket? You're crazy.'"

"Within an hour I had sold the basket for forty-five hundred dollars." McClintock had been studying ethnic art for years. "I used to be very interested in ethnic art and objects. I used to pick a topic, buy a number of objects in that area, and learn everything I could about them for several months. Then I would move on to another subject."

"I found my friend, who at the time liked to wear diamond rings. He had just bought a new one and was in the market to sell the old one. I said, 'OK, here's the thousand dollars I owe you,' and I laid down the money. 'And here's a thousand for that ring.' And I put it on and said, 'I'll never go hungry again.'"

He eventually switched to the Black Hills rings. More than once, he had pawned the rings on a Friday, then bought and sold enough over the weekend to redeem the rings on Monday and still have ample cash in his pockets.

The turnout this May is not what dealers and promoters hoped and certainly not the size of the previous May. But there are plenty of opportunities beyond Fiji walking sticks to find the rare, forgotten, and undervalued. There is the three-foot-tall corkscrew, the seven-foot-tall fun-house mirror, the seven-foot-tall barber pole, the wooden turn-of-the-century carousel horse, the gasoline pump, the bumper car, and the

Vermont tall clock with the Silas Hadley movement selling for $12,995. A note attached to the clock is dated November 15, 1925. It says: "Arthur got the grandfather clock made by Charles French and his two brothers. It was 97 years old. It will be now 125 (years). It was made at our house."

Howard Roberts's bright yellow stuffed giraffe stands a foot taller than he does. He bought it from the Palombo estate, a family that had run one of Philadelphia's most famous restaurants in the 1950s, '60s, and '70s. The estate sale had advertised five hundred gowns, five hundred hats, and five stuffed animals for sale. Roberts thought the stuffed animals would be perfect for Brimfield, preferably all five of them. They were all huge: a lion, a bear, a monkey, an elephant, and a giraffe. Then Roberts looked again at the date and realized he had to be out of town during the auction. His wife, Linda, could not make it. Then he remembered Artie, a nearby friend who was often on the flea market circuit with him. Artie did not deal in pieces like this, but he agreed to go. Afterward Roberts called Artie, who said the auction had been easy. He'd bid $50 and easily won the giraffe.

"What else did you get?" asked Roberts.

"I got the giraffe," replied Artie.

Maybe it is just as well, because the giraffe has not sold. It reminds Roberts of the buffalo head he brought a few years ago. Every kid at Brimfield loved that buffalo head and wanted his or her picture taken with it. But Roberts took it home and sold it at a loss.

Sometimes there are reasons an object remains lost or forgotten.

That may be the fate of the potentially valuable cradle, believed to be from the Hadley chest era, that Gary "Larry"

Zaczyk bought last year. Rich Conley has talked to museum curators and auction houses, hoping to lure them to Brimfield to see the cradle. But Zaczyk has placed it safely in the second floor of his antiques shop in Albion, and he really does not want to bring it back to Massachusetts simply for an appraisal. Experts who have looked at pictures of the cradle say that if it is American, it could be quite valuable. But it would be worth far less if it is English. The tip that it might have been owned by a signer of the Declaration of Independence has not been very helpful. There were five signers with a name ending in W. While none came from New York, two were from nearby Connecticut, William Williams and Oliver Wolcott. Still, tracing the cradle's provenance might be a challenge. Conley is confident that they will get answers. So is Zaczyk, who is willing to take his time. "When you own something of great value, you need to remember that you cannot take it with you when you die," he explains. "You can enjoy it only for the time you are here. For many of these pieces, we are only babysitters, sometimes watching over it and protecting it for people who may not even be born yet. At least, that's the way I see it."

Robert Lloyd has returned with his antique silver. Despite last year's burglary he has no plans to stay away from Brimfield. His insurance company did pay him for the loss—and then it dropped his coverage. That was all right, because he shopped around and found a better policy. Police have recovered one of the four hundred stolen pieces, and they may make an arrest sometime in the future. Still, it was a struggle to decide to return. "A lot of things went though my mind after the burglary," he concedes. "I started thinking, why am I doing this, is it really worth it to come here?"

Although Lloyd makes money at Brimfield, he really loves the camaraderie more than anything. One year he acquired a toy in the shape of a sunflower. It had a mechanism that caused it to wiggle and it also had a voice box. He removed the voice box, replaced it with a walkie-talkie, planted the sunflower in the ground, and had the other walkie-talkie in his van where he could watch visitors approach. When they did, the sunflower talked to them. "No one knew what to make of it," he says. At one point a thirteen-year-old boy came around. The sunflower spoke and the kid wanted no part of it. "You're not real," he told the sunflower.

"Yes, I am and I can tell you are wearing denim jeans, and a T-shirt, and you are drinking a Sprite."

The boy jumped at that, looking all around, trying to figure out who was speaking. Lloyd was covering the walkie-talkie, he was laughing so hard.

On Friday night Lloyd is planning to host a party. He has hired a band, a group of high school kids from the area that play tunes from the 1970s and '80s. He has also ordered big trays of food from Francesco's, including linguine, meatballs, clams, shrimp, and chicken marsala. Visitors will congregate behind the tent. The tent will be off limits to visitors because that's where the off-duty cops are at night.

That is another big change: Lloyd has hired off-duty police to guard his silver overnight. When he interviewed the officers, he asked them three questions: Do you own a gun? Are you licensed to use it? Are you willing to use it? "I decided that I would not give up everything here," he says. "I could have said, 'Yeah, you win, you ripped me off and I'm not coming back.' I'm a stronger person than that. These people who came to my tent, they just were not taking antique objects. They were taking food out of my kid's mouth. I feel sorry for anyone who may try and come into my tent at night now."

The police are back for the May show. Last fall the police chief, Charles Kuss, recommended that nine officers be rehired. Cheney and the board of selectmen rejected that plan, agreeing to hire only five. None of the union leaders were rehired. No one wants a union anymore. Kuss is not convinced he can police the town with so few officers, but he is willing to give it a try. "The number is a little light for a community of this size," he points out.

Rachel makes a score on Wednesday. She is walking Heart-O-The-Mart during the rush, forcing Joe for once to stay at the tent and sell, when she sees a watercolor. If there is one medium Rachel has long avoided because it will not sell, it is watercolor. People simply refuse to pay for watercolors, unless they are big names. Rarely does that kind of work show up at Brimfield. But there is something about this watercolor, a scene of a black woman standing in a cotton field under an autumnal sun. It is unsigned. The dealer wants only $20 for it. Rachel likes the composition; it is very good. On a hunch, she buys it.

When she gets back to her car, she takes the painting out of its frame and finds that it is signed by M. M. Law. She looks up the artist in several directories and discovers that Law is a listed artist from Spartanburg, South Carolina. Her work sells well. A similar watercolor four years earlier sold for $1,300. Rachel can feel it; she knows she has another winner. Joe agrees. It is better than anything he has found by the time he leaves Friday morning. He's heading home and then to the auction that will tell them so much about their future.

How can it already be Friday and the end of another Brimfield? Joel Schiff is making one last scan of J&J before leaving. He has not had much success. He gets to one booth and a boy about eight years old sees him.

"It's Joel," he yells excitedly. He begins to run out toward Schiff and then hesitates. There is an awkward moment but Schiff is delighted to see him.

"Give me a hug," he says, breaking the awkwardness.

The boy rushes into his arms.

"Where's Ruth?" Schiff asks.

"She went to a Girl Scout thing with my mom," the boy replies.

Similar scenes are occurring across the fields today. For once, Schiff suspects he has missed more than he has found at Brimfield. What he likes to call the honorable competition—others searching for cast-iron cookware—has been more resourceful than usual during this show. Sometimes he wonders why he keeps coming to Brimfield. "What is the point of coming to a show when I can find only two or three pieces for the entire week? The thing is, I was away from eBay for a week and I could have missed pieces that were there."

Then he has encounters like this one, with friends he has made over the years, and he realizes he has no choice but to return. He has so much to do, not only to look for yet another rare piece but to inventory, to look for a museum that may someday house his collection, to plan for the future. He'll be back, he says, as long as he is "still able to run."

But what will he find? Everyone seems to be worried about Brimfield. For years they have fretted that the supply of antiques is going to dry up. Dealers worry that real estate values will rise so high that the open fields will be replaced by condominiums. They grumble that they are getting older, that they can no longer handle the early-morning rushes, that the evening parties are over, that there is too much crap out on the fields, that there are too many stupid buyers. "People say Brimfield isn't what it used to be," says Walter Parker, the collector and sometime dealer who got married at J&J. "Well, nothing is the way it once was. People used to throw everything out, including things that were valuable. Now, more than ever, they save them or try and sell them."

They sell them online. While people still worry about eBay's impact, the fear seems to be lifting. Everyone is getting better at understanding the electronic market. Phillip Davies believes that ultimately it will help Brimfield. Davies, who runs the TIAS online consignment shop, used to be chased off fields by angry field promoters. Now, no one stops him as he goes from one field to another trying to interest dealers in using his site. At each booth, he offers to allow the dealer to showcase one item for free on TIAS.com. He takes a digital picture, types the relevant information into his laptop computer, and uses a cell phone to help transmit the message back to his office on Long Island. Davies discovers that many dealers already use his site or his competitors' sites. "The trend is to do multiple venues. Dealers will have a store, they will do shows, and they may use two or three websites. One might be like mine, one would be under their own domain name, another with eBay, and then with two or three more competitors. They're just becoming more sophisticated."

Tales concerning how to use the various forums to maximum benefit are proliferating. Last year Sherman Tompson found a cast-iron mousetrap at a flea market. The longtime

Maine dealer had never seen anything like it. It was in the shape of a heart and it said Royal No. 1 and was dated 1881. He paid $85 for it. A collector told him that the inventor had made it as a wedding gift for his bride. Word got out that Thomson had the mousetrap. He brought it to Brimfield last year and showed it off, but refused to sell it. Instead, he used Brimfield and other markets to advertise the mousetrap. He told everyone when the eBay auction would begin. It sold for $3,250.

Howard Roberts wonders if Brimfield has become "a dumping ground for many dealers. When dealers have something they don't know where they are going to sell it, they bring it to Brimfield. And that has been a problem. There is a lot of unusual stuff. But the quality is not as great as it once was."

It may very well be that if Brimfield has a problem, it is that the market and its dealers are getting tired and old. The fact that it grew so big is remarkable simply in itself. Brimfield began with the odds stacked against it. Kuss, the town's new police chief, has already concluded that the traffic will be his biggest challenge. "This place is horribly designed," he said. "To have this many people on each side of the road and to try to get them out of here on a single road is just about the worst possible situation." Add the fact that the market is located in a community that at best only tolerates its existence, to the point where it has failed to provide even such basics as police protection. It is located miles from the nearest hotels and restaurants. The market is controlled by more than twenty field owners who only grudgingly cooperate with each other. They pay for only a few advertisements in antiques trade publications, and they are lucky to generate stories in the local press and on a few specialized cable television channels. A more polished marketing approach would tap a far larger audience. "There are ten million people in the Northeast corridor, and if you do not get at least some of those people here, you have a problem," says Gary Sohmers, the pop-culture antiques dealer who is on *Antiques Roadshow*. Sohmers has tried to boost his own sales by bringing to Brimfield one-time television stars such as Buffalo Bob Smith from the old *Howdy Doody Show* and Jon Provost, who years ago played Timmy on *Lassie*.

For many field owners, the Brimfield market has become like a trust fund, a cash cow that will always be there. It is not that they idly sit back and let the money roll in. The field owners work hard to rent their sites and do all the daily chores to satisfy their demanding dealers. But too often their attitude is to maintain the status quo. For many at Brimfield, what worked for ten or twenty years still works today. Got a problem with security? Hire some off-duty cops. Having difficulty with the reproductions on the fields? I don't see any reproductions. Worried that there are no sidewalks or decent rest rooms or benches at Brimfield? Tough, you don't pay the taxes here. Want more publicity, want more cooperation with eBay, want more help in bringing customers into town? Do it yourself.

Some dealers are getting fed up. "Brimfield is eating itself alive," says Sandra McQuillan, a dealer from Delaware. "They have a number of problems that they don't want to face. They don't want to give anything more of themselves than they did last time, but they want more from you."

It seems that each year, as the May show approaches, dealers wonder whether the crowds will return. Then, as the white tents pop up, the traffic, people, and piles of stuff all arrive. It is as miraculous as the return of the first yellow blossoms of the forsythia each spring. There is some magic, be it the rush or the lure of a big score, or just the love of antiques and collecting, that draws everyone back. "Brimfield is like a phoenix," says Gerry Dooley, the veteran dealer who helped launch the party when Gordon Reid, Jr., thought he was going to destroy Brimfield more than twenty years ago. "Every time it looks as though it is going to crash and burn, it rises up again." Howard Roberts says that Brimfield continues to be held in high esteem by antiques dealers. "This is one of those places that you aspire to come to. There are only a few of them, and this is one. This is one of the wonders of the antiques world. In some ways Brimfield is world famous; it's a great experience."

Field owner Don Moriarty says that several years ago, as a show was ending, he felt bad for a particular dealer. It was obvious that no one was ever in his tent. No one was buying from him. On the last day Moriarty approached the dealer.

"I'm sorry business was so tough this year," he said.

"Don't worry about it," replied the dealer. "I've had my best show ever at Brimfield. It's true that I did not sell anything, but when I was going around the fields I found and bought a clock that had been made by my grandfather."

Moriarty likes to tell that story to strangers. "That's when I learned that Brimfield is not only about what you sell here."

CHAPTER 18

The Auction

JOE COMES UP the escalator that spills onto Seventh Avenue from Penn Station at 10:50 A.M. He had hoped to be here hours earlier. But he had to drive to Wilmington to pick up their two dogs from his mother, and he did not get home until late last night. He should have been here by 5 A.M. The auction of his Parrish at Illustration House does not begin until one o'clock, but he wants to spend time looking and possibly buying at the 26th Street flea market. Operating every weekend in Chelsea since around 1970, it features a few hundred dealers and draws an early morning crowd. Joe began coming here over the winter, when the wind whipped around the high-rises surrounding the asphalt lots, forcing dealers to crouch over portable heaters. Some dealers had moved much of the business inside nearby parking garages. Joe has had luck here before. One day he bought several prints by an artist named Donald Vogel. Joe was impressed with the compositions, the print numbers were low, and the prices were even better at $100 each. He has already sold two of those prints. When he gets to the garage today, he looks for that dealer but he cannot find him. A woman Joe recognizes—he thinks she is probably the dealer's wife—tells Joe that the dealer will be back later. Joe picks through the junk, knowing that he is probably hours too late to discover any bargains.

Once, Andy Warhol was a regular at this market, usually arriving in a limousine. He would pick through, looking to expand his collections, especially his cookie jar collection. Antiques and collectibles buffs still talk about Warhol's cookie jars. Warhol was a shopper in the true Brimfield spirit, and when he died unexpectedly in 1987 he left behind more than ten thousand objects in his six-story New York townhouse. The collection may have paled in comparison to that of a fanatic such as William Randolph Hearst, but it was still impressive. It was large enough that close friends said that Warhol had been crowded into using only two of his thirty rooms. Even more extraordinary was the fervor the collection created when Sotheby's scheduled it for auction in 1988.

It is still not clear what ignited the auction's popularity. Warhol had been a well-known artist as well as a celebrity, but his was not the type of fame reflected by fan clubs or groupies. At first the auction generated only the usual publicity, until the television network program 20/20 featured the upcoming auction on its broadcast one night. Whatever the cause, the result was astonishing. Sotheby's broke the collection into lots that would be sold over ten days, and it estimated that the entire amount would be sold for $10 million to $12 million. That estimate was off considerably. The segment of the auction that drew the most attention was those cookie jars. At best, they were estimated to sell for a couple of hundred dollars each. The first hint that the estimates were too low began when Sotheby's started getting pre-auction calls from all over the country. Then the auction opened and the crowd, the size of which no one had seen before at the auction house, began to arrive at Sotheby's doorstep. By the second day, when the 155 cookie jars were being sold in 38 lots, the number trying to attend swelled to an estimated 10,000. The line snaked out into the street and ran for blocks. Many bidders never did get in the door. To accommodate as many as possible, Sotheby's distributed bid forms to people in line and collected them before the bidding began. It was a nice gesture but it really did not help. Each lot sold went for thousands of dollars, often ten to twenty times the pre-auction estimate. Gasps of shock erupted repeatedly from those lucky enough to get inside. One buyer paid $23,100 for two cookie jars, a mammy and a black chef that came with a pair of matching salt and pepper shakers. A New York businessman, Gedalio Grinberg, paid more than $200,000 for most of the lots. Afterward Grinberg, who had done business with Warhol, said he just felt that it was important to keep the cookie jar collection as intact as possible. He added, "I would have gone after everything if my wife hadn't stopped me." Across the days of the auction, buyers spent $25,333,368 to purchase the Warhol collection. Joe can only hope for that kind of magic at Illustration House today. Actually, Joe is so nervous that he cannot envision much of anything good happening today. He picks at a sandwich in an antiques mall on 25th Street and talks to an art dealer in one of the shops. The dealer tells Joe that he just got back from Brimfield. Joe recognizes at least two paintings he passed on at Brimfield. The prices have more than doubled since the last time Joe saw the paintings.

Illustration House is located near the corner of 25th Street and Sixth Avenue, within sight of the flea market. It is housed in an industrial-looking brick building and its first floor measures about one hundred feet by twenty feet. It is just a little before one o'clock when Joe peeks inside. The air conditioning is blasting in the hall, which has high ceilings and raw plywood tacked to the walls. A few paintings are hung, well above eye level. Joe is shocked to find the room nearly empty. The house is scheduled to auction off several dozen pieces. Where is everyone?

Just then Rachel calls. She is checking to make sure Joe made it to New York. She has left Brimfield and is heading toward New Hampshire. She has been on the phone for less than thirty seconds when Joe's cell phone goes dead.

Joe borrows a phone and connects again with Rachel. She asks him to call her once the Parrish bidding is over. She sounds calm. He promises, assuming he can find a phone that works.

Joe is not calm. He goes back inside the auction house for a moment and fidgets. "I can't sit in there," he declares to another onlooker. "I'll go crazy."

He invents excuses to himself for leaving the gallery. He has a check he got days ago from a dealer in Brimfield. He will cash it, assuming he can find a Citibank branch. He gets lost twice looking for the bank but finally cashes the check. He finds a Starbucks where he can use the bathroom. Quietly, he is berating himself. His nerves are fraying badly. "I just know this is going to be a bust," he frets. "Anytime I have something good happen to me, it's followed by something bad. It always evens out and it's never good."

The reserve on the Parrish is $15,000. What if no one bids that much? What will they do?

He returns to Illustration House by 1:20. The auction is underway and to his surprise many of the folding chairs that were empty are now occupied. Many people have auction programs, which display the Parrish on the back cover. Joe relaxes slightly. The bidding moves rapidly. Not all the pieces are selling, but most are. He picks up a copy of the *New York Post* he bought earlier. He raises it and pretends to read.

Roger Reed watches the auction with satisfaction. He was not worried about the size of the crowd in the minutes before the auction began. True, the number of people attending has fallen in recent years. But the volume of bids has remained unchanged. Interested buyers either leave a bid or call in during the auction, and the auctioneer that the Reeds have hired, Harmer Johnson, is moving along at a good pace. Johnson is taking just as many bids from the individuals at the bank of phones as he is from the crowd.

When Lot 49 comes up for bid, for a moment Joe gives up his pretext of reading the paper and puts it down. Joe and Rachel also put this piece up for auction. It is the original art by John Falter for a magazine cover of a Christmas tree ornament in the shape of an angel. The catalog estimates its value at $3,000 to $4,000.

The bidding begins at $1,500 and moves quickly to $2,200, where it awkwardly falters. The piece has failed to reach its reserve price. After a pause, Johnson stops the bidding and with no explanation has the painting removed.

Not a good omen. Joe picks up his newspaper again.

Without the draw of something as unusual as a Warhol cookie jar collection, a good auctioneer tries to drive up prices by building excitement over the competing bidders. Charles Hamilton, a legendary proprietor of an upscale New York auction house, once described the bidding process as "auction madness." He called auctions "the world's most exhilarating game, this skirmish of wits between you and the auctioneer. Great prices are won or lost in a few seconds. Often the excitement is so intense you can hear the gasps and sighs from the audience and the bidders." Part of the thrill of an auction comes simply from the cadence of the bidding, a familiar but mysterious rapid-fire chant of figures connected by lines that are sometimes necessary but often designed only to give bidders a fleeting chance to consider whether to continue. Intense dueling between rival buyers is called "bidding fever." Psychologists and marketing professors who have studied it compare it to gambling addiction. It can happen in live auctions or online. When it occurs, buyers often pay more than the object is worth or what they originally wanted to pay. It's seductive and competitive, a fierce test of wills in which neither side wants to back down.

Joe has fallen into that frenzy before. Anytime he got sucked into a bidding contest with a competitor, he often won the battle but regretted the war. Once he found himself bidding on a painting primarily because another bidder he respected was also trying to buy it. The bidding began low, at only $25, but Joe was slightly worried because he had examined the painting and could not determine the artist. As the bidding rose higher and higher, it became evident to Joe that the painting had value. Why else would the other dealer continue to bid? Finally, at $900, the other bidder dropped out and Joe owned the painting. Later the other dealer came up to Joe, glanced at the painting, and asked, "Who is the painter?"

Joe still does not know. "Too often my emotions get the better of me," he says. "I really try to avoid bidding wars."

Rachel's cautious nature helps protect her from such contests. A former employee of two auction companies, she uses other tactics to defeat a rival bidder and the auctioneer's tactics. She likes to wait as long as possible to offer a counterbid in an attempt to disrupt flow and bring order to an otherwise threatening emotional rollercoaster ride. It slows the auctioneer's cadence and rhythm. It also forces the rival bidder to think a little bit longer as the price rises, giving Rachel more time to consider the next bid.

Today, Joe's hopes are with the auctioneer. Bidding frenzy is welcome. A few times the bidding does get more spirited; however, prices are generally low. They usually begin at a couple of thousand, rise only a few hundred with each bid, and end at $5,000, $6,000, or $7,000. That would usually be good money. But Joe is in a different league today.

Then a classic pinup, showing a secretary raising her hemline after ink has spilled on her desk and skirt, comes up for sale. It is an original by Gillette Elvgren that became a calendar illustration. Johnson has an opening bid of $40,000. The bidding moves rapidly and the pinup sells for $70,000.

Joe keeps his newspaper up during that sale and then, at Lot 76, he puts it aside, this time for good. Lot 77 is the Parrish. He can no longer hide his anticipation. In a moment he will have an answer to months of hope and anticipation. Will the Parrish score? Will it fail to sell? His hands are sweaty.

The catalog states that the Parrish has an estimated value between $20,000 and $30,000.

"Now we come to the Parrish," says auctioneer Johnson as the black-and-white drawing is placed on the easel next to him. The audience focuses on the drawing. The young man Parrish has drawn, the fairy tale character Tommy Tucker, sits placidly on a chair, one large bite out of the sandwich he holds upright in his left hand. The subject is supposed to be a self-portrait of Parrish when he was in his mid-twenties. The catalog reports that the frame was likely made by Parrish.

The bidding begins at $15,000. A bid is signified by an upraised arm holding a paddle with a number. First one arm goes up, and when Johnson responds, it is quickly followed by another, and then another. The only sounds are Johnson's voice and the roar of the air conditioner, which at times is louder.

$16,000.

$17,000.

$18,000.

$19,000.

$20,000.

There is a pause in the bidding. Joe wonders if this is the end. It wouldn't be terrible to get $20,000, although after commission they would realize only $18,000. Still, he had been willing to settle for $13,000 last November.

Then, another arm goes up. The bidding resumes and takes on new momentum.

$22,000.

$24,000.

$26,000.

$28,000.

$30,000.

$32,000.

Fran Smith's old colleague, Judy Goffman Cutler, is here in the back of the room. She had hoped to make a bid for the Parrish. Her Newport museum, the National Museum of American Illustration, has a number of Parrish originals and this would have been a nice addition. But the pace has moved so rapidly that she is already over her limit.

The competition now is among three bidders, two on the phone and one in the audience. A dealer on the phone specializes in children's illustrations, while a second dealer specializes in works by Parrish. The third bidder is only a collector, but one with a range of interests in Parrish and illustrations. As bidding continues, Roger Reed is pleased. He felt that the Parrish was valuable from the moment Joe brought it in, and now his professional estimate is being vindicated.

Joe watches almost in a trance. He feels increasingly numb and happy as the figures climb.

$34,000.

$36,000.

$40,000.

$42,000.

$44,000.

$46,000.

$48,000.

$50,000.

At this number, Johnson pauses again, as if to catch his breath. So does the bidding, but only for a second. A moment later the dealer in the audience yet again raises his paddle.

$55,000.

Quickly the paddle is raised from the phone bank.

$60,000.

Johnson looks at the dealer in the audience. The dealer does not respond. "All done?" asks Johnson. The dealer nods his head in assent.

Johnson pauses once more, just in case. "Sixty thousand, fair warning," he says. "Sold for sixty thousand."

Several weeks later both *Arts and Antiques Weekly* and the *Maine Antique Digest* will report this sale, along with the other results of the Illustration House spring auction. The final price is $67,500. Even though the auction house deducts a commission from Joe and Rachel's earnings, it is standard practice within the auction industry also to assess a fee on the buyer, thus adding to the $60,000 base price. That figure is the highest price for an ink drawing by Parrish ever achieved at Illustration House. It was one of the highest prices at the auction. The top seller was an oil and charcoal on board of a young girl standing at a sheep pen. It sold for $90,000.

These stories are not on the front pages and they are overshadowed by bigger news in the art world. Just days before, at Sotheby's, a new world art record was set when a buyer bid $104.1 million for a 1905 painting by Pablo Picasso. The Parrish price is well below the $4.29 million a buyer paid nearly a decade ago for Parrish's masterpiece, *Daybreak*.

Comparisons are relative. For Joe a truer way to gauge success is to consider what he and Rachel paid for the Parrish compared with what they are going to get from the sale. The sale price is over two hundred times what they paid. With the money they receive, finally, they can return to the middle class. They can buy not only art but also such necessities as medical insurance. The sale price represents a validation of their judgment, a reaffirmation that they were correct when they first examined the Parrish.

To Joe, that feels pretty good right now.

He steps outside. It is not yet two o'clock. The sun is shining, the dealing is still continuing at the 26th Street flea market, and the world looks no different.

Except to Joe. He whispers, almost to himself, "That was wild, wild." The smile has been edging across his face. He finds a cell phone and calls Rachel. When she comes on the line his voice is calm, almost normal, as he tells her that the Parrish was withdrawn at the last moment. It is a lame joke and Rachel is not buying it. Next he tells her it sold for $24,000. She is considering that. Should she believe him?

Days before she predicted that Joe would pull some kind of stunt, leaving her unsure about what really happened at the auction. Now her prediction is coming true.

Finally Joe tells her.

"Excellent, excellent," she says excitedly. "That was always my high estimate. I would have been happy at $45,000, but $60,000 is excellent."

Joe can't believe it. She had never told him what figure she was aiming to reach. He would have been happy at $20,000.

Rachel asks Joe if he is going to quit his job. In the buildup of the last few days, Joe has pretty much forgotten that he still works for somebody else. At the moment, he really does not care.

"Not yet," he replies. "If we get another like this, I will."

Now Joe is beginning to allow himself to think about how this sale will change their lives. First, they will pay off their bills. Then they can begin buying better paintings, art that produces a bigger return. Maybe they can buy a gallery, finally. They can get married. Life is definitely going to change.

Rachel is on country roads in southwestern New Hampshire, and she needs to get off the phone and concentrate. If that is possible. They agree to talk later tonight. Joe looks up and down at the Manhattan traffic whizzing by him on this warm, humid afternoon. The day is still young, the deal is still fresh. He begins walking toward the parking garage, hoping he can make a deal for more of the Donald Vogels.

He finds his dealer with the Vogel prints. The dealer is happy to see him.

"You got a good deal on those prints," he tells Joe.

Joe agrees.

Good enough that the price is going up. The dealer now wants $450 apiece for them. He will sell five for $2,250. Joe counters with $1,750. The dealer says he will think about it and let Joe know that night. That's all right with Joe. He leaves the garage and heads toward the asphalt lots of the 26th Street flea market. He is looking for one more deal.

Epilogue

ON THE AFTERNOON of September 28, 2004, Joe and Rachel were married under a wooden canopy at Nauset Beach on Cape Cod, Massachusetts, by a justice of the peace. Afterward Rachel and Joe walked the deserted beach. They got wet. The remnants of Hurricane Jeanne were passing over New England. They had planned and then scrapped the idea of having a big wedding at their house. The logistics became increasingly daunting, the planning draining, and the costs rising. Further, Joe had finally left his job at the gallery. Going to the Cape just felt right.

Later Rachel got a call from her father. The storm had passed Pennsylvania, and the Perkiomen was rising and would soon be lapping at the tires of Joe's 1999 Buick parked along the bank. Did she have an extra set of keys that he could use to move the car? No. By the time they got home the creek had crested without reaching the house. However, water had engulfed the car and destroyed it.

Two months later they became landlords. They bought a three-story building in nearby Phoenixville. Once it was a dry-goods store in a town so alive that the night sky was lighted by the fires of roaring iron and steel mills. Today the downtown is intact, quiet, and perhaps headed toward yet another transition. The suburban sprawl of Philadelphia is creeping into Phoenixville, with restaurants and antiques galleries replacing prostitutes and drug addicts. Joe and Rachel could never have realized their dream of opening a gallery without the $60,000 from the Maxfield Parrish drawing for the down payment. Money from the tenants in the upstairs apartments will pay the mortgage. They had enough art to open a gallery on the first floor. All they needed was the electrical wiring, plumbing, painting, and flooring that the building required.

Joe went to the Miami Beach show over the winter of 2004–2005, as did Fran Smith, Chris Smith, Mike McClintock, and Mike Pacitti. Pacitti had just gotten home after the 1,200-mile drive when he died of a massive heart attack. Pacitti's two daughters both came to Brimfield the next May to help Fran Smith and Chris Smith. The art dealers all gathered one night to remember Pacitti, the dealer who had told everyone that he was relishing whatever time he had left after his heart bypass surgery. Like all of them, he loved art.

The May 2005 Brimfield was a monster show, greater in attendance and apparently in sales than the show two years earlier, as big as any show anyone had ever seen.

Joel Schiff could not find any good cast-iron cookware, but he had found a couple of prize pieces during the winter. His graffiti-covered van died and its replacement was brown, a color considered a poor canvas by graffiti artists.

Robert Cheney mostly stayed away from the fields this time and the police seemed to be finally back in control at the show. The previous September, two Brimfield officers had arrested a Florida man whom they suspected had been stealing for days. Police said his van was filled with what they called suspicious items. Cheney's clock business was slow and he still had not had a chance to sell the Japanned clock.

Gary "Larry" Zaczyk also had not sold his Hadley-style seventeenth-century cradle. It was still up in the attic. Zaczyk periodically remembered that he should call an auction house. Somehow he never did. In the back of his mind, he wondered if it really had been a big score. "I just don't want to be disappointed," he explained. (Joe and Rachel both understood. The Alechinsky bought in May 2003 had never been checked out as to whether it was authentic or a fake. Rachel has a painting she bought five years ago that still needs verification from an expert.)

Howard Roberts had a good story about the house he had cleaned out, two years ago, of all the dirt, the leopard fur, and the grenade. The new owners had recently told the Realtor that there was something funny about the house. The owner added: "When I'm working down in the basement, I would swear there is somebody down there with me." Roberts could understand the feeling. "It was always creepy down there; I always felt uneasy." During the summer Roberts opened a new gallery, four times the size of his old one. He was not sure if it meant he would be on the road less or more.

James and Caryn Greco still have the nineteenth-century skeleton in their dining room, except on each Halloween when it makes an appearance for the night on their porch, much to the delight of the neighboring children.

As summer ended and another Brimfield season closed, Joe and Rachel were struggling to open their gallery and were on the cusp of more developments. During the winter Joe had gone to preview a book auction and had found a red scrapbook in a box with other books. Inside the scrapbook were seven loose sheets of paper, watercolors, drawings, and a collage. The signatures included Paul Klee and Wassily Kandinsky, two European-born artists who helped define abstract art in the twentieth century. Joe spent a restless, nervous, suspenseful twenty-four hours waiting for the auction. Bidding on the box began at $5 and ended at $40. Joe won. A New York auction house was working to authenticate the seven art pieces. If genuine, the minimum score would be $50,000.

Joe and Rachel knew they would transfer all their paintings out of the house on Perkiomen Creek. Then the question was, what should they hang on the walls of the gallery? They wanted to make a dramatic statement, to draw the biggest crowds, to make the most money. As they talked about it, they both began to realize that the biggest attraction would be the dozen or so Philadelphia Ten paintings. To Rachel, the idea of selling them cut like a knife. She loved these paintings; they had become part of her over the years. But she was also pragmatic. She knew she and Joe had more bills. It took a month before the idea was no longer painful, before she could not only accept it but embrace it. And so the decision was made: Griffin's Gallery would open featuring the lost art of the Philadelphia Ten. Rachel was ready for the next step, whatever it was.

"It's time," she said.

Acknowledgments

First and foremost I would like to thank all the individuals both at Brimfield and in the antiques business who offered their time and their guidance to make this book possible. Many were helpful in opening up not just their businesses but their lives. The debt I have to some simply cannot be repaid.

Several libraries were very helpful, particularly the Brimfield Public Library, which has an extensive historical collection devoted to the flea market. The staffs at the University of Connecticut library and the Providence Public Library also provided assistance. At Brimfield, David Lamberto was helpful in making it easier for me to do my job during the shows.

I would like to thank the University of Connecticut and my colleagues in the Journalism Department for their support and guidance, including Marcel Dufresne, Tim Kenny, John Breen, and Patricia Bukowski. I especially want to thank Wayne Worcester and Maureen Croteau, department chair, for reviewing drafts, making suggestions, and encouraging me to persist in some of the darkest days of this project.

Others who assisted include Bruce Butterfield, Lynn

Arditi, Bob Chiappinelli, Tim Barmann, Laura Meade Kirk, Karen Lee Ziner, Andy Burkhardt, and Jean Plunkett. My friend and colleague Brian Jones was particularly helpful in reading drafts and making countless suggestions.

I owe a huge debt of gratitude to Webster Bull, editor and publisher of Commonwealth Editions, who was the first to recognize the value of this story and make the commitment to publish. His guidance has gone a long way in making this a better book. I also want to thank other staff members at Commonwealth, including Katie Bull, Jill Christiansen, Anne Rolland, and Marian Bull.

Finally, I want to thank my family for putting up for three years with all my stories about the antics of Brimfield. They all gave me the support to continue. In particular two family members stepped to the forefront and became my two best editors. My daughter, Cate Paolino, read and edited every word. My wife, Dianne Sprague, not only read and edited every word of every draft, but she also lived through and helped immeasurably with the reporting.

Source Notes

THIS BOOK IS a work of nonfiction. It is the result of three years of research and is based primarily on interviews of sources named throughout the book and on personal observations and reporting between July 2002 and August 2005.

Most of the sources are named and information they supplied is clearly attributed. Among the other sources who are not named in the book but who contributed are Bob Adams, Paulette Andrew-Smith, Jill Baldarelli, Beth Brennan, Kim Brewer, Jeff Bridgeman, Bob Burgess, Bob Cahn, Bill Campisi, Ann Charters, Joe Collins, Don Decker, Tom DiPippo, Terry Duffy, Angie Fergione, Howard Gehrke, Ron and Diane Heagney, Harry Hepburn, Bill Heuring, Herb Klatchman, Jim and Christie Wilson Krusz, Jennifer LeFleur, Joni Lima, Ian Lynch, Rob McElroy, Nancy Moore, Marion Ough, Wanita Paolino, Darryl and John Peters, Penny Phaneuf, John Polito, Kevin Quinlan, Al and Tenny Roches, Ekhard Schwad, Esther Singleton, J. J. Smith, Elizabeth Stoudt, Liam Sullivan, Don Treworgy, Emma Lee Turney, Jeff Turney, Robert Waite, Ken Woodbury, Jody Young, and Gale Zernick.

Newspaper and magazine articles, books, and public records provided background material that enhanced my understanding of the accounts given by my sources. Below is a listing of additional resources used in the chapters and a bibliography.

Chapter 1—Background on Alechinsky, Waugh, and McCurdy is from *Davenport, Who's Who,* and other art references.

Chapter 2—The history of the Reid family and the development of the Brimfield market is partly based on the Brimfield Library's archive and includes articles published between 1970 and 2005 by, among others, the Associated Press, the *Brimfielder, Cigar Aficionado, Country Journal,* the *New York Times, Palmer Journal, Palmer Journal Register, Southfield News, Springfield Daily News, Springfield Union,* and *Worcester Telegram and Gazette.* Information on First Monday Sales in Ripley, Mississippi, is partially based on an article by the Center for the Study of Southern Culture at the University of Mississippi. The discussion of the origins of the term "flea market" derives partly from *The Jersey Devil's Official Flea Marketeer's Manual.* The eBay statistics are from eBay press releases and SEC filings.

Chapter 4—Background on Wachter, Helder, Coolidge, and Enneking is from *Davenport, Who's Who,* and other art references.

Chapter 5—Background on Nevelson and Catlin is from *Who's Who* and other art references.

Chapter 6—Some material about the Dunlap Broadside, its discovery and sale, comes from the *Maine Antique Digest, Christian Science Monitor,* and *Lancaster New Era.* The research by Frederick Goff comes from his book.

Chapter 7—Information about Bernstein comes from her book on Meyerowitz and three books on Bernstein, none of which listed authors, published in 1985 and 1990 by Smith-

Girard and 2000 by Joan Whalen Fine Art. Other Bernstein information comes from articles in *American Artist,* the *Boston Globe,* the *New York Times,* and the *Palm Beach Post.* Background on the Philadelphia Ten artists is partly from the book by Talbott and Tanis. Supplemental information on Colton is from Mangum's *One Woman's West.*

Chapter 8—The Parker wedding story is taken partly from *Palmer Journal.* The "Brimfield Is Back" reference is from *Brimfield Antiques Guide.*

Chapter 9—Supplemental information about the Brimfield police dispute and Gillespie burglary is from such publications as the *Worcester Telegram and Gazette, Southbridge Evening News, Springfield Republican,* and the Associated Press. Cheney's article about clocks is from *The Magazine Antiques.*

Chapter 10—Background information on William Randolph Hearst's collecting obsession comes from several biographies, including *The Chief* by Nasaw. Details of the sad fate of Langley and Homer Collyer are from Carmichael's *Incredible Collectors.* The story of Thomas Phillip's book collecting obsession is from several sources, including Muensterberger's *Collecting.*

Chapter 11—Background on Schofield and Peto is from *Davenport* and *Who's Who* and other art references. Supplemental information about historical crime problems at Brimfield comes from the *Palmer Journal, Southbridge Evening News,* and *Brimfielder.* The background information on the arrest of Leighton Deming is from the Associated Press.

Chapter 12—Supplemental background information on the Onassis and Windsor sales is from *Antiques and the Arts Weekly* and the Associated Press.

Chapter 13—eBay corporate officials declined repeated requests to cooperate or to answer almost any questions. The background information about the company's positions is from Cohen's *The Perfect Store*, corporate press releases, and filings with the SEC, as well as from published remarks in writings by the Associated Press and in the *New York Times, Providence Journal, San Francisco Chronicle,* and *USA Today*.

Chapter 14—Supplemental background on the Kovels and Rinker is from Internet sites barnesandnoble.com and annonline.com. The Kenos have discussed their Brimfield experiences in their book, *Hidden Treasures*. Some details on the Taubman conviction are from the Associated Press.

Chapter 15—Background information on Richards, Newman, and Bye is from *Who's Who* and other art references. Background on Parrish is from several references including Cutler's *Maxfield Parrish*, Bharucha's *Buried Treasures*, and Ludwig's *Maxfield Parrish*.

Chapter 16—Background on Irving, Lovel, Whitcomb, and Dohanos is from *Who's Who* and other art references. Additional background on Parrish is from Cutler's *Maxfield Parrish*, Bharucha's *Buried Treasures*, and Ludwig's *Maxfield Parrish*.

Chapter 17—The Black Hills gold story is from goldoutlet.com and other sources.

Chapter 18—Some information on the Warhol auction comes from the *Maine Antique Digest*. Background on bidding is partly from Hamilton's *Auction Madness*.

Bibliography

BOOKS

American Federation of Arts. *Who's Who in American Art*. New York: American Federation of Arts, 2002.

An American Tradition: The Pennsylvania Impressionists. New York: Beacon Hill Fine Art, 1995.

Bernstein, Theresa. *William Meyerowitz: The Artist Speaks*. Philadelphia: Art Alliance Press, 1986.

Bharucha, Fershid. *Buried Treasures: The Black and White Work of Maxfield Parrish, 1896-1905*. San Francisco: Pomegranate, 1992.

Blom, Philipp. *To Have and to Hold: An Intimate History of Collectors and Collecting*. Woodstock, N.Y.: Overlook Press, 2002.

Brown, Robert E. *Brimfield: The Collector's Paradise*. Brimfield, Mass.: Brimfield Publications, 1996.

Carmichael, Bill. *Incredible Collectors, Weird Antiques, and Odd Hobbies*. Englewood Cliffs, N.J.: Prentice Hall, 1971.

Cohen, Adam. *The Perfect Store*. Boston: Little, Brown, 2002.

Cutler, Lawrence, and Judy Goffman Cutler. *Maxfield Parrish: A Retrospective*. New York: Gramercy Press, 1999.

Davis, Fritz. *The Jersey Devil's Official Flea Marketeers Manual*. New York: Arco Publications, 1982.

Folk, Thomas. *Edward Redfield: First Master of the Twentieth Century Landscape*. Allentown, Penn.: Allentown Art Museum, 1987.

Goff, Frederick R. *The John Dunlap Broadside*. Washington, D.C.: Library of Congress, 1978.

Hamilton, Charles. *Auction Madness*. New York: Everest House, 1981.

Harvey, Miles. *The Island of Lost Maps*. New York: Random House, 2000.

Haynes, Colin. *The Complete Collector's Guide to Fakes and Forgeries*. Greensboro, N.C.: Homestead Book Co., 1988.

Hume, Ivor Noel. *All the Best Rubbish*. New York: Harper and Row, 1974.

Jeppson, Lawrence. *The Fabulous Frauds*. New York: Weybright and Talley, 1970.

Keno, Leigh, Leslie Keno, and Joan Barzilay. *Hidden Treasures: Searching for Masterpieces of American Furniture*. New York: Warner Books, 2000.

Lacey, Robert. *Sotheby's Bidding for Class*. Boston: Little, Brown, 1988.

Ludwig, Coy. *Maxfield Parrish*. New York: Watson-Guptill, 1973.

Mangum, Richard, and Sherry G. Mangum. *One Woman's West: The Life of Mary-Russell Ferrell Colton*. Flagstaff, Ariz.: Northland Publishing, 1997.

McMurty, Larry. *Cadillac Jack*. New York: Simon and Schuster, 1982.

Muensterberger, Werner. *Collecting: An Unruly Passion*. Princeton, N.J.: Princeton University Press, 1994.

Nasaw, David. *The Chief*. New York: Houghton Mifflin, 2000.

Nochlin, Linda. *Women, Art, and Power, and Other Essays*. New York: Harper and Row, 1988.

Reinhardt, Lisa, ed. *Davenport's Art Reference and Price Guide 2003/2004*. Phoenix, Ariz.: Gordon's Art Reference, 2003.

Rinker, Harry L. *How to Make the Most of Your Investments in Antiques and Collectibles*. New York: Arbor House, 1988.

Sack, Harold, and Max Wilk. *American Treasure Hunt*. Boston: Little, Brown, 1986.

Savage, George. *Forgeries, Fakes, and Reproductions: A Complete Guide for the Art Dealer and Collector*. New York: F.A. Praeger, 1964.

Sheehan, Susan, and Means, Howard. *The Banana Sculptor, the Purple Lady, and the All-Night Swimmer*. New York: Simon and Schuster, 2002.

Sloan, John. *Gist of Art*. New York: American Artists Group, 1939.

Solis-Cohen, Lita, ed. *Maine Antique Digest: The Americana Chronicle*. Philadelphia: Running Press, 2004.

Talbott, Page, and Patricia Tanis Sydney. *The Philadelphia Ten: A Women's Artist Group, 1917-1945*. Kansas City: American Art Review Press, 1998.

Theresa Bernstein. Stamford, Conn: Smith-Girard, 1985.

Theresa Bernstein (1890-): An Early Modernist. New York: Joan Whalen Fine Art, 2000.

Theresa Bernstein: Expressions of Cape Ann and New York, 1914-1972, A Centennial Exhibition. Stamford, Conn: Stamford Museum and Nature Center and Smith-Girard, 1990.

Turney, Emma Lee, and Beverly Harris. *Denim and Diamonds: The True Story of Emma Lee Turney's Round Top Antiques Fair*. Newport, R.I.: Going Press, 1998.

Yates, Raymond E. *Antique Fakes and Their Detection*. New York: Gramercy Publishing Co., 1950

NEWSPAPERS, PERIODICALS, AND OTHER RECORDS

Allen, Greg. "The X Factor." *New York Times*, May 1, 2005, AL-2.

Axtman, Kris. "The Price of Independence: $8.1 Million." *Christian Science Monitor*, July 3, 2000, 1.

Bailey, Michael J. "Theresa Bernstein at 111, Realist, Painter, Author." *Boston Globe*, February 15, 2002, B-14.

Beall, Pam. "Fleas Draw Cons and Crime." *Southbridge News*, November 8, 1983, 1.

_____ "The Girls of the Brimfield Flea Market." *Southbridge News*, June 20, 1983.

_____ "Three Flea Markets Get Adverse Decision." *Southbridge News*, August 16, 1977.

Biography, Harry Rinker, www.annonline.com.

Black Hills Gold History, www.goldoutlet.com/history.html.

Burgess, Robert. "Brimfield Faces Division over Police Issue." *Southbridge Evening News*, July 9, 2003, 1.

Cheney, Robert C. "Roxbury Eight-Day Movements and the English Connection, 1785-1825." *The Magazine Antiques*, May 2000.

Crable, Ad. "Local Antique Find May Sell for $4 Million." *Lancaster New Era*, June 2, 2000, 1.

De Thuin, Richard. "Jessie Wilcox Smith Oil Tops Illustration Auction." *Maine Antique Digest*, September 2004, D-1.

Dole, Fred. "Twenty Acres of Antiques." *Country Journal*, May 1973, 50-55.

eBay Annual Report, U.S. Securities and Exchanges Commission, April 13, 2005.

Farr, Sheila. "Fake Antiques Are a Tradition in China." *Seattle Times*, January 27, 2003, A-7.

"Find Could Make Man Independently Wealthy." *St. Petersburg Times*, April 3, 1991, 1A.

First Monday Sale and Trade Days Ripley Mississippi. Center for the Study of Southern Culture, University of Mississippi, 1999.

Fortier, Bill. "Brimfield Show Weathers Dispute." *Worcester Telegram and Gazette*, July 13, 2003, A-1.

"Gordon Reid Dies; Noted Auctioneer." *Palmer Journal Register*, November 28, 1974.

Grady, Marie P. "Brimfield Fears 'Poison Ivy' Trend of Flea Markets." *Springfield Daily News*, May 7, 1985.

Hall, Trish. "A Painter with a New Lease on Fame." *New York Times*, February 17, 1991, 61.

Hoses, Jennifer. "Invasion of the Sofa Snatchers." *Washington Post Magazine*, May 3, 1992, W-43.

Jacobs, Sally. "Still Painting after All These Years." *Boston Globe*, September 9, 1998, C-1.

"Judge Orders Transfer of Geronimo Headdress to Interior Dept." Associated Press, November 10, 2001.

Kientz, Renee. "The Thrill of the Hunt." *Texas Magazine*, March 24, 2002, 6.

Lyman, Ruth. "Brimfield's Famous Antique Flea Market Operator Sets Sights on New York Location." *New England Country Antiques*, May 1983.

MacDonald, Veronica. "Brimfield Dealers Dry Out, Sell On." *Springfield Union-News*, September 18, 1999.

"Madelyn Reid, 75, Operated First Brimfield Flea Market. *Southbridge News*, March 10, 1987.

McClaim, Erin. "Auction Houses Settle Antitrust Suit in Price-Fixing Case." Associated Press, March 11, 2003.

McEntire, Mac. "Brimfield Makes Do without Local Force." *Southbridge Evening News*, July 7, 2003, 1.

McFadden, Robert D. "Life, Liberty and the Pursuit of Oratory." *New York Times*, July 4, 2001, E-1.

Meade Kirk, Laura. "Sold on eBay." *Providence Journal*, May 1, 2005, Lifestyles 6.

Meet the Writers, Ralph and Terry Kovel. www.barnesandnoble.com.

Milgrom, Melissa. "America's Yard Sale." *Cigar Aficionado*, July/August 1997.

Movalli, Charles. "A Conversation with William Meyerowitz and Theresa Bernstein." *American Artist*, January 1980, 62-67.

Murphy, Carol. "Police Seize Phony Dealer Passes." *Springfield Union-News*, May 14, 1998.

Osterman, Elsie. "It Only Took One. Brimfield's Flea Market Frenzy Just Isn't What Gordon Reid Had in Mind." *Springfield Daily News*, September 5, 1980.

Picard, Jennifer. "Officers Bag Game at Shows." *Springfield Republican*, September 6, 2003, B-1.

Poole, Robert M. "Ripped from the Walls (and the Headlines)." *Smithsonian*, July 2005, 92-103.

"Reid Faces Mountain of Regulations in New York." *Southbridge News*, June 10, 1983, 1.

Ring, Kim. "Dealers Worried about Safety." *Springfield Republican*, July 8, 2003.

_____. "Jewelry Stolen from Show Tent." *Springfield Republican*, September 9, 2003.

_____, "Thieves Get Silver in Show Heist." *Springfield Republican*, July 11, .2003, B-1.

Rivlin, Gary, "eBay's Joy Ride: Going Once..." *New York Times*, March 6, 2005, BU-1.

Russell, James, "Skeleton Crew Patrols Flea Market." *Worcester Telegram and Gazette,* July 9, 2003, 1.

Ryan, John. "Dealer Stuck with Bad Checks." *Southbridge News*, July 14, 1997, 1.

Said, Carolyn. "Online Auction Scams Soar." *San Francisco Chronicle*, February 2, 2005, A-1.

Saunders-Watson, Catherine. "Sotheby's Auctions the Jacqueline Kennedy Onassis Estate." *Antiques and the Arts Weekly*, electronic entry of December 5, 2000, states date unknown.

Schlatter, Laurie. "New Restrictions on Brimfield Flea Market." *Southbridge News*, February 23, 1982.

Schwan, Gary. "Long-Lost Modernist Best Left Forgotten." *Palm Beach Post*, December 2003, 63.

"Sotheby's Chief Gets Year in Jail." BBC News, April 23, 2002.

Steiner, Ina. "AuctionBytes Releases 2003 Price Index of eBay Collectibles." *AuctionBytes*, May 18, 2003.

Swartz, Jon. "eBay Faithful Expect Loyalty in Return." *USA Today*, July 1, 2002, B-1.

Taylor, Lucy. "Residents Speak Out about Flea Market." *Palmer Journal*, September 23, 1999.

_____. "Wedding Bells at the Brimfield Flea Market." *Palmer Journal Register*, September 14, 2000.

"This Flea Market Could End an Era." *Worcester Telegram and Gazette*, September 8, 1983.

Trainor, Karen. "Brimfield Is Back!" *Brimfield Antiques Guide*, Summer 2003, 14.

About the Author

BOB WYSS is a journalism professor at the University of Connecticut. He was a writer and editor at the *Providence Journal* for 28 years, covering the environment, energy, and business issues. He has contributed award-winning work to publications such as the *New York Times, Christian Science Monitor, Boston Globe, Yankee,* and *Rhode Island Monthly.* Born and raised in California, he is a graduate of California State University Long Beach and Kansas State University. He lives with his wife in Cranston, Rhode Island.